LANGUAGE AND LITERACY SERIES

Dorothy S. Strickland, FOUNDING EDITOR
Celia Genishi and Donna E. Alvermann, SERIES EDITORS
ADVISORY BOARD: *Richard Allington, Kathryn Au, Bernice Cullinan, Colette Daiute,*
Anne Haas Dyson, Carole Edelsky, Mary Juzwik, Susan Lytle, Django Paris, Timothy Shanahan

continued

For volumes in the NCRLL Collection (edited by JoBeth Allen and Donna E. Alvermann) and the Practitioners Bookshelf Series
(edited by Celia Genishi and Donna E. Alvermann), as well as other titles in this series, please visit www.tcpress.com.

Language and Literacy Series, *continued*

Amplifying
the Curriculum

Designing Quality
Learning Opportunities
for English Learners

Aída Walqui
George C. Bunch

EDITORS

TEACHERS COLLEGE PRESS

TEACHERS COLLEGE | COLUMBIA UNIVERSITY
NEW YORK AND LONDON

WestEd.org

Published simultaneously by Teachers College Press, 1234 Amsterdam Avenue, New York, NY 10027 and WestEd, 730 Harrison Street, San Francisco, CA 94107

Copyright © 2019 by Aída Walqui and George C. Bunch

Cover design by David K. Kessler. Cover illustration by CSA-Printstock / iStock by GettyImages.

Library of Congress Cataloging-in-Publication Data is available at loc.gov

ISBN 978-0-8077-6119-9 (paper)
ISBN 978-0-8077-6120-5 (hardcover)
ISBN 978-0-8077-7685-8 (ebook)

Printed on acid-free paper
Manufactured in the United States of America

To the students, teachers, and student teachers we have worked with over the years. You have demonstrated, beyond any doubt, the possibility and power of amplifying the curriculum.

Contents

Preface

This book is about how teachers can design high-quality, intellectually challenging, and well-supported learning opportunities that move from *simplification* to *amplification* as the guiding principle for the education of all students, but especially students classified by their schools as English Learners. The shift to amplification, which includes enhancement and elaboration of language and content for English Learners instead of reduction and simplification, is particularly important in light of efforts to strengthen the quality of education available for all students through the "deeper learning" and "21st-century skills" necessary for our complex times. Such a shift is also necessary for English Learners—and other students who have been identified as in need of language and literacy support—to meet the more rigorous content standards and assessments recently adopted in many states, especially since these standards have increased the English language and literacy required to access the core curriculum.

The book is written for current and future teachers across the subject areas—primarily for those who teach at the high school and middle school levels, but also with relevance for teachers in elementary school, especially in the upper grades. It is also intended for those who support teachers in preparing for and doing this challenging and rewarding work, including preservice teacher educators, providers of professional learning opportunities for in-service teachers, educational leaders, other curriculum and instructional materials developers (including open source initiatives and textbook companies), and those who design assessments.

Given the growing numbers of English Learners attending schools throughout the United States, the increasing language and literacy demands across the subject areas, and the fact that disciplinary instruction can serve as an ideal context for language development, it can no longer be the case that the development of English for academic purposes remains the sole responsibility of English as a Second Language teachers. This responsibility has to be understood as belonging to every teacher, in every discipline. The good news is that, as the discussion and examples throughout the book will demonstrate, the kinds of amplification we argue for, while particularly crucial for English Learners, are also helpful for all students, including "mainstream" students who speak only English and former English Learners who have been reclassified as fluent English speakers.

It is, we hope, uncontroversial to argue that English Learners should have access to the educational "goods" increasingly being advocated for all students in the 21st century. As aspirations shift for what public education should look like for all students, it is essential to include English Learners in that vision. And so it is obviously necessary to keep our "eyes on the prize" as we consider approaches to working with English Learners. But we frame the book in this way not just to remind teachers and others responsible for the education of English Learners that the ultimate goal—developing capacities for meaningful engagement in 21-st century civic, economic, and social life—is the same for these students as for all others. We also argue that English Learners bring all the necessary capabilities to participate in instruction with such goals *right now*—if units, lessons, and instructional strategies are designed in ways that allow them to leverage their capacity. In other words, it is not the case that English Learners are not "ready" for deep learning, but rather that learning environments as often conceived currently are not ready to maximize English Learners' potential.

Rather than describing isolated, disconnected "methods" or "strategies" for teachers to choose from on an ad hoc basis, this book focuses on how teachers and those working with them can design integrated tasks, lessons, and units of study that are based on coherent theory and research on learning and language development. For those teachers who are still required to use curricular materials developed by others, the book also provides guidance for how teachers can move toward amplifying those materials, at first perhaps in modest ways, and over time with increasing agency and autonomy.

In sum, the central goal of this book is to prepare teachers to design instruction that provides access to and support for English Learners to engage in conceptually rich and analytically challenging disciplinary content—while simultaneously developing the language and literacy inherently connected to this content. In articulating the ideas outlined in the book, we build on theory and research in learning, language development, disciplinary literacy, pedagogy, and teacher preparation. We also draw on our own experiences as educational professionals over several decades—first as classroom teachers ourselves and later as teacher educators, professional development providers, curriculum developers, educational researchers, and scholars of language and literacy issues in education. Aída was born and raised in Peru, taught in indigenous bilingual education settings in Latin America as well as in middle schools in California, and has educated preservice teachers at universities in Latin America, California, and the United Kingdom. For the past two decades, as director of WestEd's Teacher Professional Development Program and the Quality Teaching for English Learners (QTEL) initiative, she has worked with colleagues to develop curriculum and provide professional learning opportunities for teachers across the United States.

Meanwhile, George grew up in New Mexico, decided to become a teacher while volunteering in Nicaragua, and taught high school Spanish, English for Speakers of Other Languages (ESOL), and social studies in the Washington, DC, area. As a professor at the University of California, Santa Cruz, he conducts research on language and literacy issues relevant to English Learners, and he prepares future teachers for working with this population.

When we began collaborating together in 2010 as part of the Understanding Language Initiative, we realized that we shared visions, practices, and commitments in or work across the varied geographical, grade level, and linguistic contexts in which we had worked with K–12 students, teachers, and educational leaders. We also realized we had been grappling throughout our careers with a similar set of problems:

- deficit views of what language learners can do both intellectually and linguistically as they develop their home and additional languages;
- reductive pedagogical approaches based on these assumptions that often leave some students without access to high-quality, intellectually rich, discipline-based curriculum and pedagogy;
- the relegation of content-area instruction for English Learners to language teachers who lack the appropriate content and pedagogical content knowledge in the disciplines they are teaching;
- guidance for teachers that emphasizes discrete "strategies" or "methods" for English Learners that do not cohere theoretically and are disconnected to the key practices in the various disciplines;
- teachers being viewed and treated merely as the *deliverers* of curriculum developed by others rather than as *designers* of lessons, units, and instructional materials themselves.

It was without hesitation, therefore, that George agreed when Aída approached him about collaborating on a book that would provide guidance— through highly practical and well-illustrated exemplars grounded in a coherent conceptual framework and principles for design—for addressing the concerns we had been working on throughout our careers. We were particularly excited about the opportunity to share work that Aída and her colleagues at WestEd had been developing for years—grounded in a view of learning as socially constructed, of English Learners as immensely capable individuals, and of schooling as an energizing future-oriented endeavor for all. Most of the examples in this book come from lessons and units created with and for classroom teachers by the QTEL team, all of whom themselves are experienced teachers and in-service teacher educators, building on Aída's work on the development of ambitious, well-supported invitations for English Learners to develop their academic potential. An exception is the chapter on science (Chapter 5), which was written by Tomás Galguera, a long-time collaborator of the QTEL team, and colleagues outside of QTEL who have integrated the ideas developed in the book with their own approaches as preservice teacher educators, professional development providers, and science curriculum developers. Chapter 9 reports on teachers' and students' perspectives from the implementation of a unit designed by Aída and her team at QTEL for the Understanding Language initiative, a unit that George had been involved with since its inception as the chair of the Understanding Language working group that commissioned it and as a "critical friend" throughout the process of its development.

The ideas explored in this book are therefore the joint products of collaborative work among a number of teachers, teacher educators, and scholars. Unlike many edited volumes, which consist of a compilation of loosely connected chapters around a central theme, this book is the product of deep and sustained collective activity conducted by the editors and authors over several years. Following established conventions, each chapter bears the names of those most centrally relevant to its content, but all the chapters have benefitted from extensive conceptual and editorial support from the team as a whole.

We can say from our own professional experience that, despite the challenges, engaging in the design of the kind of amplified learning tasks, lessons, and units described in this book—those that are simultaneously inviting, challenging, and supportive for English Learners—is not only possible, but also inspiring and rewarding. Our hope is that the book provides a solid foundation, as well as practical guidance and helpful examples, for teachers and those who prepare and support them as they move toward more ambitious instruction for English Learners in the 21st century.

—*A. W. and G.C.B.*,
February 9, 2019, New York, NY, and Santa Cruz, CA

Acknowledgments

We are appreciative of the hard work, patience, and good cheer among all the chapter authors throughout the many rounds of conversation, drafting, revision, and editing that we collectively undertook. Unlike many other edited books, this one was mostly written by a team that has worked together for over a decade, and it attempts to present a shared and coherent view of curriculum design. All authors worked on their chapters while also working full time on other professional learning and design endeavors. In spite of that, their dedication to sharing lessons learned with educators nationwide propelled them to work diligently and graciously through reviews and multiple drafts to arrive at this publication.

With such a large number of "cooks in the kitchen," this project could not have been completed without a trusted, thoughtful, and meticulous internal editorial colleague to help us enhance our arguments, gain coherence, stay organized, attend to details, and generally maintain our sanity. Peggy Mueller served in this capacity magnificently, reading every word of multiple drafts of the manuscript, her unfailing eye helping us see through redundancies and inconsistencies and considerably strengthening the book's coherence. She deserves our gratitude for having carried out that work with patience, determination, and grace. Thanks also to Patricia López-Hurtado, who assisted in making several copies of the manuscript presentable, as well as finalizing all of the tables and figures for publication. Without the careful and timely work of these colleagues, the book would not have seen the light of day.

We extend special thanks to Emily Spangler, our editor at Teachers College Press, who supported the idea for the book from its inception and patiently encouraged us to continue through our multiple missed deadlines. We realize how wonderful it is to have editors who are aware of the importance of fanning the fire just right, so that it keeps going without the threat of extinction. Emily's feedback included an ideal combination of encouragement and critique, and the final draft has benefitted measurably from her suggestions.

We also want to thank colleagues and friends who carefully read one or more chapters during the development of the book and who gave us thoughtful, honest, and helpful feedback. These "critical friends" (critical both in the sense of providing critique and also in the sense of being essential to a successful outcome) include Cindy Pease-Alvarez (who also generously provided us a home for several key writing retreats), Kathi Bailey, Sarah Beck, Cory Buxton, Hongying Chen, Ana England, Amanda Kibler, Tatyana Kleyn, Nora Lang, César Larriva, Okhee Lee, Tom Levine, Daisy Martin, Jeremy Shonick, Guadalupe Valdés, and Bill Zahner. A special thanks also to the teachers, administrators, and other leaders who read chapters and provided feedback as they participated in QTEL institutes and professional development across the country. It was inspiring to hear you talk about how the book might help your efforts to amplify instruction for English Learners, and we appreciate your feedback regarding how to make the book inviting for teachers and administrators who are in a position to do this work.

Finally, on a personal note, we wish to express deep appreciation to family, friends, and colleagues for their patience, understanding, and support during the many hours (days, months, years!) it took us to complete this project.

CHAPTER 1

Educating English Learners in the 21st Century

George C. Bunch and Aída Walqui

A growing number of students throughout the United States come to school speaking languages other than English. Although some are assessed as having sufficient English proficiency to do grade-level work in English without targeted language preparation and support, many others are deemed to be in need of assistance. Schools refer to this latter group using a number of different terms, including *English Learners* and *English Language Learners*. In some places, the term *Multilingual Learners* or *Emergent Bilinguals* is used to emphasize the importance of students' continuing development of language and literacy in their home languages as well as in English. In this book, we use the term English Learner, an imperfect label for reasons we will discuss later, but the one that is most recognizable across the country and appears in federal education legislation outlining schools' responsibility for meeting the needs of this population.[1] We also note that the approach we lay out, because it is designed to support students wherever they currently are in their linguistic and academic journeys, is applicable to teachers' efforts to design learning opportunities for *all* students, including speakers of nondominant varieties of English and others who may be identified as in need of language and literacy support.

Identifying English Learners—along with addressing their specific needs—was mandated by the U.S. Supreme Court over 40 years ago (*Lau v. Nichols*, 1974). But neither the courts nor the federal government have stipulated exactly *how* English Learners should be supported, leaving those decisions up to states, districts, schools, academic departments, and individual teachers. Unfortunately, the preparation and support provided for English Learners have often ended up restricting both content learning and language development in ways that diminish—rather than enhance—their opportunities to learn important subject matter, enrich understandings, engage in careful analysis, and advance compelling arguments (Gamoran, 2017; Gebhard & Harman, 2011). At the same time, these reductive approaches have denied English Learners opportunities to develop

[handwritten margin note: Most policy is by state, not federal]

1

the language and literacy resources needed to communicate effectively with a variety of audiences for a variety of purposes in an increasingly complex and interconnected world.

In contrast to the ways that instruction has been *simplified* for English Learners in the past, in this book we present a vision for how teachers and other educators can design activities, instructional materials, lessons, and units that *amplify* opportunities for students to engage with rich, meaningful, and challenging language and content. Moving from reduction to elaboration as the foundation for the education of English Learners is especially important given increasing emphasis on the need for *all* students to develop multifaceted and sophisticated competencies for life in the 21st century.

Schools across the country are being called upon to change their instructional practices in order to promote what some have called "deeper learning" (Heller, Wolfe, & Steinberg, 2017; Pellegrino & Hilton, 2012) and what we refer to as "quality learning" (Walqui & van Lier, 2010). English Learners should have the same right other students have to deep and high-quality learning opportunities. But improving the education of English Learners is not only an act of advocacy for this particular population. It is also in society's collective self-interest to include this large and growing segment of the U.S. population in efforts to strengthen the public education on which our economic health and participatory democracy rely. Fortunately, the deep and quality learning at the heart of current educational reform can provide optimum contexts for language and literacy development (Lee, Quinn, & Valdés, 2013). Further, it is clear that English Learners bring to the table a wide range of multilingual and multicultural resources that make them not only candidates for the kind of learning increasingly advocated for in the 21st century, but also essential actors in efforts to create a more equitable and just society.

THE PLAN FOR THE BOOK

In this book, we offer the following advice to those responsible for the education of English Learners—content teachers, English language development specialists, administrators, curriculum developers, teacher educators, and professional development providers: *"Amplify, don't simplify!"* (Walqui & van Lier, 2010, p. 38). Drawing on definitions of amplification that include "enhancement," "elaboration," "augmentation," "extension," and "expansion"—and theories of learning and language development where these concepts are paramount—we present a vision and blueprint for designing classroom instruction for English Learners. We elaborate the rationale for amplification, provide guidance for designing it, and share examples of what it looks like in practice. Because the demands of both subject area material and language and literacy increase throughout the grades, we focus on instruction at the secondary level (middle and high schools), although the principles we discuss can be adapted to elementary contexts as well, especially in the upper grades.

Crucially, instruction cannot be amplified in the classroom without careful consideration of the larger curriculum—that is, the fundamental goals of instruction and how those goals are to be manifested through the organization of learning activities, lessons, and units. Effectively educating English Learners, or any students for that matter, must go beyond the implementation of discrete instructional "strategies," no matter how compelling those individual strategies are. But to be clear, *curriculum,* as we use the term in this book, does not refer to something that is merely handed to teachers for them to follow.

Ultimately, we argue, classroom teachers are the most important curriculum developers, both in terms of creating their own materials and adapting those created by others, and so we envision teachers as the most important audience for this book. At the same time, because many current teachers have never been asked to participate in designing curriculum, they may feel overwhelmed, not knowing where to begin. Thus, we have written this book also for those who work closely with teachers: preservice teacher educators, professional developers, coaches, and school administrators. We also write for those engaged in curriculum design at larger scales, who continue to play a critical role in influencing the education of English Learners: district-level curriculum developers, commercial and open-source publishers, governmental and nongovernmental organizations, assessment specialists, and educational researchers involved in curriculum development.

Over the course of the chapters that follow, we invite readers to join us through the journey of designing challenging, interesting, relevant, interconnected, and valuable learning opportunities for English Learners across the subject areas. After presenting a rationale for our approach and a description of English Learners in this introductory chapter (Chapter 1), we describe tenets that ground our vision of amplification in Chapter 2. That is followed in Chapter 3 by design features to guide the development of lessons, units, and the broader curriculum.

Chapters 4 through 8 present illustrations of specific units, lessons, and learning activities that provide opportunities for students to encounter important concepts, engage in complex analysis, and use and develop a range of language and literacy practices. Written by educators who collectively have experience as classroom teachers, preservice teacher educators, providers of professional development, and curriculum developers, these chapters invite readers to envision the kind of amplification that we propose must be at the heart of effective instructional design for English Learners.

The lessons and units described in these core chapters demonstrate ways to engage and support English Learners in doing things like analyzing original language from Shakespeare's *Macbeth* in an English language arts unit

(Chapter 4), conducting science experiments to understand germ theory and disease treatment (Chapter 5), engaging with mathematical concepts such as steepness and slope (Chapter 6), and exploring 15th- and 16th-century maps that provide historical context for the Age of Exploration (Chapter 7). Chapter 8 presents examples from a unit designed for a small but important subpopulation of English Learners: beginning-level English Learners who have recently arrived in the United States, sometimes called "Newcomers." Each chapter guides the reader through the process of deciding on key concepts that the unit will explore; selecting high-quality texts, problems, or phenomena for students to grapple with; developing tasks that will guide students' analysis; facilitating students in developing relevant language and literacy practices; and organizing all of the above into coherent instructional sequences, lessons, units, and larger curricular scopes and sequences.

Lest readers get the impression that the kinds of challenging curriculum we are describing is unrealistic in the "real world," we provide examples of materials, activities, and lessons that we have seen teachers across the United States use successfully with English Learners from a wide variety of backgrounds. For example, Chapters 2 and 3 include samples of student talk and written work from these activities, and Chapter 9 shares the voices of teachers and students in three different states as they implemented a unit developed using the same tenets and design features as the ones described in the previous chapters. The book concludes with a discussion of what teachers can do to immediately begin to move in this direction, as well as the role of teacher preparation and professional development in working with teachers to design the kind of amplified instruction described throughout the book (Chapter 10).

The remainder of this introductory chapter is organized into two main sections. The first situates our vision for deep, quality learning for English Learners in the context of the current movement in U.S. public education calling for learning opportunities that better prepare students for the competencies required in the 21st century. The second part provides an introduction to students often classified as English Learners and discusses the benefits and liabilities associated with that label. We conclude Chapter 1 by re-emphasizing how, given demographic shifts likely to continue, improving the education of English Learners helps unleash not only their potential for individual success, but also their contributions to a more vibrant, equitable, and sustainable world.

Before proceeding, it is important to point out that there are numerous cognitive, social, and economic benefits of bilingualism in the 21st century (Callahan & Gándara, 2014; National Academies, 2017; Orellana, 2009; Valdés, 2003), and students' home languages can serve as an important resource for their learning in school (García & Kleifgen, 2018). We are heartened that states such as California and Massachusetts have recently rescinded their "English-only" restrictions for schools, and we support efforts to prepare teachers for leveraging students' home language resources

ASSET-BASED PEDAGOGY [handwritten margin note]

even when the teachers themselves do not speak those languages (García & Kleyn, 2016). At the same time, the fact is that most English Learners in U.S. schools still receive content area instruction and assessments predominantly in English. Because this is unlikely to change in the foreseeable future, in this book we focus predominantly on examples where English is the medium of instruction. Nonetheless, the tenets and design features we present in Chapters 2 and 3 are also applicable to contexts that include instruction in languages other than English and so will be of use to teachers in a range of bilingual settings.

LEARNING FOR THE 21ST CENTURY

If students and society are to thrive in the 21st century, learners will need to develop a range of competencies. As Mehta and Fine (2017) point out:

> Successfully navigating twenty-first-century adult life requires far more than basic academic knowledge and skills. On the personal front, adults need to be able to navigate among plural identities, to confront complex ethical questions, and to make informed decisions in the face of uncertainty. On the civic front, they need to be able to articulate and advocate for their perspectives, to engage in productive dialogue across ideological divides, and to decide among imperfect options. On the professional front, they need to be able to tackle open-ended problems in critical, creative, and collaborative ways and to engage in ongoing learning that allows them to adapt to the needs of a rapidly changing job market. (p.11)

Perhaps recognition of this wide range of necessary competencies is why there are signs that, at long last, the "basic skills" movement that has gripped U.S. educational policy and practice on and off throughout its history may be losing some of its purchase. As anyone involved in U.S. public schools over the last decade and a half can attest, basic skills were what counted in U.S. public education under the No Child Left Behind Act (NCLB, 2001), and proficiency in these skills was judged predominantly by scores on standardized achievement tests in reading and mathematics. Now, however, the focus is shifting. The emphasis—by federal policy, national educational foundations, and new standards in many states—is increasingly on competencies that go well beyond the basics.

To be sure, testing and accountability still constitute the centerpiece of federal education policy, and many teachers still feel pressure to focus on increasing students' scores on end-of-year standardized tests. But new state content area standards and frameworks are redefining the goals of education for students across the country. As states implement the Every Student Succeeds Act (ESSA), which replaced NCLB as federal education law in 2015, some states are moving toward broader systems of content-area assessment intended to measure students' performance on a wider range of tasks than in the past, including reading for diverse purposes, constructing arguments using evidence, and solving problems (Bennett, 2015; Conley, 2017; Heller et al., 2017). Concurrently, English language proficiency standards—and the tests that measure them—are being redesigned to meet federal requirements calling for them to align with states' content area standards and assessments (Council of Chief State School Officers, 2012; Heritage, Walqui, & Linquanti, 2015).

As a result of these new emphases, *all* teachers are being called upon to focus their instruction on competencies different from those they have taught in the past. These competencies, and the goals of instruction that prepare students for them, are referred to by different terms, including *deeper learning, 21st century skills, college and career readiness,* and *next generation learning* (Chow, 2017, p. v; Pellegrino & Hilton, 2012). While the competencies are defined slightly differently in each case, it is clear that curriculum and instruction in the United States will need to change dramatically, for English Learners and all students, in order to attend to new standards and the larger competencies they are designed to foster. Recent reviews of research on success during the early years of college has demonstrated the importance of understanding key concepts and "big ideas" of core content areas, but also of developing cognitive strategies, student ownership of learning, and the ability to navigate complex institutions (Conley, 2017, p. 205; Pellegrino & Hilton, 2012). And research on workplace settings has highlighted the need to communicate and collaborate with diverse colleagues, to solve problems of increasing complexity, and to adapt to ever-changing contexts (Heller et al., 2017).

Of course, many past reform efforts have also challenged the idea that "basic skills" should be the primary goal of U.S. public education (Ladson-Billings, 2006; Oakes, 1985; Tyack & Cuban, 1995). There are, however, two critical differences in the 21st century. One is the "rapid and irreversible transformations to the landscape of modern life" that make these competencies even more necessary today than in the past (Mehta & Fine, p. 13). And the second is that *everyone*—not just those in the "elite" classes—is called upon to use such competencies: in the workplace, in civic spaces, in social networks, and even at home (Pellegrino & Hilton 2012). We live in such rapidly changing times that we cannot fathom the jobs that will be available when those currently in middle school will seek them. What skills inside and outside of the workplace will be needed in this new landscape? While many are impossible to predict, certainly the ability to observe critically, ask questions, understand diverse points of view, advance arguments, and negotiate solutions will be among them.

It is also important to remember that in a democratic society, preparing students to be successful in higher education and enabling their development for productive careers are not the only goals of public education (Gutmann, 1987; Noddings, 2013). Westheimer (2015) poignantly challenges us to consider what might distinguish classroom teaching and learning in a democratic society compared with a totalitarian regime:

> [D]o students in democratic countries learn how to participate in public decision making (the kind of participation that is required for democracy to function properly)? Are they taught to see themselves as individual actors who work in concert with others to create a better society? Are they taught the skills they need to think for themselves and to govern collectively? (pp. 11–12)

Deeper Learning for Whom?

Classroom environments that foster the deep and rich learning necessary for development of the 21st-century competencies described above have been scarce throughout the history of U.S. public education, particularly for students from minoritized, immigrant, and low-income backgrounds. Noguera, Darling-Hammond, and Friedlaender (2017) describe a "vicious cycle" during the No Child Left Behind era that exacerbated longstanding inequities (p. 84). Many schools serving low-income students, in an effort to improve their students' performance on standardized reading and math tests, reduced access to learning opportunities in history, science, writing, and the arts. At the same time, test scores were used to assign students differentially either to courses with opportunities to engage in "higher order thinking skills" or those focused on "remedial, rote-oriented, and often scripted courses of study" (p. 84). In many cases, students were assigned to the kind of instruction they had already experienced in the past, perpetuating a cycle of inequitable learning opportunities and expectations.

Schools' provisions of opportunities for students to develop active citizenship have also been inequitably distributed. Westheimer (2015) points out that, where initiatives do exist that "sharpen students' thinking about issues of public debate and concern," they are disproportionately available to already-high-achieving students, often from economically privileged backgrounds (p. 14). The result is a "civic opportunity gap" leading to disparate opportunities for practicing democratic engagement in schools (p. 14).[2]

An inequitable curriculum, of course, exacerbates societal inequities, with more affluent students having opportunities to further develop "problem-solving" competencies often associated with "managerial classes" while others are given "rule-following tasks that mirror much of factory and other working class work" (Mehta, 2014, quoted in Noguera et al., 2017, pp. 83–84). This arrangement replicates power differentials, maintaining the status quo of who has access to higher level jobs (Anyon, 1980; Bowles & Gintis, 1976). It also denies those presumed to be "managers" opportunities to develop multifaceted perspectives and civic responsibility, while withholding opportunities for future "workers" to engage in the kind of intellectual and literacy practices that will lead to deep and enduring participation in the full range of opportunities available in 21st-century life.

The general move toward deeper learning and the specific goals of new standards in many states offer potential opportunities to disrupt the vicious cycle mentioned above. Promising evidence suggests that shifting school practices toward those that support deep learning can benefit all students. For example, Noguera et al. (2017) report that schools adopting practices to promote deeper learning (including inquiry-based learning and group-work; performance-based assessments; curricula relevant to the world beyond school; and supports for reflection, collaboration, and professional development for teachers) had better outcomes across a wide range of indicators (academic performance, attendance, student behavior, dropout rates, graduation rates, college attendance, and perseverance) for low-income and minority students than schools serving similar student populations that did not implement these practices (Noguera et al., 2017).

Such change will not happen automatically, and much attention has been placed, legitimately, on the obstacles that will need to be overcome in implementing quality instruction for deep learning at a large scale. Some of these are outside of the individual classroom teacher's control and must be undertaken at the school, district, or even state or national level (Bryk, 2015; O'Day & Smith, 2016). However, if schools are going to have any chance of moving toward more intellectually substantive and socially relevant practices for all students, it will be teachers who ultimately make it happen. This book, therefore, is about what teachers can do, directly within their sphere of influence and with the support of others, as they envision, plan, and enact quality instruction for English Learners and for all of their students.

Quality Learning in the Classroom

Our model of promoting quality learning for English Learners shares features with—and adds to—those of others calling for opportunities for deep learning for all students. As Lampert (2017) argues, if students are going to be expected to "learn deeply" (master core content, collaborate with others, communicate well, and develop "academic mindsets"), then what teachers are asking them to do in classrooms will also have to change. Unfortunately, students in most classrooms are still expected to learn predominantly in two ways: listening to the teacher and reading textbooks. "Deeper learning" will require what Lampert calls "deeper teaching" (p. 149).

Such teaching, which is often contrary to the classrooms that teachers themselves experienced as students and unwittingly replicate (Lortie, 1975), must center on goals that are more "intellectually and socially ambitious"

(Lampert, 2017, p. 150). For example, Lampert describes mathematics class-rooms where teachers

- build on what students already know in order to invite them into challenging and interesting conversations around key central concepts;
- construct these conversations as a collective endeavor that the whole class is engaged in; and
- provide opportunities for students to converse with each other as they work through their thinking. (p. 157)

As Lampert (2017) points out, although these kinds of learning activities and talk are often quite different from what most students are used to doing in school, they are consistent with theory and research about how best to support student learning (Bransford, Brown, & Cocking, 1999; National Academies, 2018).

At the same time, as schools and teachers contemplate the kinds of citizens they are helping their students become, Westheimer (2015) urges teachers to draw on their own and their students' interests, passion, and knowledge to focus on students' own questions; to encourage students to evaluate core subject matter in substantive ways (rather than as "facts" that they are asked to regurgitate); to create contexts in which students can ana-lyze and discuss various viewpoints (including those that are controversial); to ground instruction in local contexts; and to encourage participation in community projects that encourage personal responsibility, engaged partici-pation, and critical analysis (pp. 80, 99).

Our conception of quality learning, introduced in Chapters 2 and 3, shares many of the same goals as those described above. With a particular focus on English Learners, we offer a vision—and a map—for how teachers, in concert with others, can design curriculum that provides opportunities for students to engage with each other and the teacher in learning through participation in conceptual, analytic, and language practices in disciplines across the curriculum (Valdés, Kibler, & Walqui, 2014). Doing so requires revisiting and rethinking the traditional structures of lesson plans and de-sign in ways that are informed by theories of how learning takes place and how language is implicated in that learning (Bruner, 1996; Vygotsky, 1962, 1978). Therefore, the book does not present a list of discrete teaching strat-egies or activities to be replicated ad hoc in classrooms, but rather a prin-cipled *framework* for designing learning opportunities for English Learners and other students, with many examples of activities that could reside within that framework depending on a multitude of contextual variables. Collectively, the activities are designed to promote students' consideration of powerful ideas that are interconnected and discussed critically through interactions that engage everybody in sustained intellectual conversations and academic work.

ENGLISH LEARNERS IN THE 21ST CENTURY

The term *English Learner* is fraught with multiple meanings, underlying complexities, and dilemmas relevant to prospects for the education of this population. The almost 5 million students in U.S. schools currently designated as English Learners come from different geographic, demographic, linguistic, educational, and socioeconomic backgrounds. And the range of their developmental stages of English is considerable. In fact, the National Academies of Sciences, Engineering, and Medicine (2017) recently concluded that "a defining characteristic" of English Learners is the diversity among them (p. S-1).

Demographic Diversity

Students designated as English Learners include young people who arrived in the United States from countries around the globe, some very recently (including in the middle of the school year) and some years ago. Some arrived with their families, others with distant relatives, and still others by themselves, as "unaccompanied minors." Contrary to common assumptions, the majority of English Learners were born in the United States and are, therefore, U.S. citizens. Others are protected by the U.S. government as refugees, some hold work or family visas, and others are without legal papers. The U.S. Supreme Court ruled over three decades ago that all children and youth have a right to public education while living in the United States (*Plyler v. Doe*, 1982). Yet many immigrant families face continuing—and recently increasing—fear and uncertainty regarding their status and safety.

Students classified as English Learners also vary with regard to their prior education. Some have had high-quality previous schooling, but many have attended under-resourced schools (either in the United States or other countries), and some have had interrupted or even no previous formal education due to war, economic crises, frequent migration, or other circumstances barring them from access to school. English Learners also vary considerably in terms of their parents' socioeconomic status, educational levels, and literacy backgrounds (Walqui, 2005). Finally, it is not uncommon for English Learners and their families to travel back and forth between the United States and other countries, pursuing economic opportunities or attending to family needs, over the course of one or more academic years.

Spanish is spoken at home by a large majority of English Learners (73%), while hundreds of other languages are spoken by smaller numbers of students. Perhaps surprising to many teachers, most English Learners were born in the United States (between 55% and 65% of English Learners in the secondary grades were born in the United States, and between 70% and 90% in the elementary grades were born in this country). Among English Learners born outside of the United States, over 40% were born in Mexico, with smaller but significant percentages born in China, Korea, the Philippines, Haiti, other Latin American countries, Europe, and Africa (National Academies, 2017).

English Language Proficiency

Students classified as English Learners also have widely different proficiencies in English, from those newly arrived in the United States speaking virtually no English to students who appear to speak fluent English but are still designated as English Learners due to reading and writing or other academic challenges. Effective instruction will look different for English Learners at different places along the continuum of their English language development (Valdés, Bunch, Snow, & Lee, 2005), but the principles, approaches to developing curriculum, and structure of lesson design advocated in this book apply to all English Learners.

It is important for teachers to understand that the bureaucratic categories or English language proficiency "levels" that students are assigned by schools are the result of imperfect tests, classification procedures, and accountability mandates that may not be valid indications of what students can actually do in the classroom with appropriate curriculum and scaffolding. Beyond the idealized progressions through different language proficiency "levels," individuals are undergoing the "extraordinarily complex" process of developing an additional language (Valdés, Capitelli, & Alvarez, 2011). In fact, some scholars have argued that language instruction and assessment should focus on how learners become productive "users" of more than one language, rather than solely on how they develop internal linguistic systems (Cook, 2007; Kibler & Valdés, 2016). As Valdés et al. (2011) have put it, the goal of learning a second language from this perspective "is not to become like native speakers of the language but to use the language to function competently in a variety of contexts for a range of purposes" (p. 23).

While many debates continue among scholars about the nature of second language development and the best conditions to support it, Valdés, Poza, & Brooks (2014) point out important areas of agreement: that language acquisition is not linear, that it is highly variable and individual, that the highest attainment for most does not result in perfectly balanced bilingualism, that formalized language instruction does not necessarily lead to language development, and that developing additional languages is "a slow and time-consuming process" (Valdés et al., 2011, p. 17; see also VanPatten, 2003). These understandings, as Valdés et al. (2011) point out, have profound implications. They mean that English Learners will need to use English for school learning before they have fully acquired the linguistic system. It also implies that their teachers must learn to support students' content area learning during this process.

The Limits of Assessment and Classification

It is thus important for teachers to understand that the information they receive from schools and districts, both about students' English Learner classification in general and about their language proficiency "levels" in particular, are at best approximations—and at worst distortions—of what students are capable of doing with their developing English language resources. Standardized tests continue to dominate efforts to classify language learners, place them in courses, and measure how teachers and schools are doing in educating them (Valdés et al., 2014). Yet problems have persisted in assessing both the content learning and language development of English Learners, leading experts on testing to question the validity of such assessments (Cumming, 2008; Valdés et al., 2011).

The fact that "proficiency levels" that schools assign English Learners may distort what students can actually do leads to a larger point about the English Learner classification itself. It, too, is a construct based largely on testing, not only on students' English language proficiency but often also on students' ability to demonstrate their knowledge of subject matter on standardized tests given (in most states) in English. In fact, for several years there has been mounting criticism of the use of the term *English Learner* itself. Increasingly, some researchers and educators use the term "Emergent Bilingual" or "Multilingual Learner" instead of English Learner, as a means of emphasizing the importance of the maintenance and development of students' home language as well as English, and the need for instructional settings that allow students to use and build on their full range of linguistic competencies (García, 2009; García & Kleifgen, 2018).

Given all of the above, why do we, in this book and elsewhere, continue to use the term *English Learner*? It is true that the term is an invention—an abstraction that admittedly has a number of problems associated with it. On the other hand, the label has concrete, material, and tangible consequences for students assigned it. It represents a statutory category in federal law that requires state and local educational agencies to test and classify some students and provide differential treatment for them compared with fluent English speakers. The impact on students is obviously intended to be positive: to mandate the provision of appropriate support and instructional environments. And sometimes this is the case. However, there is also evidence that the label can lead to a number of possible deleterious consequences: a stigma leading to low expectations by teachers and classmates; lack of access to a rigorous, college preparatory curriculum, either due to "watered-down" sheltered content courses or not being enrolled in a content courses altogether to accommodate English as a Second Language (ESL) classes; exclusion from arts education and "gifted and talented" programs; and disproportionate referrals to special education (Callahan, 2005; Gamoran, 2017; Kanno & Kangas, 2014). For all these reasons, we can't just wash the term away, pretending that the construct and its consequences—positive or negative—do not exist.

Challenges and Opportunities for English Learners

Moving beyond the "basics" to include opportunities for deep thinking, problem solving, and intellectual and civic engagement presents language and literacy challenges for all students, but especially for those called upon to engage in these new practices in a language they are in the process of developing (Bunch, Walqui, & Pearson, 2014; Duhaylongsod, Snow, Selman, & Donovan, 2015; Fillmore & Fillmore, 2012; Lee, Quinn, & Valdés, 2013; Moschkovich, 2012). But the heightened language and literacy *demands* represent simultaneous *opportunities* for language and literacy development. These opportunities suggest that the primary challenge for educators is not to find ways to eliminate the demands but rather to support English Learners in meeting them (Bunch, Kibler, & Pimentel, 2012).

The good news for teachers is that English Learners bring a wealth of resources (Ruiz, 1984) that can allow them both to flourish in the kinds of classrooms called for by the new standards and to participate actively in complex and dynamic 21st-century communities—when these resources are acknowledged and leveraged. As Gándara (2017) has argued, when the skills they bring to the classroom are viewed as resources and opportunities for development rather than deficits to overcome, students from immigrant families are especially well-suited to thrive in the kinds of instructional environments advocated for in this book. In addition to the advantages of bilingualism mentioned earlier, English Learners often bring nuanced perspectives on history and politics by virtue of their multicultural and multinational backgrounds; belong to cultures that value collaboration; share the motivation, resilience, and self-reliance often exhibited by immigrant families; and have experience with intercultural communication and teamwork (Gándara, 2017, p. 133).

The families of English Learners also have what Yosso (2005) calls "community cultural wealth." Yosso describes the various kinds of "capital" (Bourdieu, 1973), often unrecognized and untapped by schools, that members of communities of color have developed in response to marginalization in the United States. These include *aspirational capital* to maintain hope for the future even in the face of daunting obstacles; *familial capital* that leverages community knowledge and traditions for emotional support and for educational and professional advancement; *social capital* that helps leverage community networks; *navigational capital* to negotiate institutions that are often not designed with their needs in mind; and *resistant capital* used for challenging inequitable structures in order to transform them (pp. 78–81). All of these can serve as resources for supporting English Learners in navigating the competencies required in the 21st century and the kinds of learning opportunities described in this book.

English Learners also bring communicative resources that, albeit different from their teachers and classmates from dominant groups, can be used to engage effectively in learning activities and demonstrate their understandings when teachers recognize them as resources (Valdés et al., 2005). In addition to students' home languages, such resources include English Learners' still-imperfect but developing English (Valdés, Capitelli, & Alvarez, 2011); nondominant varieties of English such as Chicano and African American English (Fought, 2003; Green, 2004); "informal" English commonly used when discussing ideas and working on problems even by scholars at the highest levels of academia (Bunch, 2014; MacSwan & Rolstad, 2003); and paralinguistic semiotic resources (gestures, graphical representations, other visual designs) recognized in many disciplines as being associated with high-level conceptual engagement (van Lier & Walqui, 2012). Teachers can build on these resources as students expand their repertoires to also include more "standard" forms of expression in English used for different audiences and purposes (Bunch, 2014; Valdés et al., 2005).

A host of possibilities arise, therefore, when we shift the lens away from perceived deficits in English Learners' abilities toward questions such as those proposed by Orellana and Gutierrez (2006): "'What *do* our students know?' 'What *can* they do?' 'What are their skills, contributions, or experiences that can be useful for them or for the world?'" (p. 120, emphasis in original; see also Gutierrez & Rogoff, 2003). As we will discuss throughout the book and especially in Chapter 9, we have found that many teachers find that English Learners, when given the opportunity and support to do so, can engage productively with complex and challenging texts and ideas in ways that teachers previously would not have thought possible.

Our intention is not to minimize the significant obstacles, linguistic and otherwise, that English Learners may face in achieving academic success—including, depending on the learners and the context, the effects of poverty, racism, interrupted schooling, frequent migration, limited formal educational attainment among their parents, and unsettled immigration status (Gándara, 2017; National Academies, 2017). But the experiences of English Learners and their families navigating these very obstacles are also the source of significant resources that—when understood and acted upon—can be leveraged for precisely the kind of learning called for in the 21st century.

Why English Learners Matter for Everyone

How students from immigrant and English learning backgrounds fare in the coming years will determine to a large extent how the larger U.S. society fares. Immigrants and their descendants are expected to represent almost

90% of all U.S. population growth between now and 2065 (López, Bialik, & Radford, 2018). In light of an aging workforce, children of immigrants are also projected to become the primary source of growth among all U.S. workers, beginning as early as 2020 (Singer & Myers, 2016). In California, over half of all K–12 students now have at least one foreign-born parent (Sugerman & Geary, 2018), and the largest states will continue to have a disproportionate number and concentration of immigrants and children of immigrants. But the United States as a whole is also experiencing an "unprecedented geographic diversification" of immigrants and their families (Callahan & Muller, 2013, p. 15). The Hispanic population in 15 states more than doubled between 2000 and 2012, including Tennessee, Alabama, Kentucky, and North and South Dakota (National Academies, 2017). And while the education of immigrant students and English Learners has often been seen as an "urban" issue, immigrants are increasingly also settling in rural areas, small towns, and suburbs previously unaccustomed to this kind of diversity (Callahan & Muller, 2013).

With an enhanced commitment to providing high-quality education for English Learners, models for curriculum and instruction to realize this commitment, and support for teachers in implementing them, we see the current demographic trends as hopeful—not alarming—for the future of the country. Given what we have outlined above about the assets that English Learners and immigrant families bring to the table, it becomes obvious that English Learners are not burdens to bear, but rather bearers of remarkable, often untapped, societal resources. In fact, who better than English Learners and others from immigrant families to help lead the way in preparing *all* students for 21st-century challenges?

By virtue of their own experiences, such students are already developing real-life expertise as they encounter situations where, returning to the 21st-century competencies shared earlier from Mehta and Fine (2017), they are called upon to "navigate among plural identities, . . . make informed decisions in the face of uncertainty, . . . engage in productive dialogue across ideological divides, . . . decide among imperfect options, . . . [and] tackle open-ended problems in critical, creative, and collaborative ways" (p. 11). In short, English Learners bring precisely the kinds of diverse life perspectives and experiences needed for an intellectually, culturally, and socially vibrant 21st-century milieu. We offer this book as one possible roadmap for how teachers and other educators can help to realize this potential.

NOTES

1. The Elementary and Secondary Education Act defines *English Learners* as those students speaking languages other than English "whose difficulties in speaking, reading, writing, or understanding the English language may be sufficient to

deny the individual (i) the ability to meet the challenging State academic standards; (ii) the ability to successfully achieve in classrooms where the language of instruction is English; or (iii) the opportunity to participate fully in society" (U.S. Department of Education, 2016, p. 43).

2. This is not to say, of course, that young people, especially those from marginalized backgrounds, are not engaged in other sorts of civic engagement. As Mirra and Garcia (2017) point out, young people of color are often deeply involved in "connected learning" through digital media, participatory "hashtag" movements such as #BlackLivesMatter and #Occupy (p. 147), and, in fewer cases, participatory action research in school or after-school programs. For the most part, however, such opportunities are neither acknowledged nor developed in U.S. schools and classrooms.

REFERENCES

Anyon, J. (1980). Social class and the hidden curriculum of work. *Journal of Education, 162*(1), 67–92.

Bennett, R. E. (2015). The changing nature of educational assessment. *Review of Research in Education, 39*, 370–407.

Bourdieu, P. (1973). *Cultural reproduction and social reproduction in knowledge, education, and cultural change.* London, UK: Tavistock.

Bowles, S., & Gintis, H. (1976). *Schooling in capitalist America: Educational reform and the contradictions of economic life.* New York, NY: Basic Books.

Bransford, J., Brown, A., & Cocking, R. (Eds.). (1999). *How people learn: Brain, mind, experience, and school.* Washington, DC: National Academies Press.

Bruner, J. (1996). *The culture of education.* Cambridge, MA: Harvard University Press.

Bryk, A. S. (2015). Accelerating how we learn to improve. *Educational Researcher, 44*(9), 467–477.

Bunch, G. C. (2014). The language of ideas and the language of display: Reconceptualizing "academic language" in linguistically diverse classrooms. *International Multilingual Multicultural Research Journal, 8*(1), 70–86.

Bunch, G. C., Kibler, A., & Pimentel, S. (2012, January). Realizing opportunities for English learners in the Common Core English Language Arts and Disciplinary Literacy Standards. Paper presented at the Understanding Language Conference, Stanford, CA. Retrieved from https://ell.stanford.edu/papers/practice

Bunch, G. C., Walqui, A., & Pearson, D. P. (2014). Complex text and new common standards in the United States: Pedagogical implications for English learners. *TESOL Quarterly, 48*(3), 533–559. doi: 10.1002/tesq.175

Callahan, R. (2005). Tracking and high school English learners: Limiting opportunities to learn. *American Educational Research Journal, 42*(2), 305–328.

Callahan, R. M., & Gándara, P. C. (Eds.). (2014). *The bilingual advantage: Language, literacy, and the US labor market* (pp. 286–297). Bristol, UK: Multilingual Matters.

Callahan, R. M., & Muller, C. (2013). *Coming of political age: American schools and the civic development of immigrant youth.* New York, NY: Russell Sage Foundation.

Chow, B. (2017). Foreword. In R. Heller, R. E. Wolfe, & A. Steinberg (Eds.), *Rethinking readiness: Deeper learning for college, work, and life* (pp. v.–vii). Cambridge, MA: Harvard Education Press.

Conley, D. T. (2017). Toward systems of assessment for deeper learning. In R. Heller, R. E. Wolfe, & A. Steinberg (Eds.), *Rethinking readiness: Deeper learning for college, work, and life* (pp. 195–219). Cambridge, MA: Harvard Education Press.

Cook, V. (2007). The goals of ELT: Reproducing native speakers or promoting multicompetence among second-language users? In J. Cummins & C. Davison (Eds.), *International handbook of English language teaching, Part I* (pp. 237–248). New York, NY: Springer.

Council of Chief State School Officers (CCSSO). (2012). Framework for English language proficiency development standards corresponding to the Common Core State Standards and the Next Generation Science Standards. Retrieved from ccsso .org/resource-library/english-language-proficiency-development-elpd-framework

Cumming, A. (2008). Assessing oral and literate abilities. In E. Shohamy & N. Hornberger (Eds.), *Encyclopedia of language and education: Language testing and assessment*. New York, NY: Springer.

Duhaylongsod, L., Snow, C. E., Selman, R. L., & Donovan, M. S. (2015). Toward disciplinary literacy: Dilemmas and challenges in designing history curriculum to support middle school students. *Harvard Educational Review, 85*(4), 584–608.

Fillmore, L. W., & Fillmore, C. (2012, January). What does text complexity mean for English learners and language minority students? Paper presented at the Understanding Language Conference, Stanford, CA. Retrieved from http://ell .stanford.edu/papers/language

Fought, C. (2003). *Chicano English in context* (pp. 1–10). New York, NY: Palgrave Macmillan.

Gamoran, A. (2017). *Engaging English learners with rigorous academic content: Insights from research on tracking*. New York, NY: William T. Grant Foundation.

Gándara, P. (2017). Deeper learning for English language learners. In R. Heller, R. E. Wolfe, & A. Steinberg (Eds.). *Rethinking readiness: Deeper learning for college, work, and life* (pp. 123–144). Cambridge, MA: Harvard Education Press.

García, O. (2009). *Bilingual education in the 21st century: A global perspective*. Malden, MA; Oxford: Wiley-Blackwell.

García, O., & Kleifgen, J. A. (2018). *Educating emergent bilinguals: Policies, programs, and practices for English language learners* (2nd ed.). New York, NY: Teachers College Press.

García, O., & Kleyn, T. (2016). *Translanguaging with multilingual students: Learning from classroom moments*. New York, NY: Routledge.

Gebhard, M., & Harman, R. (2011). Reconsidering genre theory in K–12 schools: A response to school reforms in the United States. *Journal of Second Language Writing, 20*(1), 45–55.

Green, L. (2004). African American English. In E. Finegan & J. R. Rickford (Eds.), *Language in the USA: Themes for the twenty-first century* (pp. 76–91). Cambridge, UK: Cambridge University Press.

Gutiérrez, K. D., & Rogoff, B. (2003). Cultural ways of learning: Individual traits or repertoires of practice. *Educational Researcher, 32*(5), 19–25.

Gutmann, A. (1987). *Democratic education.* Princeton, NJ: Princeton University Press.

Heller, R., Wolfe, R. E., & Steinberg, A. (2017). Introduction. In R. Heller, R. E. Wolfe, & A. Steinberg (Eds.), *Rethinking readiness: Deeper learning for college, work, and life* (pp. 1–8). Cambridge, MA: Harvard Education Press.

Heritage, M., Walqui, A., & Linquanti, R. (2015). *English language learners and the new standards: Developing language, content knowledge, and analytical practices in the classroom* (pp. 1–21). Cambridge, MA: Harvard Education Press.

Kanno, Y., & Kangas, S. E. N. (2014). "I'm not going to be, like, for the AP": English language learners' limited access to advanced college-preparatory courses in high school. *American Educational Research Journal*, 1–31. doi: 10.3102/0002831214544716

Kibler, A. K., & Valdés, G. (2016). Conceptualizing language learners: Socioinstitutional mechanisms and their consequences. *The Modern Language Journal* 100, 96–116.

Ladson-Billings, G. (2006). From the achievement gap to the education debt: Understanding achievement in U.S. schools. *Educational Researcher, 35*(7), 3–12.

Lampert, M. (2017). Ambitious teaching: A deep dive. In R. Heller, R. E. Wolfe, & A. Steinberg (Eds.), *Rethinking readiness: Deeper learning for college, work, and life* (pp. 147–173). Cambridge, MA: Harvard Education Press.

Lau v. Nichols, 414 U. S. 563 (1974).

Lee, O., Quinn, H., & Valdés, G. (2013). Science and language for English Language Learners in relation to Next Generation Science Standards and with implications for Common Core State Standards for English language arts and mathematics. *Educational Researcher, 42*, 234–249.

López, G., Bialik, K., & Radford, J. (2018, September). *Key findings about U.S. immigrants.* Washington, DC: Pew Research Center. Retrieved from http://www.pewresearch.org/fact-tank/2018/09/14/key-findings-about-u-s-immigrants/

Lortie, D. C. (1975). *Schoolteacher: A sociological study.* Chicago, IL: University of Chicago Press.

MacSwan, J., & Rolstad, K. (2003). Linguistic diversity, schooling, and social class: Rethinking our conception of language proficiency in language minority education. In C. B. Paulston & G. R. Tucker (Eds.), *Sociolinguistics: The essential readings* (pp. 329–340). Malden, MA: Blackwell.

Mehta, J., & Fine, S. (2017). How we got here: The imperative for deeper learning. In R. Heller, R. E. Wolfe, & A. Steinberg (Eds.), *Rethinking readiness: Deeper learning for college, work, and life* (pp. 11–35). Cambridge, MA: Harvard Education Press.

Mirra, N., & García, A. (2017). Civic participation reimagined: Youth interrogation and innovation in the multimodal public sphere. *Review of Research in Education, 41*, 136–158.

Moschkovich, J. (2012, January). Mathematics, the Common Core, and language: Recommendations for mathematics instruction for ELs aligned with the Common Core. Paper presented at the Understanding Language Conference, Stanford, CA. Retrieved from http://ell.stanford.edu/papers/practice

National Academies of Sciences, Engineering, and Medicine. (2017). *Promoting the educational success of children and youth learning english: Promising futures.* Washington, DC: National Academies Press. doi:10.17226/24677

National Academies of Sciences, Engineering, and Medicine. (2018). *How people learn II: Learners, contexts, and cultures.* Washington, DC: The National Academies Press. doi:10.17226/24783

No Child Left Behind Act of 2001, P.L. 107–110, 20 U.S.C. § 115 Stat.1425 (2002).

Noddings, N. (2013). *Education and democracy in the 21st century.* New York, NY: Teachers College Press.

Noguera, P., Darling-Hammond, L., & Friedlaender, D. (2017). Equal opportunity for deeper learning. In R. Heller, R. E. Wolfe, & A. Steinberg (Eds.), *Rethinking readiness: Deeper learning for college, work, and life* (pp. 81–104). Cambridge, MA: Harvard Education Press.

Oakes, J. (1985). *Keeping track: How schools structure inequality.* New Haven, CT: Yale University Press.

O'Day, J. A., & Smith, M. S. (2016). Quality and equality in American education: Systemic problems, systemic solutions. In I. Kirsch and H. Braun (Eds.), *The dynamics of opportunity in America: Evidence and perspectives* (pp. 297–358). Springer Open and Educational Testing Service. Retrieved from https://link .springer.com/chapter/10.1007/978-3-319-25991-8_9

Orellana, M. F. (2009). *Translating childhoods: Immigrant youth, language and culture.* New Brunswick, NJ: Rutgers University Press.

Orellana, M. F., & Gutierrez, K. D. (2006). What's the problem? Constructing *different* genres for the study of English Learners. *Research in the Teaching of English*, *41*(1), 118–123.

Pellegrino, J. W., & Hilton, M. (2012). *Education for life and work: Developing transferable knowledge and skills in the 21st Century.* Washington, DC: National Academies Press.

Plyler v. Doe, 457 U.S. 202 (1982).

Ruiz, R. (1984). Orientations in language planning. *NABE Journal, 8*(2), 15–34.

Singer, A., & Myers, D. (2016, September). *Labor force growth increasingly depends on immigrants and their children.* Washington, DC: Urban Institute. Retrieved from https://www.urban.org/urban-wire/labor-force-growth-increasingly -depends-immigrants-and-their-children

Sugerman, J., & Geary, C. (2018, August). English Learners in California: Demographics, outcomes, and state accountability policies. Washington, DC: Migration Policy Institute. Retrieved from https://www.migrationpolicy.org/research /english-learners-demographics-outcomes-state-accountability-policies

Tyack, D., & Cuban, L. (1995). *Tinkering toward utopia: A century of public school reform.* Cambridge, MA: Harvard University Press.

U.S. Department of Education. (2016). Non-regulatory guidance: English Learners and Title III of the Elementary and Secondary Education Act (ESEA), as amended by the Every Student Succeeds Act (ESSA). Retrieved from https://www2.ed .gov/policy/elsec/leg/essa/essatitleiiiguidenglishlearners92016.pdf

Valdés, G. (2003). *Expanding definitions of giftedness: The case of young interpreters from immigrant communities.* Mahwah, NJ: Lawrence Erlbaum.

Valdés, G., Bunch, G. C., Snow, C. E., & Lee, C. (2005). Enhancing the development of students' language(s). In L. Darling-Hammond, J. Bransford, P. LePage, K. Hammerness, & H. Duffy (Eds.), *Preparing teachers for a changing world: What teachers should learn and be able to do* (pp. 126–168). San Francisco, CA: Jossey-Bass.

Valdés, G., Capitelli, S., & Alvarez, L. (2011). Realistic expectations: English language learners and the acquisition of "academic" English. In *Latino children learning English: Steps in the journey*. New York, NY: Teachers College Press.

Valdés, G., Kibler, A., & Walqui, A. (2014). *Changes in the expertise of ESL professionals: Knowledge and action in an era of new standards*. Alexandria, VA: TESOL International Association. Retrieved from http://www.tesol.org/docs/default -source/papers-and-briefs/professional-paper-26-march-2014.pdf?sfvrsn=4

Valdés, G., Poza, L., & Brooks, M. (2014). Educating students who do not speak the societal language: The social construction of language learner categories. *Profession*. Retrieved from https://profession.mla.hcommons.org/2014/10/09 /educating-students-who-do-not-speak-the-societal-language/

van Lier, L., & Walqui, A. (2012). Language and the Common Core State Standards. Paper presented at the Understanding Language Conference, Stanford, CA. Retrieved from http://ell.stanford.edu/papers/language

VanPatten, B. (2003). Some givens about second language acquisition. In *From input to output: A teacher's guide to second language acquisition* (pp. 9–24). Boston, MA: McGraw-Hill.

Vygotsky, L. (1962). *Thought and language*. Cambridge, MA: MIT Press.

Vygotsky, L. (1978). *Mind in society*. Cambridge, MA: Harvard University Press.

Walqui, A. (2005). Who are our students? In P. A. Richard-Amato & M. A. Snow (Eds.), *Academic success for English language learners* (pp. 7–21). White Plains, NY: Longman.

Walqui, A., & van Lier, L. (2010). *Scaffolding the academic success of adolescent English language learners: A pedagogy of promise*. San Francisco, CA: WestEd.

Westheimer, J. (2015). *What kind of citizen? Educating our children for the common good*. New York, NY: Teachers College Press.

Yosso, T. (2005). Whose culture has capital? A critical race theory discussion of community cultural wealth. *Race, Ethnicity, and Education, 8*, 69–91.

CHAPTER 2

What Is Quality Learning for English Learners?

Aída Walqui and George C. Bunch

How can teachers design and enact stimulating, demanding, well-supported lessons to transform what is currently offered to many English Learners, which too often consists of simplified, discrete, and superficial work; teacher-dominated patterns of instruction; and unenticing materials? In this chapter, we provide classroom examples to anchor discussions of the significant changes in thinking that teachers and schools need to undertake to *amplify* the curriculum and instruction available to English Learners and to address the 21st-century competencies laid out in Chapter 1. When these changes are enacted, they result in offering English Learners powerful learning opportunities that realize their full potential and develop the knowledge, dispositions, and skills they need to live productive and socially responsible lives. This chapter also elaborates on the theoretical framework for designing quality learning opportunities that we will unpack in Chapter 3 and illustrate in the remaining chapters of the book. While the chapter—as well as the book as a whole—focuses on English Learners' opportunities to engage in substantive and generative subject matter learning in English, the ideas presented here also apply to classes being taught in students' home languages.

QUALITY LEARNING FOR ENGLISH LEARNERS

To realize English Learners' immense potential, we promote an ambitious, amplified, "high challenge, high support" pedagogy. This approach offers a way of bringing together consistent ideas from multiple, overlapping orientations to illuminate a process through which students learn under optimal circumstances. More specifically, our pedagogical stance builds from the coherent weaving of several perspectives emanating from second language acquisition (Ortega, 2008, 2016), sociocultural theory (Kozulin, Gindis, Ageyev, & Miller, 2003; Lantolf & Thorne, 2006; van Lier, 1996, 2001; Vygotsky, 1962, 1976, 1978), educational sociolinguistics (Gibbons, 2009;

Hammond, 2014), the ecology of learning and the concept of affordances (Larsen-Freeman, 2013, 2014; van Lier, 2000, 2004), and general education theory and research (Schwab, 1996; Shulman, 1996; among many others).

Central to this process is the design and enactment of lessons that have students working at the edge of their ability (Bruner, 1996), *beyond* their level of comfort, participating in activities that offer them support and that eventually enable them to appropriate important intellectual tools they will be able to use independently in other relevant contexts in the future. This proposal also assumes that language learners bring valuable resources to the educational encounter and that—if provided the right invitations and support—they will willingly engage and learn. It also assumes that the role of educators is *proleptic*, meaning that teachers anticipate in advance the realization of students' potential and treat students accordingly. To use Leont'ev's phrase, education helps learners "become who they are not yet" (as quoted in Bronfenbrenner, 1979). This stance contrasts sharply with orientations toward teaching and learning that assume that English Learners should not engage in difficult tasks until they are "linguistically ready" to do so.

In this ambitious pedagogy, teachers are pivotal in several ways:

1. In *designing* environments and opportunities for students to engage in activity that develops learners' autonomy, agency, and voice within democratic, participatory contexts;
2. In *enacting* these plans while at the same time observing how students take the invitations, interpreting evidence from their students as learning takes place;
3. In *reflecting on* what is working, what is no longer needed, and what assistance must be provided next in order to keep students growing in intended (and unexpected) ways; and
4. In *creating* equitable environments in their classes and school, environments that support students' backgrounds, value their contributions, and build on them to advance their multilingualism, interculturalism, and participation in society.

We elaborate on three of these aspects in this chapter: *design, enactment,* and *reflection,* including the process of observation and assessment in which teachers continuously engage to redesign and enact instruction in order to ensure learners meet the goals.

English Learners, like all students, apprentice attitudes and abilities in classrooms through meaningful participation that provides opportunities to "appropriate" ideas and skills. Thus, making concepts, practices, and language their own will make it possible for students individually to re-create them in future opportunities to use them in powerful, responsive, and creative ways. Students' appropriations, their ownership and personal use of newly developed practices, and their future performances will manifest their growing *autonomy*—that is, their ability to stand on their own two feet while continuing to learn in school and beyond. The sense of feeling in control as they participate in novel applications of knowledge and practice builds students' *agency*. As students exercise their agency and growing autonomy, they develop unique, personal ways of engaging in the practices of the community with whom they are interacting and the right to be heard; that is, they grow their *voice*. Participation, engagement, a sense of belonging, gradual development of competencies, joy, the building of stamina and perseverance—all these feelings and actions characterize classes where quality learning is alive.

KEY TENETS

What, then, defines quality learning for English Learners? In the remainder of this chapter, we discuss key tenets that inform the construction and enactment of quality learning opportunities and provide classroom examples that illustrate them.

1. Development emerges in social interaction. It is a consequence of, not a prerequisite for, learning.
2. Quality learning is deliberately and contingently scaffolded.
3. Quality school learning focuses on substantive and generative disciplinary practices.
4. During learning, English Learners simultaneously develop conceptual, analytic, and language practices.
5. When it comes to the development of language practices, quality learning opportunities for English Learners focus on form in contextual, contingent, and supportive ways.

1. Development Emerges in Social Interaction. It Is a Consequence of, Not a Prerequisite for, Learning.

The notion of "readiness" is deeply ingrained in American education. It assumes that learning proceeds in predetermined sequences, each of which is required before the next one is attended to. Applied to learning in a second language, that process is considered as linear, one in which students grow linguistically in lockstep fashion, with learning mostly being constructed in the "black box" of the student's head. Talk and interaction are perceived as mere demonstrations that learning is taking place. If learners do not develop as the sequence intends them to, something must be at fault with the students. In those cases, three solutions are offered: courses are repeated, students are "remediated" via alternative arrangements (for example during pull-out sessions), or the intellectual expectations of classes are reduced.

Then, to complicate the situation, if "remedial" instruction is chosen, it tends to be similar to that which did not render positive results in the first place. In this sequential and deterministic view, knowledge and teaching are fixed, and teachers impart it in stages, not necessarily in interconnected ways. This learning leads to superficial, inert knowledge.

Our position on learning builds on Vygotsky's idea of the Zone of Proximal Development (ZPD) (Vygotsky, 1978) and on the work of many others who based their work on notions proposed by the influential Russian psychologist in the early part of the 20th century, especially Leo van Lier (2004). Vygotsky asserted that there is no learning that does not take place ahead of development and that this development is premised on social activity and talk. Consistent with this view, our first tenet proposes that all learners' development in school unfolds because students are offered opportunities to participate in carefully designed interactions that place them beyond their current ability to respond on their own and that support their engagement with practices, with each other, and with the teacher. This proleptic approach emphasizes ripening students' potential and building their futures, rather than lamenting their pasts or being constrained by their current abilities. It also requires deliberate attention to the construction of social engagements that will support and push development.

In our view, classroom talk is much more than the simple manifestation of learning; it *is* learning. Human beings are meaning-makers, and meaning is created through communication. In communication, human beings do not only interpret isolated linguistic elements, such as words and phrases, they also perceive and use paralinguistic (intonation, stress, rhythm) and extra-linguistic features (gesture, distance, pictures, graphics, etc.). Together, these features constitute the affordances offered by the learning context. As students listen to others and perceive their surroundings, they respond in ways that have been modeled for them directly or indirectly in the process of communication. That is, learners approximate ways of thinking and acting in specific contexts that their community models for them. In the process, they find and refine conceptual understandings, practice ways of using them, and enhance their use of phrases, words, texts, and action. Teachers' and classmates' responses to learners' participation in oral activity encourage— or discourage—students' further learning and sense of belonging. From their first words, and through schooling and life, English Learners, and all other students, keep making sense of the world, building knowledge, and evaluating the value of participating through the use of language and interaction. As they do, if welcomed and supported, they become full-fledged members of specific communities of practice.

Consequently, working with the carefully designed supports provided, as well as with peers and their teachers, English Learners grow and gradually become experienced at the concepts and processes intended as the goal for learning. As Vygotsky wrote, "an essential feature of learning is that it creates the zone of proximal development, that is, learning that is placed beyond students' ability to act on their own, awaken[ing] a variety of developmental processes that are able to operate only when the child is interacting with people in his environment and in collaboration with his peers" (Vygotsky, 1978, p. 90).

Importantly, and counter to many American educators' understanding of the term, the zone of proximal development in pedagogical settings is not a fixed attribute of the individual learner, but rather a dynamic, interactive space created to afford a group of learners the opportunity to construct needed understandings. Teachers consider where their students are—in their multiple developmental places—and place learning ahead of all of them. Some students will be faced with immense challenge, while for others the challenge may be closer to their developed ability. However, interacting with each other, learners will support each other's understanding and will grow in tandem, although they will not all develop in exactly the same way. In this view, "mastery" is neither a possible nor desired outcome; rather, the goal is gradual approximations to the ideal knowledge and performance envisioned.

Scaffolding provides students the needed support for engaging in interactive meaning-making (semiotic) activities that begin to realize their potential. The learner in this view is not construed as a passive recipient of knowledge, but as an active "negotiator of meanings, of pathways, of stances, and of identities" (Kramsch, 2003). Education, in this sense, is no longer about *teaching* (as transmission), but about promoting and supporting *learning* as it unfolds.

To be able to grow and begin to appropriate disciplinary language practices, students need purposeful, dynamic, semiotically negotiated supports, including those that focus on linguistic structures of a language, such as grammar and vocabulary, but also on paralinguistic and extralinguistic tools that mediate communication. Elaborating on Gibson's notion of affordances (1979), van Lier (2004) proposed that what learners are exposed to is not "input," a fixed construct, but "affordances" from which they perceive and select those that best fit their experience and the activity in which they are engaged. Affordances present possibilities for action that yield opportunities for the learner, stimulate intersubjectivity (the tacit agreement between interlocutors to make every effort to understand each other), joint attention, and various kinds of linguistic commentary. Affordances do not *cause* development, but they provide learners *opportunities* for development as they perceive, act, interpret, and eventually appropriate ideas, as we will see in action in an activity we describe later on. In van Lier's words:

> The environment is full of meaning potential, especially if it has a rich semiotic budget, which may not be true of all classrooms, textbooks, or pedagogical interactions. The . . . learner . . . has certain abilities, aptitudes, effectiveness, fitness. . . . Affordances are those relationships that provide a "match" between

something in the environment (whether it's a chair or an utterance) and the learner. The affordance fuels perception and activity, and brings about meanings— further affordances and signs, and further higher-level activity as well as more differentiated perception. (p. 96)

In order to design quality opportunities and lessons for English Learners, teachers place their focus on the potential for growth that students carry with them, on the experiences and linguistic repertoires (including their family languages) students bring with them to school, as well as on the intentional provision of supports and affordances that will make specific growth possible.

2. Quality Learning Is Deliberately and Contingently Scaffolded.

As already discussed, English Learners develop discipline-specific practices as a consequence of participating in learning experiences. If these experiences are expertly designed and implemented, they provide students with multiple points of entry, action, and growth. Some of the tasks students are offered will be more routine in structure, although novel in content, while others may be more novel in structure and specifically designed for the learning moment. Whichever the case, tasks provide the temporary supports needed by learners to engage in substantive activity and develop autonomy.

The concept of scaffolding derives from Jerome Bruner's readings of Vygotsky's work. Bruner (1976) proposed the scaffolding metaphor to indicate the pedagogical support offered to assist learners in performing beyond their current development, enabling them in the process to develop further. Scaffolding is temporary assistance grounded on a clear sense of where learning needs to be headed and what efforts and supports need to be invested to get there. Scaffolding *amplifies* the opportunities students have to negotiate meaning and action, working proleptically, constructing what students will be able to do in the future.

Scaffolding is both planned and responsive (Walqui & van Lier, 2010). It is deliberately constructed in lessons as tasks that offer students support to participate successfully in a given activity to accomplish a specific purpose. It is also unplanned, offered the moment an unanticipated need arises. It is planned insofar as it is the pedagogical design that supports students' exploration beyond what they know and are able to do; it is responsive because scaffolding is also the contingent support offered after observing how learners engage in the planned scaffolding, determining what is developing well and what requires further assistance to mature.

The design of rigorous and enticing lessons that include the right kind of scaffolding is a complex professional endeavor, one that can be an enriching professional enterprise for teachers. It also presents educators with challenges. One such challenge is the mandate in some schools or districts that teachers move their instruction along "pacing guides" or follow other sorts of predetermined curricular progressions. If the provision of learning opportunities for students must respond to their needs, pacing should not be mandated.

Successful scaffolding ultimately renders itself unnecessary as learners grow and develop their autonomy. When specific scaffolds are no longer needed, however, other scaffolds will be necessary to support further learner development. Thus, scaffolding always requires that teachers engage in close observation of their students' actions to ascertain how it is working, and whether it is still needed as it stands or needs to be modified to respond to emerging needs and ongoing development.

Although the concept of scaffolding was first proposed in the late 1970s and has been widely used in education since that time, it is still a construct that invites misunderstandings. Scaffolds are often construed as a way of reducing or simplifying the complexity of the task at hand. For example, in some curricular approaches, scaffolding is interpreted in closed, mechanistic ways such as asking students to practice a linguistic form by filling in blanks in sentences that require the specified target form. The same repeated fill-in-the-blanks activity takes place across multiple, disconnected sentences, thus promoting atomistic, superficial, inert learning. This is neither the process nor goal of scaffolding.

Other misunderstandings of the concept have resulted in conceptual and linguistic simplifications or in the offering of exercises that have students repeatedly apply discrete linguistic forms singled out for attention, without engaging their agency or creativity. In this sense, scaffolding has been wrongly interpreted to mean *any* assistance, even teacher-driven "steps" to get students from point A to point B without fostering students' autonomy.

Scaffolding is best conceived as the support that assists students in gaining increasingly deeper and more complex understandings, simultaneously promoting their agency, the sense of knowing what to do in specific academic situations. Agency develops as a result of inviting students to apply practices in meaningful, collaborative environments. Through this engagement, students gain awareness of the (subject-specific) practices that constitute the goal of the lesson, the way they work, and their purposes. The goal is for students to eventually gain conscious control of practices and to finally appropriate them and apply them independently to novel, relevant situations (Walqui & van Lier, 2010).

Practical demonstrations throughout this book will highlight two aspects of scaffolding that are important to teachers' work: structure and process.

Scaffolding Structures. These structures—which propose the way in which students will interact—invite students to build their understanding as they work with each other and offer opportunities for all students in a class to actively participate. Structures create predictability since they entail students' participation in routine moves. Structures translate into tasks, the specific routines used for a purpose that are offered students to actively participate, and thus develop. For example, the task we call The Oral Development Jigsaw, described next, has as its goals the development of students' ability to understand the difference between two different types of genre: descriptions and narratives, and generate two different types of text. The task ensures that all students develop awareness of work entailed in understanding and crafting the two genres, and that all students begin to gain familiarity with each.

To understand the work of planned scaffolding, let us analyze the structure of The Oral Development Jigsaw, a learning task designed by Aída for use in her language and content courses when she was a high school teacher. The structure can be used in multiple disciplines, including science and social studies. As described here, it involves students working with four pictures depicting characters involved in action (such as those shown in Figure 2.1).

The Jigsaw starts with students seated in groups of four called Base Groups. In our example, which comes from a combination English as a Second Language (ESL)/English Language Arts (ELA) class, the teacher does the following:

1. Explains the *purpose* of descriptions (e.g., to paint pictures with words so that somebody who has not seen a scene can imagine it); their *organization* (setting and the details: where the scene takes place, who is present, what characters look like, what they are doing, other interesting relevant details); and offers *formulaic expressions* that are typically used in descriptions (*The picture we have shows . . . The scene takes place in . . . In this picture we can observe . . .*).

2. In order to practice using these guidelines in their descriptions, new groups of four students are formed by sending each member of the Base Group to a new group, known as Expert Groups. Four different pictures will be simultaneously described in the class by Expert Groups. Students within Expert Groups work together to come up with a joint description of their scene. While students negotiate the description collaboratively, each student will be responsible for describing their picture when they go back to their Base Group. This step simulates real-life descriptions, in which interlocutors usually have not seen what is being described to them. To prepare students for this task, the teacher collects the pictures and invites them to rehearse the descriptions to see if they need extra support from peers or the teacher.

3. Back in their original Base Groups, students describe their pictures to their teammates using words and body language to enhance their descriptions.

4. To explore the four descriptions further, students are invited to ask each other questions as they mentally connect ideas and ask for elaborations.

5. Up to this point, students have engaged in practicing descriptions minimally three times: as they construct them, during rehearsal, and when they communicate their description to their Base Group that has not seen their picture.

6. Next, to move into narratives, teacher and students discuss the *purposes* for narratives (stories, myths), how they are *usually organized* in English, and *typical phrases* that signal event transition in a story (once upon a time, then, after that, meanwhile, finally, etc.) are offered.

7. To practice their new understanding of narrative texts, students are now asked to construct a story in their Base Groups, using the same pictures. As they link scenes and add details to construct their narrative, students have to be creative, understanding that their story has to be interesting, coherent, and make sense.

8. So far, the activity has been oral, but once the story is completed, all students write their team's full narratives. Their stories will be read to their classmates—taking turns—so that the whole class can appreciate the varied stories that emerged from the same set of pictures.

This Oral Development Jigsaw structures the activity so that all students participate, having clear rules that move them from simpler (static descriptions) to increasingly more complex practices (dynamic descriptions and abstract construction of stories).

Scaffolding Process. The second critical aspect of scaffolding is what it makes possible: dynamic interactions that, while more or less predictable, are unique. What any student may suggest, and what the group may agree to accept, is not to be dictated by the teacher nor by one student alone. Affordances—pictures, suggestions to use their hands, gestures that accompany utterances—are built into the environment for students to perceive, act on, participate, and learn. However, what causes learning is not scaffolding nor affordances, but the active engagement of students. As a team decides how to construct their description, and later on their narrative, each student advances from where they were before, developing more robust conceptual, analytic, and language practices as a result of their collaborative work with peers and their environment.

Observe the following interaction as a team of four in an Advanced Beginner English as a New Language/ELA class puts together a story based on the four pictures depicted in Figure 2.1. The transcript comes from Ms.

Ng's English as a New Language combination Beginners/Intermediate class at MS 131 in Chinatown, New York City. Reading the transcript, it will be evident that a student called Chen talks the most, while Hue talks the least. However, when they write their story, and practice presenting it, Hue will get at least two more opportunities to practice the newly gained ability to construct narratives, and by the end of the 45-minute class she, and all her classmates, will have grown:

> *Chen:* Yeah, he looks sad, right? walking on the street, hands in his pocket. Found ten-dollar bill, then go to market. And he, they buy books—
>
> *Xi:* Yeah, buy some—
>
> *Chen:* Buy cartoon books—
>
> *Xi:* No, I think, I think this is the first one (signaling to partner who was responsible for describing a different picture), the one on the street, and he saw ten-dollar bill, and then he went to market and—
>
> *Chen:* How about sad first, sad first—
>
> *Ben:* No, not really—
>
> *Chen:* Sad first—
>
> *Ben:* Not really—
>
> *Chen:* Walking on the street—
>
> *Xi:* Yeah—
>
> *Chen:* Yeah, on the street, right? He sad, he sad, right? and he on the street. On the street he found—
>
> *Xi:* Ten-dollar bill.
>
> *Chen:* And . . .
>
> *Xi:* Went to the market to buy something.
>
> *Chen:* Buy the books!
>
> *Xi:* To buy books and, happy ending! There, "Lucky Boy" (the name for the story they agreed on).
>
> *Chen:* Sad first, found money—sad, money, market, books.
>
> *Ben:* No, it's like a street—
>
> *Xi:* I don't think it's a market.
>
> *Hue:* Yeah—A lot of people selling stuff on the street.
>
> *Xi:* It is like a bookstore, isn't it?
>
> *Chen:* Uh, book market—
>
> *Hue:* No, they sell different kinds of stuff.
>
> *Chen:* Okay. Book market.
>
> *Ben:* No! No, it's not book market!
>
> *Chen:* What's it then? That's where you're selling a book.
>
> *Ben:* It's bigger than selling books, many things are selling. It's not book market.

Students' interactions as they try to organize their stories are made possible because the structure of the task supports their work. It assists them in understanding the features of two different genres and crafting them collaboratively. Without the structure, such rich process would not have been possible. As we will see below, this structure also makes possible their ability to construct a narrative.

Another essential aspect of scaffolding is that it promotes the emergence of novelty. Students use what they learned in new contexts. In our example, the stories emerging from class are unique and rich in diverse details, although they are based on the same four pictures. This makes the task exciting for students, and as they listen to their peer's stories, they learn new details they may incorporate in future narratives. We include one story as read by the students:

> *Ben:* The title of our story is "Lucky Boy." The setting is on the street, in the neighborhood. The characters are Danny and Bobby. One summer day, Danny go out to buy a gift for his brother named Bobby. They are twins; today is their birthday.
>
> *Xi:* Bobby stayed at home. Meanwhile, Danny is walking on a street. He saw a ten-dollar bill, and he was so surprised.
>
> *Chen:* He's thinking about how to use the money to buy a birthday gift for his brother. He goes to the outdoor market to look for a gift.
>
> *Hue:* Then he buy a book, he buy a comic book, and bring the book to his brother. And then, he shared the book, and they are very happy to have these books.

As illustrated in Figure 2.1, pictures required for the Oral Development Jigsaw must each present the same character, while the setting, activity, and other characters depicted have to vary.

The examples above evidence that English Learners learn and develop along different trajectories, thus teachers need to adjust scaffolding contingently based on a continuous stream of specific and timely evidence gathered through observation and interaction during instruction (Walqui & Heritage, 2012). As students' emerging understandings and misconceptions are revealed, this awareness of their current performance relative to the lesson goal guides the teacher's next actions and supports.

Although widely misunderstood, the ZPD is the area where *interpersonal* activity, with the support of deliberate scaffolding, engages learners in substantive disciplinary, focused interaction that leads to *intrapersonal* development and the appropriation of conceptual understandings, analytical skills, and the language required to express them.

It is also important in scaffolding and formative assessment that teachers be selective in addressing errors and contingent in providing feedback

Figure 2.1. Pictures for the Oral Development Jigsaw

(Walqui & Heritage, 2018). Had Ms. Ng corrected students as they were enthusiastically constructing their stories, she would have stopped the flow of communication and their enjoyment. New invitations should be directed to ripening what is budding growth, and to redirect what may be misconstrued. This may mean teacher action does not need to be immediate but can wait until the next class. During Ms. Ng's 45-minute class, all the steps in the Jigsaw get done. After teams of four students constructed their narratives and wrote their stories, each team was invited to share their story with the class, with each student reading a part. Having developed new practices, each student during the next class wrote their own new narrative about other situations, which was edited by the team and shared with the whole class in a classroom publication.

3. Quality School Learning Focuses on Substantive, Generative Disciplinary Practices.

Realizing the potential that English Learners bring to school requires that teachers see their students both for who they are at the moment, full of resources and immense potential, and for who they will be at the end of a unit of teaching, at the end of a course, at the end of their school studies, and in productive and responsible life in their communities and the world (Walqui & van Lier, 2010). Successful growth in classes with English Learners entails reciprocal responsibility. Students make the effort to do their best in terms of rigorous participation and, understanding the goal of their learning, keep working to meet their goals. Teachers, on the other hand, have the responsibility to provide students with supportive and safe environments where the fear of failure is mitigated by the sense that with errors come new opportunities to learn. This tacit agreement also requires that as teachers teach, they increase their own depth of subject matter knowledge and disciplinary understanding and the ability to translate them into pedagogical action that builds students' conceptual, analytical, and linguistic strengths while fostering their agency and autonomy (van Lier, 2008).

In our model, the teacher's job is to "teach" less (i.e., lecturing from the front of the room) and instead to create more opportunities for students to engage in carefully crafted activity and thus learn—while the teacher formatively assesses how learning is unfolding to prepare new learning opportunities that will support new growth.

We propose that a rigorous lesson focuses on the understanding of key concepts, texts, problems, and phenomena related to an important theme in the discipline being studied. As students engage with pivotal concepts and their interconnections that build the discipline, anchor concepts become clearer to them, enabling them to deepen and expand their knowledge in an organized, productive manner.

As the examples throughout the book illustrate, teachers' depth of disciplinary understanding becomes essential as they select what to teach, what to emphasize, and how to structure learning opportunities for students. Not everything in the curriculum can be taught, nor should it be, when what teachers are after is quality learning opportunities for English Learners (and other students). To move beyond what has been characterized by many as curriculum that is "a mile wide and an inch deep," teachers need to focus on the key constructs and relationships in the theme studied.

If English Learners' learning has to focus on key conceptual understandings as well as analytic and language practices, then accomplishing deeper, increasingly interconnected knowledge and the ability to use it creatively requires a spiraling, rather than a linear, curricular organization. With this model, key ideas are introduced with the expectation that they will not be understood fully by every student in class. However, because these ideas are so important in the discipline, they will reoccur time and time again, with each reoccurrence affording students the opportunity to revisit and expand these ideas and practices through different contexts, solidifying and deepening their understandings. Examples of spiraling curriculum are presented and explored in this book.

4. During Learning, English Learners Simultaneously Develop Conceptual, Analytic, and Language Practices.

The traditional separation of language and content, which offers simplified content to English Learners who have not yet "mastered" English, has not proved productive for them. Nor has it promoted quality learning opportunities that focus on important ideas in a subject area, unpack how these ideas interconnect, and introduce students to practices engaged in by disciplinary experts.

We propose then that conceptual understandings, analytic skills, and the language required to express them develop simultaneously, as a result of apprenticeship into disciplinary practices, which entails participation in activity (Valdés, Kibler, & Walqui, 2014; see Figure 2.2). In the Oral Development Jigsaw described earlier, *conceptually* students needed to understand first the nature of descriptive texts and then that of narrative texts. They also needed to become aware of how both genres differ in terms of purpose, organization, and preferred language use. In terms of purpose, a description has an interlocutor painting pictures with words to illustrate for someone else what they saw. Thus, it was important to convey the setting of the picture first (the landscape against which characters and actions will be depicted). *Analytically,* students needed to know how these two different types of texts are organized. In the description, for example, following the establishment of the setting, characters needed to be introduced, as well as their characteristics and activities. The sequence in which these elements are announced makes a difference in terms of the interlocutor's ability to imagine the picture. Thus, having a sense of audience is essential for the analytical practice of description. Finally, specific *language* is routinely used to convey the different scenes, the organization of events and the marking of the sequence of events by—as seen in the examples—using connectors of time.

In their final products, we see the emerging proficiency of the students. Throughout human history, the purpose of narratives has been both to entertain and to teach lessons. Stories are typically organized sequentially: a setting and a character are introduced, the character is portrayed as possessing certain characteristics, then something happens to the character and the resolution to the situation changes the character. Typical expressions that move the action include terms such as *one day, because, suddenly,* and *then.* We see this process unfolding in the following story constructed by a second group in Ms. Ng's class:

> *Jade:* The title of our story is "The Lucky Day." The setting is out on the street. The character is Alex and Mike.
>
> *Alex:* One day Alex went walking alone in the street. He look sad, bored, because he saw, he saw a comic book and he couldn't buy it because he used his allowance, and all his money, in clothes. He wants to buy comic books but don't save one cent to use the money and buy unnecessary things.
>
> *Roger:* Suddenly a ten-dollar bill popped into Alex's sight. It's like a wick in the darkness. His face full of happiness, he pick it up and put the bill inside his pocket. But he didn't put away his money completely—the half ten-dollar bill stuck out his pocket. Then he walked out of crowded market and into the bookstore.
>
> *Mike:* He can't wait to tell his best friend Mike what happened to him today. He shared the comic book with him when he gets back home. The happiness, the big smile hanging in their face all day long.

As seen in the excerpt above, conceptual, analytic, and language development function as sociocultural formations, resulting from the interactions of students with each other, with teachers, with constructs, with a budget of environmental affordances, and with the culture that is constantly established in the class. Learning takes place in the space between students' current and planned development, and it is made possible by teachers who deliberately build opportunities that assist learners in approximating the set destination: the acquisition of conceptual, analytic, and language practices. In the transcript above, the four students involved are at different places in their development, but in their collaborative interactions they support each others' growth in terms of understanding the concepts of description and narrative, analytical practices such as the organization of events, and language such as the expressions that will convey events and transitions.

Figure 2.2 illustrates the relationship among the conceptual, analytic, and language practices we have been discussing, and shows how disciplinary experts share conceptual understandings that are key in their field, run

Figure 2.2. Disciplinary Practices

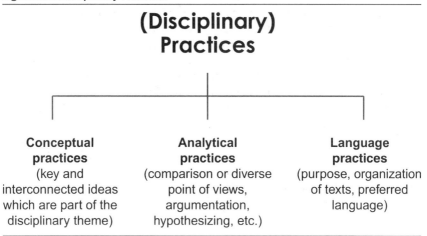

(Disciplinary)
Practices

Conceptual practices	Analytical practices	Language practices
(key and interconnected ideas which are part of the disciplinary theme)	(comparison or diverse point of views, argumentation, hypothesizing, etc.)	(purpose, organization of texts, preferred language)

Source: Valdés, Kibler, & Walqui, 2014.

ideas through distinct mental operations, and tend to use language in a specialized way. Building on conceptions of "communities of practice" originally proposed by Lave & Wenger (1991), apprenticeship into disciplinary communities entails a context in which (1) learners are gradually introduced into the disciplinary community of practice, one that shares understandings, norms, beliefs, actions, artifacts, and specific ways of expressing itself; (2) apprentices are considered capable, and they are supported and validated by masters and peers as they approximate their full engagement in communities of practice; (3) apprentices—while approximating masters—have full view of what the community considers accomplished performance of the discipline; and (4) apprentices are not expected to develop in exactly the same way nor at the same time, and they are offered multiple contingent opportunities to keep enhancing their new practices. While students' growing sense of autonomy is the goal, "autonomy in an ecological approach does not mean independence or individualism. . . . It means having the authorship of one's actions, having the voice that speaks one's words, and being emotionally connected to one's actions and speech . . . within one's community of practice" (van Lier, 2004, p. 8).

Users of new languages, apprenticing into specific practices in that language, are surrounded by a community that models those practices and invites them to use their nascent language with an emphasis on participation in exchanges that aim for them to be increasingly more successful. Success, in this sense, is defined by meaning-making through engagement in effective action (i.e., students accomplish the purposes of the task), although their responses may be expressed with some formal imperfections in language production. Paralinguistic and extralinguistic affordances help students perceive, convey, understand, and eventually appropriate ideas. During this performance by learners, it is important to value what students can do, and it is equally important—both for learners and for teachers—to develop a clear understanding of what remains ahead to be worked on. If interlocutors value English Learners' meaningful communication, their responses confer legitimacy on students (i.e., they belong in the encounter, they have the right to participate and the right to speak—errors and all). In the process, students' agency is fostered, as we saw in the transcript from Ms. Ng's ESL class.

Viewing disciplinary practices as encompassing conceptual understandings, analytic tasks, and the language required to develop them and engage successfully in academic activity does not eliminate the possibility of focusing on one of the subcomponents when needed, in very situated, contingent ways. An explicit focus on conceptual understandings and how to compare, analyze, and the like is essential, as is a focus on language features. However, such a focus must occur together with, and in the service of, subject-matter learning (Kelley, Lesaux, Kieffer, & Faller, 2010).

5. When It Comes to the Development of Language Practices, Quality Learning Opportunities for English Learners Focus on Form in Contextual, Contingent, and Supportive Ways.

As the most important tool for learning, language mediates the development of valued practices in a subject matter area and, as such, it needs to be attended to purposefully. This attention, however, cannot be at the center of learning opportunities, since language is *the vehicle* for learning concepts, and using those concepts through analytic tasks constitutes the central goal of these efforts. However, when language, the tool that mediates work and builds disciplinary and conceptual understandings and practices, stands in the way of expression, a focus on its specific, contextually relevant use is essential. In other words, the redirection needs to focus on the concrete expression that impedes understanding and not be an excuse for a lesson on decontextualized language.

Two decades ago, Michael Long (1996) drew a useful distinction between approaches to learning English as a second language: they either focused on *forms* or they focused on *form*. Applying the distinction to our situation, a focus on *forms* results when the goal of education for English Learners is to learn how language works in general with a focus on the production of well-formed sentences. As a result, language forms are taught for their own sake, and the emphasis and organization of a course—and of teachers' actions—prioritize grammatical, lexical, or morphological structures. In contrast, a focus on *form* occurs when the emphasis is placed on specific meaningful social activity. In this case, the focus on language is limited to work on an erroneous form that impedes understanding. In these situations, which are part of a larger effort at meaning-making, "the formal knowledge remains connected and can bear fruit in terms of further learning" (van Lier, 2001, p. 259).

An example of a nonproductive focus on forms occurs in the common practice of "frontloading" vocabulary at the beginning of a lesson that dedicates prime time to "teach" a list of isolated words before conceptual understandings are addressed. This focus on lexis—or on grammatical structures—runs the risk of producing superficial knowledge that remains inert, or, even worse, the shoehorning of content lessons to produce artificial opportunities for students to practice the vocabulary (Bruna, Vann, & Escudero, 2007).

Another example of a common practice derived from curricula focused on forms is the explicit "teaching" (i.e., explanation) of when to use a specific verb tense, followed by applications of the rule that ask students to fill in the blanks with the correct form of the verb in a list of eight or ten sentences that are unrelated. In this case, students spend time quietly doing busy work that is superficial, nongenerative, and lacking context or meaning.

This tenet highlights the need for shifting conceptions of language teaching and learning more generally. Starting in the 1950s and influenced by structural linguistics, ESL classes were designed around a sequential development of syntactic and lexical aspects of English, an orientation that still dominates some ESL and world language instruction, both at the K–12 and post-secondary level. The underlying assumption was that there were simpler syntactic forms (the present simple, for example) and more complex ones (present and past perfect) and that this "natural" order suggested the organization of curricula from easier to more complex structures (Mackey, 1967). Having selected the grammatical forms, curriculum developers and the teachers who worked with these materials looked for examples of texts that used them or created those texts.

Instead, as explored through the Oral Development Jigsaw, students need to get a sense of general aspects of the "text" (whether written or oral discourse), including the purpose that guided its creation, the way different types of texts (stories, speeches, instructions) tend to be organized (what typically comes first, next, and how these texts tend to end), and the usual language used to present and link ideas. To use a common expression, they need to know they are in a forest first to then start making sense of and analyzing the trees. This sense of going from the broader understanding of a text to the specific is not a new idea. It is just one that has not taken much hold in schools.

English Learners learn to use their new language investing all the devices they have at their disposal to make sense of what is said and to express themselves. For them, language is *action* (Walqui & van Lier, 2010), which involves the use of affordances. Furthermore, their ability to express themselves and understand others is always evolving, thus the term used for this process: *languaging* (Tocalli-Beller & Swain, 2007). As we will see when we discuss planning and responsive implementation of plans in the subject matter areas, students' products are never static; they are always in the process of becoming increasingly more accomplished. Languaging is an accurate verb to describe their efforts to increasingly approximate the norm and surpass it.

The most important concept we are trying to convey is that language is a semiotic tool that enables human beings to develop higher mental processes (Vygotsky, 1978). While cognitive theory emphasized the role of the individual and activity in the "black box" of the mind, sociocultural theorists following Vygotsky placed learning squarely in interactional activity:

> Human development is the product of a broader system than just the system of a person's individual functions, specifically, systems of social connections and relations, of collective forms of behavior and social cooperation (Vygotsky, 1978, p. 41).

Examples of how teachers can provide students with an explicit focus on form that is integrated into meaning-making and is not atomistic are provided in the following chapters as we and our colleagues demonstrate and explain how to amplify the curriculum in subject matter areas.

REFERENCES

Brofenbrenner, U. (1979). *The ecology of human development: Experiments by nature and design.* Cambridge, MA: Harvard University Press.

Bruna, K., Vann, R., & Escudero, M. (2007). What's language got to do with it? A case study of academic language instruction in a high school "English Learner Science" class. *Journal of English for Academic Purposes, 6*(1), 36–54.

Bruner, J. (1976). Prelinguistic prerequisites of speech. In R. Campbell & P. Smith (Eds.), *Recent advances in the psychology of language*, 4a, 199–214. New York, NY: Plenum Press.

Bruner, J. (1996). *The culture of education.* Cambridge, MA: Harvard University Press.

Gibbons, P. (2009). *English Learners, academic literacy and thinking: Learning in the challenge zone.* New York, NY: Heinemann.

Gibson, J. J. (1979). *The ecological approach to visual perception.* Hillsdale, NJ: Erlbaum.

Hammond, J. (2014). *The transition of refugee students from intensive English centres to mainstream high schools: Current practices and future possibilities.* Sydney, NSW: Department of Education and Communities.

Kelley, J., Lesaux, N., Kieffer, M., & Faller, S. (2010). Effective academic vocabulary instruction in the urban middle school. *Reading Teacher, 64*(1), 5–14.

Kozulin, A., Gindis, B., Ageyev, V., & Miller, S. (Eds.). (2003). *Vygotsky's educational theory in cultural context.* Cambridge, UK: Cambridge University Press.

Kramsch, C. (Ed.). (2003). *Language acquisition and language socialization: Ecological perspectives.* London, UK & New York, NY: Bloomsbury Academic.

Lantolf, J. P., & Thorne, S. L. (2006). *Sociocultural theory and the genesis of second language development*. Oxford, UK: Oxford University Press.

Larsen-Freeman, D. (2013). Complex, dynamic systems and technemes. In J. Arnold Morgan & T. Murphey (Eds.), *Meaningful action: Earl Stevick's influence on language teaching*. Cambridge, UK: Cambridge University Press.

Larsen-Freeman, D. (2014). Saying what we mean: Making the case for second language acquisition to become second language development. *Language Teaching/* FirstView Article/April 2014, 1–15.

Lave, J., & Wenger, E. (1991). *Situated learning: Legitimate peripheral participation*. New York, NY: Cambridge University Press.

Long, M. (1996). The role of the linguistic environment in second language acquisition. In W. C. Ritchie & T. K. Bhatia (Eds.), *Handbook of second language acquisition* (pp. 413–468). San Diego, CA: Academic Press.

Mackey, W. (1967). *Language teaching analysis*. London, UK: Longman.

Ortega, L. (2008). *Understanding second language acquisition*. New York, NY: Routledge.

Ortega, L. (2016). Foreword. In R. Blake & E. Zysik (Eds.), *El español y la lingüística aplicada*. Washington, DC: Georgetown University Press.

Schwab, J. J. (1996). The practical four: Something for curriculum professors to do. In E. R. Holli (Ed.), *Transforming curriculum for a culturally diverse society*. Mahwah, NJ: Erlbaum.

Shulman, L. S. (1996). Paradigms and research programs in the study of teaching: A contemporary perspective. In M. C. Wittrock (Ed.), *Handbook of research on teaching* (3rd ed., pp. 3–36). New York, NY: MacMillan.

Tocalli-Beller, A., & Swain, M. (2007). Riddles and puns in the ESL classroom: Adults talk to learn. In A. Mackey (Ed.), *Conversational interaction in second language acquisition* (pp. 143–167). New York, NY: Oxford University Press.

Valdés, G., Kibler, A., & Walqui, A. (2014, March). *Changes in the expertise of ESL professionals: Knowledge and action in an era of new standards*. Alexandria, VA: TESOL International Association.

van Lier, L. (1996). *Interaction in the language curriculum: Awareness, autonomy, and authenticity*. London, UK: Longman.

van Lier, L. (2000). From input to affordance: Social-interactive learning from an ecological perspective. In J. P. Lantolf (Ed.), *Sociocultural theory and second language learning* (pp. 155–177). Oxford, UK: Oxford University Press.

van Lier, L. (2001). The role of form in language learning. In M. Bax & J. Zwart (Eds.), *Reflections on language and language learning*. Amsterdam, NL & Philadelphia, PA: John Benjamins Publishing.

van Lier, L. (2004). *The ecology and semiotics of language learning: A sociocultural perspective*. Dordrecht, NL: Kluwer Academic.

van Lier, L. (2008). Agency in the classroom. In J. P. Lantolf & M. E. Poehner (Eds.), *Sociocultural theory and the teaching of second languages* (pp. 136–186). London, UK: Equinox.

Vygotsky, L. (1962). *Thought and language*. Cambridge, MA: MIT Press.

Vygotsky, L. S. (1976). Play and its role in the mental development of the child. In J. Bruner, A. Jolly, & K. Sylva (Eds.), *Play: Its role in development and evolution* (pp. 537–554). Harmondsworth, UK: Penguin Books Ltd.

Vygotsky, L. (1978). *Mind in society*. Cambridge, MA: Harvard University Press.

Walqui, A., & Heritage, M. (2012, January). Instruction for diverse groups of English language learners. Paper presented at the Understanding Language Conference, Stanford, CA.

Walqui, A., & Heritage, M. (2018, Fall). Meaningful classroom talk: Supporting English learners' oral language development. *American Educator*, *42*(3), 18–23.

Walqui, A., & van Lier, L. (2010). *Scaffolding the academic success of English Language Learners. A pedagogy of promise*. San Francisco, CA: WestEd.

CHAPTER 3

Designing the Amplified Lesson

Aída Walqui

In the same way that architects design buildings and use blueprints to achieve their design goals, teachers plan lessons to meet the interests, educational needs, and personal, intellectual, and civic growth of their students. Buildings, as culturally symbolic constructed artifacts, are determined through blueprints based on the purpose for the building, the desires of the future owner, the shape and function of the different rooms to be built, how light and landscape will be used, and other contextual elements. A lesson plan, also a culturally symbolic constructed artifact, selects what students will learn based on the nature of the disciplinary practices to be developed, curricula and standards, the support students will need to apprentice into the selected goals for the lesson, the time available, and other contextual factors.

Teachers make decisions as to how to use what is available, what else will be needed, and how to organize resources and activities so that their deliberately designed lessons render expected results. Furthermore, in the same way in which architectural blueprints for buildings start with consideration of the characteristics of the land where the building will be constructed, a lesson plan must account first for who the learners are and what they bring to the learning activity. These considerations are placed against where the lesson will take them. The lesson constitutes the space between—that is, the road that will lead students from where they are to their destination, the lesson's established goals.

In this chapter, we discuss key elements and decision points in the planning of lessons that seek to develop students' future academic practices in their emergent English. In an increasingly globalized world, the work of developing students' additional language, English in the context we focus on in this book, is equally important to that of continuing the growth of their home languages, be it through coursework or extracurricular activities. Multilingual and intercultural environments are increasingly the norm in school, work, and life. Thus, the design ideas proposed here are equally relevant to the development of academic practices in English Learners' other languages.

We propose that teachers never design accomplished lessons in the abstract. Lessons are uniquely and specifically situated to satisfy particular goals with specific students, under specific situations in a class, school, and time. We also address the choice of texts, the architecture of lessons, and the role and sequence of tasks. Our extensive work with teachers has offered us the opportunity to design, enact, and refine multiple lessons, and we share some scenarios and transcripts from our portfolio of work.

Our use of the construct "lesson" merits elaboration here. As used in this book, a lesson focuses on developing a small set of interrelated key disciplinary practices through deliberately designed tasks that scaffold students' growth through interaction. As discussed in Chapter 2, such practices encompass conceptual, analytic, and language dimensions. To provide an example, we will consider a lesson where the conceptual goals are for students to understand the role of power, the possible rewards and consequences of taking a stand or not when faced with unjust situations, and the notion that protest can bring about societal change. Analytic practices developed in the same lesson center on the critical reading and analysis of multimedia texts and the use of metacognition during reading. Students thereby learn to track their own evolving understanding of texts, solve reading difficulties, self-assess what they understand and don't understand about a text, and learn about what they can do to solve gaps in understanding. The language practices to be developed involve the understanding and formulation of ideas and processes involved.

Given the magnitude of the goals that have to be accomplished, a single lesson cannot be synonymous with a class period. It is not likely for students, and English Learners in particular, to develop deep, substantive, and generative practices in the short time usually allotted to one class period. A lesson's sustained and spiraled revisiting of key themes through analytic, interactive activities invites students to apply the practices time and time again through novel contexts over the course of several days. This sustained engagement makes it possible for students to gradually gain a stronger and clearer grasp of the ideas and their interconnections, as well as to increasingly appropriate higher-order thinking and more precise and eloquent language.

Our comments about the situated nature of lessons so far beg the question of the role of published curricula in creating quality learning opportunities for English Learners and other students. In the United States, published educational materials, and, more recently, open access curricula available online, often constitute the tools teachers work with in class. We take the stance that even the best preexisting curriculum needs to be adapted by teachers to meet the needs of the particular students in their classes. Even if the architecture of the materials and the development of lessons are optimal, one or two tasks will need to be changed to meet the interests, maturational levels, and budding developments of students. If the existing lessons leave much to be desired, then it will take as much or more work to modify them for the kinds of ambitious and supportive goals we are arguing for than the time it would take to start a new design.

While lesson design is a strategic and time-consuming activity, the teacher's responsibility is to craft good lessons and units that follow an inviting, robust, and flexible design in order to facilitate multiple adaptations and successful situated enactments. We recognize that teachers in the United States are typically given curriculum to use in their classes; however, we propose that the hallmark of an accomplished educator is creating and adapting quality curricula. Lesson design is an immensely sophisticated and rewarding professional activity, one that we believe teachers can embrace and grow into if they are provided guidelines and support. With that goal in mind, we propose a framework for lesson design—a task that is ideally carried out in collaboration with peers—and discuss the ways in which it can come to life in classes. At the same time, we believe that much of what this book presents can be used by teachers immediately, including in their efforts to modify—perhaps in small ways at first—the existing and sometimes mandated curriculum that they are expected to teach. We discuss these ideas more fully in Chapter 10.

GETTING STARTED: CONSIDERATIONS AND GUIDELINES

We now elaborate on the situated nature of good lessons. Those of us who have taught in K–12 classrooms and were given the same course to teach two or three times a day, for example an introductory world history class, know that it is impossible to teach the same lesson in exactly the same way, with the same tasks, and at the same pace to different cohorts of students. Each group of students presents unique characteristics and displays idiosyncrasies that need to be met if we want the lesson to be successful. A concept may have already been clarified in one class because either the idea emerged spontaneously or a question was asked, while in another class the concept needs to be introduced for the first time. In one first period class, the pace of activity is faster and students accomplish more, not requiring the revisiting of practices from new perspectives. In the same class, in the fifth period, while students are engaged and attentive, activities take longer and more invitations are required for them to make ideas and practices their own. It is, in fact, these accommodations that make lessons successful, and this responsiveness renders students who are motivated, engaged, and willing to remain invested. They know lessons were created for them specifically and appreciate this fact.

But before discussing the complexities of lesson design, our proposed architecture, and construct for units and lessons, let us focus on some general guidelines for that design—addressing its advantages for English Learners as well as for other students. A lesson is an invitation teachers issue students to embark on a discovery and knowledge-building journey. Several requirements are needed for this journey to be successful.

Desirable and Motivating Learning Goals and Activities

The goal of the lesson—the destination—needs to be understood and felt as desirable. English Learners are motivated as a result of being offered invitations to engage in activities that are interesting, authentic, present a challenging problem or significant idea, and include propositions or questions that in themselves serve as magnets to student interaction and engagement. Valuable, challenging activity that provides the needed support motivates students. Student motivation is not a prerequisite for learning, but rather a consequence of being offered valuable learning opportunities. Motivating students becomes easier to accomplish when prior learning experiences have taught students how stimulating learning can be, even when it entails hard work.

A good lesson surrounds students with possibilities for meaning-making and growth. These opportunities do not constitute "input," that is segments of a ready-made, fixed language code provided by the teacher to the students—a perspective that was prevalent in the education of English Learners for many years and is still evident in some classrooms. Rather, what facilitates learning is the offering of rich *affordances*—particular properties designed into the environment from which students perceive and select those that best fit in their experience and the activity in which they are engaged (van Lier, 2000, 2004). As introduced in Chapter 2, affordances provide learners the opportunity to notice, engage, and thus develop important understandings and skills they find to be worthwhile, for example video clips, photographs, notes, and texts. Affordances do not cause learning in and of themselves. Thus, an important part of a teacher's role is to surround students with a rich semiotic (meaning-making) budget and to "structure the learners' activities and participation so that access is available and engagement encouraged" (van Lier, 2000, p. 253).

Over half a century ago, Jerome Bruner wrote that interest in the material to be learned, rather than external goals such as grades or later competitive advantage, is the best stimulus to learning: "In an age of increasing spectatorship, motives for learning must be kept from going passive . . . they must be based as much as possible upon the arousal of interest in what there is be learned, and they must be kept broad and diverse in expression" (1960, p. 14).

Coherence Across Activities, Lessons, and Units

Goals for learning can be considered at three levels: *macro goals* (to be reached at the end of a unit of study lasting a few weeks and composed of several lessons centered on a generative theme); *meso objectives* (to be reached at the end of a lesson taking several class periods, a component of the generative theme addressed in the unit but which stands on its own); and *micro objectives* (to be addressed by the specific tasks that constitute the fluid and organic steps in a lesson and that support students' activity). A task, a lesson, and a unit are interrelated and move the students from simpler understandings of a theme to increasingly more complex, interrelated, deeper ones. Once again, Bruner provides important insight into this concept: "If earlier learning is to render later learning easier, it must do so by providing a general picture in terms of which the relations between things encountered earlier and later are made as clear as possible" (1960, p. 12).

Tasks as Purposeful Steps Toward a Learning Goal

In the same way that steps in a journey help travelers move forward toward reaching their destination, the role of *tasks* is to help students move toward the goals of a lesson. Tasks are concrete instantiations of individual support manifested through interactions that engage students in structured participation, unpacking a bit at a time the concepts, skills, and language that are in the process of being apprenticed, while linking them and building on prior encounters with such disciplinary practices. Throughout the book, we present multiple examples of tasks, their purposes and place, and how they should—in any good design—follow each other seamlessly, each one representing a step forward in the accomplishment of predetermined objectives.

Self- and Peer-Assessment as Part of the Learning

Finally, as a preamble to unpacking the architecture of a lesson, a lesson needs to invite students to be actively engaged in their own self-assessment and in the assessment of peers. The more aware students are of what counts as quality performance of a task and whether they have reached goals, the clearer it will be to them whether results are being accomplished, in what measure, and what to do about improving their performance. Using clear examples of prior student work, rubrics, and self-reflection charts, students can own the work of assessing themselves.

PEDAGOGICAL DESIGN

With these key considerations in mind, we present a framework for this pedagogy that supports learners' simultaneous conceptual, analytic, and linguistic development. We focus here on the architecture of units and lessons in which tasks are embedded and stress once again the importance of coherence, purpose, and progression at micro (task), meso (lesson), and macro (unit) levels of development.

Unit Design

As discussed earlier, a unit consists of three to five lessons focused on un-packing one large, powerful theme. For example, the unit we will discuss in this chapter to illustrate the design choices teachers engage in is called *Power, Protest, and Change*. This specific unit, designed for about 4 weeks of work, is comprised of three lessons (see Figure 3.1). The first one centers around the role children played in social protest, and the theme and texts used come from the period of the American school desegregation movement in the South. The second lesson, which we will consider in more detail, focuses on the role of protest during current popular sport activities in the United States and abroad. The final lesson considers the role of children in international protests and includes several texts around Malala Youzafsai (a biography, a speech to other adolescents, and a speech she gave to the United Nations General Assembly). Throughout the unit, students move from vague to more precise understanding of concepts such as power, con-trol, status quo, bystander, upstander, heroic acts, and consequences. They learn to read and analyze the author's perspective and to analyze language

Figure 3.1. Spiraled Unit on *Power, Protest, and Change*

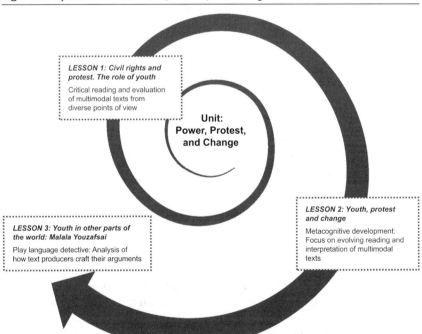

for tone and positionality. They also simultaneously become increasingly more comfortable and precise with their language use on these topics.

Lesson Design

We use the example of Lesson 2: "Youth, Protest, and Change" from the unit outlined in Figure 3.1, cowritten by Yael Glick (a teacher at Voyages Academy in New York City), and Aída Walqui. Ms. Glick's school is for "over-age" students (up to 21 years old) who abandoned or were expelled from their regular school. Ms. Glick's classes consist of mainly "bureaucratically labeled Long Term English Learners" (Valdés, 2018). In the example we elaborate, these students come from a variety of places (Colombia, the Dominican Republic, Mexico, Namibia, Puerto Rico, and Russia). As Ms. Glick planned her unit, her first major decision had to do with what theme she would focus on in the lessons and unit. She realized her students were very smart; they just had not been treated as such in school. They had to recover credits to be able to graduate as soon as possible, but they did not trust school; they had found their prior experiences to be boring and diminishing. In order to get an equivalency diploma, they needed to write texts that presented a position and supported it with well-developed ideas. What theme would move her students to write such essays? What types of texts would they be interested in interacting with and learning from along the way as they developed important discipline-specific academic practices? At the time of writing her unit, the story of Colin Kaepernick—the San Francisco 49ers football player who knelt in silent protest as the national anthem played during games to signal his solidarity with the Black Lives Matter movement—was prominent. Ms. Glick had heard her students refer to Kaepernick's protest, expressing many different opinions. She had also noticed that in school and in the neighborhood, in the same way in which Black and Latino people had negative stereotypes about minority groups, many also believed negative overgeneralizations made about White people. She knew that in the broader context there were strong feelings for and against Kaepernick's protest representing a variety of interpretations. That gave her a thematic link for her lesson, which addresses issues that are not only central to the operation of a democratic society, but are also very close to the contexts and concerns within which immigrant students live: how diverse groups in society perceive each others' actions, and how to engage in debate without prejudging others.

Having chosen a theme that would be relevant and compelling for her students, Ms. Glick's next big decision was to find the right texts for her lesson. She wondered how she may surround her students with multimodal texts that would help them select from the created pedagogical context, perceive, engage, and grow. She recalled having read an article online written by James Montague (2012) about an event at the 1968 Olympics that had a profound impact on her. Furthermore, she had at the time looked for videos of the event, the 200 meters race, and been impressed by the joint power of the article and the video. She decided to make Montague's piece the center text of her lesson and to provide other visual texts as affordances for her students.

THREE MOMENTS IN A LESSON

We propose that lessons be designed along three key Moments named after what students accomplish with concepts or texts: Preparing Learners, Interacting with Text (or Concept), and Extending Understanding (see Figure 3.3 later in the chapter). A lesson may unfold over five or six periods in a middle or high school class and consists of a coherent set of tasks that support students' deepening understanding and appropriation of central—and interrelated—concepts or texts interconnected to the theme of the unit.

Preparing Learners

First, students need to be readied to undertake sustained productive academic work by focusing their attention, activating prior knowledge that is relevant to the lesson at hand, and increasing their familiarity with a few new terms needed in context.

Focusing. A million things happen between one class period and another, and not all students are ready to start anew picking up where the last class left off. To start the exploration of ideas when everybody is in a different mental space will not create the best circumstances for the development of new disciplinary practices.

Activating Prior Knowledge or Building the Field. Learning in school entails building meaningful interconnections between what students know and that which will be explored in the new lesson. In addition, if students do not have relevant contextual knowledge where new ideas and processes may be anchored, then "building the field" is necessary to create the basic contextual understandings for students to make sense of novel ideas. For example, Chapter 4 outlines some building the field tasks that are needed for English Learners to read *Macbeth* with understanding.

Focusing students' attention, activating their prior relevant knowledge, building the field, and introducing key terms in context are carried out through the implementation of interactive tasks intended to build students' zone of proximal development. We will now discuss the tasks Ms. Glick designed and enacted to prepare her students to read Montague's *The Third Man: The Forgotten Black Power Hero.*

Because the issues to be addressed in the article had to do with athletes taking a stand against injustice, Ms. Glick decided to begin her lesson with a topic that was polemic and present in her students' minds. She wanted her students to have the time to express their thoughts and feelings unencumbered by having to present them orally. To accomplish this first step, she chose an activity she calls Silent Graffiti. The task invited students, working in groups of four or five, to spend 2 minutes, each with a different color marker, silently and simultaneously writing down their reactions and questions on a big piece of paper, which at the center has Colin Kaepernick's picture. After studying the picture, all students in the team recorded their reactions, writing them down at the same time, and then proceeding to sign their reactions with their color marker. Then, Ms. Glick invited students to move around the table and, still silently, to read their partners' thoughts and add their reactions and questions to the comments for the next 2 minutes. Students were asked to sign with their color markers their initial thoughts as well as their reactions to others' ideas. Students engaged in the task with high interest, as they read and responded to their classmates' reactions. Photo 3.1 shows students working through the activity and Photo 3.2 shows a product that emerged from these highly productive 4 minutes.

As a result of participating in Silent Graffiti, the class had been given the opportunity to manifest their perspectives and had focused on the themes that would be further unpacked during the lesson.

Ms. Glick focused on a second goal of Preparing Learners and decided to continue directing students' attention to some of the meaningful connections to be developed in the lesson. After students had a short time to discuss

Photo 3.1. Students in Ms. Glick's Class Work on Silent Graffiti

Photo 3.2. Silent Graffiti Comments

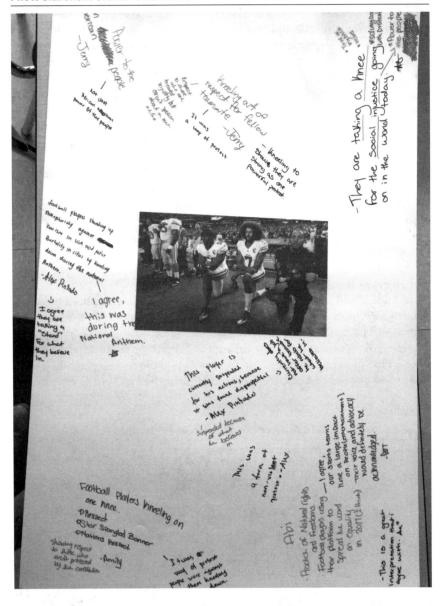

Photo 3.3. Olympic Award Ceremony

orally their similar or different reactions to the picture of Kaepernick, they were then invited to view another photograph engaging in a different task: Guided Reading of a Picture, which would get them closer to the Montague text. They were directed to notice particular details in the iconic sports photograph (Photo 3.3) taken during the 1968 Olympic Games and showing three athletes at the podium: two African American runners and a White runner—who won second place.

Ms. Glick knew that the photograph would probably not be familiar to her students, since none of them, and probably not even their parents, were alive at the time. But she intended for them to study the picture, notice details in it, and record their responses to the first three questions posed: what they knew about the picture, what they noticed, and questions that the picture suggested to them. They then shared their answers orally in a Round Robin (a task that gives each student the floor to express the ideas they jotted down without being interrupted). When one student was done, the next one continued, acknowledging ideas already expressed and adding ideas they had not thought of in the Iconic Photograph to their charts (Table 3.1).

A third goal of Preparing Learners has to do with the selective introduction of new terms that will be indispensable to understand in order to begin to make sense of a text or a concept. If this is necessary, the terms should be

Table 3.1. An Iconic Photograph Notetaker

Take a couple of minutes to examine this photograph. Then jot down answers to the questions in the chart.	
What do you observe in the picture?	What do you know about this picture?
Personal questions What questions do you have as you look at this picture?	
Other interesting questions my teammates asked:	

minimal in number (4 to 6) and introduced in meaningful contexts. Those contexts already begin to focus students' attention to the theme at the heart of the lesson, without directly addressing the specific content of the text. In Ms. Glick's class, students were directed to watch a brief video showing the race (https://www.youtube.com/watch?v=bWI9raEM1-4) and to notice terms they were not familiar with. The terms and phrases that students tended to notice were *overshadow, gesture, raise their fists, symbolize, black socks represent Black poverty,* and *human rights.* As an added support, the video has English subtitles, which can be helpful for students among a variety of other meaning-making supports.

Together, the activities described here from the "Youth, Protest, and Change" lesson activate students' prior knowledge and build new knowledge, preparing them to critically read the article at the center of the lesson.

It is important to note, however, that the Preparing Learners tasks do not "pre-teach" ideas. These tasks are not mini-lessons that preview the content of the central lesson. In fact, students are directed to notice and form opinions. Affordances are offered learners to perceive, interpret, and use in further learning. Ms. Glick does not correct what her students notice, or their opinions, but she does track what interpretations or misconceptions come up in order to use that information to design ways of exploring these issues further throughout the lesson. Students themselves will then be invited to check their original understandings, and whether, after having explored the lesson in its totality, they still agree with them or have changed their mind, indicating the reasons for their responses. Illustrating this point, the following exchange was recorded during a rich dialog in Ms. Glick's class during the Round Robin:

> *Abi:* This is not something I know, this is something I am inferring, there's still inequality because even though the guy in the middle is in a higher position, he's still behind the white guy, and the white guy is in third place. If the white guy is in third place, he should be standing behind the second black guy, but regardless, he's still in first place, because he's the only white man there.
>
> *Amily:* I agree with that.
>
> *Abi:* [nodding] Yeah, I see where you're coming from.
>
> *Eric:* I agree with Abi that, it's also what I get from this picture is there's still going to be inequality, but as a unit, we'll still be able to take huge steps and achieve many things; this was one of the first ones that we took.

It is evident that the students at this point thought the white athlete is American and that, in spite of coming in second in the race (there is confusion here because Abi mistakenly thought that he came in third), he stands in a more prominent place. All these confusions will be revised as they begin to read the article at the center of this lesson. Throughout, they expand their understanding of the sacrifices social protest usually entails (which they started working on in Lesson 1 of this unit, focused on the role of children in protest during the Civil Rights movement and school desegregation in the 1960s).

Interacting with a Text, Concept, Problem, or Phenomenon

During this second Moment of the lesson, students are guided to (1) examine individual components (episodes) of a text to make sense of them; (2) to reconnect them, linking them in meaningful clusters of understanding; and (3) to develop critical and metacognitive stances as students. Tasks focus on students' gradually going through a text, exploring its meaning components, noticing—guided by teachers' invitations to engage in specific activity—aspects of text and content that are important to understand in terms of the destination of the lesson, and skipping others that may not be essential for the lesson objectives. As students explore key pieces, they establish conceptual interconnections, practice analytical thinking, and simultaneously, through constant dialogue with their peers, develop the English required to express their ongoing work. This work entails the learning of structure (triggered by teacher design and moves), rather than simply the limited mastery of discrete facts or techniques. As Bruner (1996) reminded us, to build new practices it is necessary that new learning be placed against a general picture already discussed and that students be invited to interweave connections between earlier and later understandings.

Earlier in this chapter we also discussed that pivotal to the success of a lesson is the careful and deliberate choice of a text or concept. Only a strong text can support a complex pedagogical architecture intended to engage both a wide variety of English Learners and more proficient speakers of English. Quality of texts matters. Ms. Glick's chosen article tracks three athletes through acts of solidarity, punishment, and lasting friendship. Because Montague's text is rich, robust, and complex, the teacher has "engineered" it. She does not want to water it down, but she has introduced minor indicators in the text that will alert students to what they are reading (see Figure 3.2).

Back in Ms. Glick's class, students were now invited to start reading the engineered article called *The Third Man: The Forgotten Black Power Hero* (Montague, 2012). To make sense of how the article portrays the three athletes a bit at a time, Ms. Glick asked her students to track what they were learning about the two American runners, Tommie Smith and John Carlos, and their Australian counterpart, Peter Norman, using a task called The Double-Entry Journal (Table 3.2). Two students in a group of four tracked Smith and Carlos, while the other two worked on Norman, the Australian runner who won second place. This was not the first time the teacher had worked with Double-Entry Journals with these students, so she asked students to spend 5 minutes individually, reading the first two pages of the article, taking notes from the perspective of their assigned runner. After 5 minutes, dyads—who read from the same perspective—shared their notes, agreed on important information, and then shared it with the other two partners who had a different focus, to then end the interaction with the other dyad sharing the notes they agreed on.

The Double-Entry Journal asks students to generalize characteristics of the men assigned in the left-hand side of the organizer (e.g., bold, self-assured, fast runner) and then to identify evidence that supported their generalizations. As students share notes, each group of four in the classroom is actively engaged in asking whether the evidence supports the generalization or not.

Once students were immersed in the reading of the article, the teacher asked them to read the next two sections working silently, adding anything of relevance to their Double-Entry Journals. After 5 minutes of busy silence, Ms. Glick conducted a brief discussion with the entire class on the ideas students were finding out so far. Dyadic interaction restarted with

Figure 3.2. Excerpt from Engineered Text—Adaptation of *The Third Man: The Forgotten Black Power Hero* (Montague, 2012)

notes

raft of **prejudicial** laws against its **indigenous** aboriginal population, including a policy of taking Aboriginal children from their birth parents and handing them to white couples for adoption, a practice that continued until the 1970s.

prejudicial: Showing an unfair feeling of dislike for a person or group because of race, sex, religion

indigenous: The original people born to a particular place, native

Unexpected threat

Although Norman was a **staunch** anti-racism advocate, no one expected him to take a stand in Mexico. The Australian Olympic Committee had laid out just three rules for him to follow. The first was to repeat his qualification time before the Games.

staunch: Very devoted to a cause

"Rule number two: don't finish last in any round," Norman recalled.

"Third, and under no circumstances, don't get beaten by a Pom (a British runner)."

Norman had previously been ignored by the U.S. team, who had assumed they'd win a clean sweep of medals in the 200 meters, but he burst on to their radar when he broke the Olympic record in one of the early heats.

"When I first saw Peter, I said, 'Who's this little white guy?'" Carlos told CNN.

He would soon regret the oversight. When the 200 meters final arrived, all eyes were on the U.S. duo. Smith was expected to win easily ("You wouldn't be able to catch him on a motorbike," was Norman's assessment) but the speculation centered on what political gesture the American athletes might make on the podium.

The starting pistol was fired and Smith powered to gold. But out of nowhere Norman stormed down the last 50 meters, taking the line before a shocked Carlos. Norman's time of 20 seconds flat would have won gold four years later at the Munich Olympics and at the Sydney Games in 2000.

A fateful decision

Smith and Carlos had already decided to make a statement on the podium. They were to wear black gloves. But Carlos left his at the Olympic village. It was Norman who suggested they should wear one each on alternate hands. Yet Norman had no means of making a protest of his own. So he asked a member of the U.S. rowing team for his "Olympic Project for Human Rights" badge, so that he could show solidarity.

"He came up to me and said, 'Have you got one of those buttons, mate,'" said U.S. rower Paul Hoffman. "If a white Australian is going to ask me for an Olympic Project for Human

the reading of the next section she had labeled through her chunking of the text, A Fateful Decision. Ms. Glick had determined that this was going to be a difficult section to understand because it refers to what happened to the Australian runner, Peter Norman, when he was unexpectedly flown back to Australia. To assist students in their work through the text, she invited them to use the Clarifying Bookmark.

The Clarifying Bookmark, a metacognitive activity, provides students with six strategies they may use as they work on making sense of complex

Table 3.2. Double-Entry Journal

What do you learn about Tommie Smith and John Carlos from what you read in the next pages?	Supporting quotes from the text
What do you learn about Peter Norman from what you read in the next pages?	Supporting quotes from the text

written text (see Table 3.3). It assumes that English Learners are bound to have questions and not understand specific terms, and it helps them express those difficulties. As the Clarifying Bookmark is used in a course, students are introduced to two of these strategies at a time. Later on, two more are added as students appropriate the ones that they have practiced several times, until all strategies are used. In this class, Ms. Glick practiced for the second time the use of all six strategies at once. Working in dyads and taking turns, her students each read a paragraph at a time, pausing to consider which one of the strategies may be more appropriate for them to explore sections of the paragraph they just read aloud (and others already read) that they needed to clarify. The student announces which strategy s/he is going to use and then explores the passage. On the right-hand side of the bookmark there are three formulaic expressions from which students can choose, if needed, to initiate their discussion of text. Dyads engage in the activity working together for the next four paragraphs.

Formulaic expressions are different from sentence frames, which are basically fill-in-the-blanks activities that have only one right answer. Formulaic

Table 3.3. Clarifying Bookmark

Clarifying Bookmark I	
What I Can Do	**What I Can Say**
I am going to think about what the selected text may mean.	*I'm not sure what this is about, but I think it may mean . . .*
	This part is tricky, but I think it means . . .
	After rereading this part, I think it may mean . . .
I am going to summarize my understanding so far.	*What I understand about this reading so far is . . .*
	I can summarize this part by saying . . .
	The main points of this section are . . .
Clarifying Bookmark II	
What I Can Do	**What I Can Say**
I am going to use my prior knowledge to help me understand.	*I know something about this from . . .*
	I have read or heard about this when . . .
	I don't understand the section, but I do recognize . . .
I am going to apply related concepts and/or readings.	*One reading/idea I have encountered before that relates to this is . . .*
	We learned about this idea/concept when we studied . . .
	This concept/idea is related to . . .
Clarifying Bookmark III	
What I Can Do	**What I Can Say**
I am going to ask questions about ideas and phrases I don't understand.	*Two questions I have about this section are . . .*
	I understand this part, but I have a question about . . .
	I have a question about . . .
I am going to use related text, pictures, tables, and graphs to help me understand unclear ideas.	*If we look at this graphic, it shows . . .*
	The table gives me more information about . . .
	When I scanned the earlier part of the chapter, I found . . .

Source: Walqui, 2008.

expressions are phrases that are typically used time and time again in academic engagements and mark beginnings or transitions between ideas; thus they are immensely useful for English Learners (Walqui & Heritage, 2018). Ellis (2005) discusses formulaic expressions as generative phrases that introduce a type of relationship or comment. They are learned by students as unanalyzed chunks, almost as one word, and only later on, as the students learn more English, they begin to realize it is formed by several words.

We include a transcript of one of several interactions students engaged in during the "Youth, Protest, and Change" lesson (Photo 3.4):

> *Carmen:* [Reading text under A Fateful Decision. Looking at the Clarifying Bookmark] What I can do, I'm going to apply related concepts. One idea I have a concept for that relates to this is the photo where it shows that it's obvious that Smith and Carlos are wearing black gloves for black power. I also can now answer one of my questions from yesterday: Why is one guy raising his right arm and the other one the left arm?
>
> *Maria:* I agree with that. Also in the previous lesson when we looked at the photo, and it didn't really show that—it wasn't obvious that Norman was part of the act. Okay. [Reading text] So [looking at the Clarifying Bookmark], what I can do is I can summarize my understanding. My understanding of this is that during this time period when the Olympics took place, segregation still had its toll and people were still agreeing with it. So when people made this movement, they weren't really supportive of it, and they were probably more surprised than anything, that's why they were quiet.
>
> *Carmen:* I agree with what you're saying because segregation was at its highest at that time, because why is it when someone decides to speak out and fight for what they think is right, no one else has anything to say and stand up with them. Like, leaving them out on their own.

Ms. Glick carefully listened to see how students themselves were gradually changing their original opinions. She took notes to remind herself of what she needed to keep in mind in order to provide students with further opportunities to arrive at their own understanding about protest, the individual costs of taking a stance, and human solidarity, all of them immensely important themes for their current and future lives as immigrant students in the United States.

The examples also indicate that no ideas are discussed in isolation. In Ms. Glick's class, as should be the case in any class with English Learners, chunks of text are discussed to then be interwoven into larger networks of understanding.

Photo 3.4. Using the Clarifying Bookmark

Extending Understanding

The third Moment, Extending Understanding, is the part of a lesson where students, having completed the examination of a text or sets of texts, connect their new understandings to ideas beyond the lesson to form increasingly more complex understandings and reach the preset objective for the lesson. It invites students to apply their knowledge—both longstanding (sometimes corrected) and new—and involves them in the participation in new tasks that enhance newly developed practices. For example, they produce new texts—which may be written or multimodal, conduct research on the topic that has become enticing to them, engage in debates—where teachers assign what position to take and prepare for, and in general expand their understanding of ideas, processes, and language learned in the lesson to another context. Inequality, power, protest, and the need to engage in change will always be themes that ignite students' interests and are thus especially appropriate for English Learners.

When students complete their reading of the central article in Lesson 2, Ms. Glick's lesson is not done. She wants her students to make connections. She has designed tasks that ask students to draw on one page a Compare/Contrast organizer (Table 3.4) that now links the first text in the lesson, Kaepernick's photograph, to what they learned through the reading of *The Third Man: The Forgotten Black Power Hero*. Students' focus is directed to key dimensions of the two athletes that they will have to address in their writing.

Then, before students are invited to connect their newly developed understandings to other lessons, using other texts, they are directed to first discuss and then write about acts of heroism. Groups of students come up with definitions of what makes an act heroic and when a person merits the

Table 3.4. Compare/Contrast Organizer

In preparation to write a short essay, I want you to compare the two athletes at the center of our lesson.

	Peter Norman	Colin Kaepernick
Who are they?		
What did they do? Why?		
What were the consequences of their actions?		
Comments		

label "hero." Students are then invited to write about someone they know about who engaged in a heroic act or merits being called a hero. At the request of one student in Ms. Glick's class, the writing included another option, presenting the case of someone who has been called a hero but does not deserve the name. Finally, for this lesson, students are invited to assess orally the development of their own understanding, taking turns in their groups of four. The following reflection comes from Abi, a young woman from Eritrea in Ms. Glick's class:

> Originally when I saw this picture, I thought that um that Carlos and Smith originally were on one team and they were working together and knew how they were going to do and um Norman was just there because he was receiving his award. I also originally thought that he had something against them because he didn't look, and from my thinking I just didn't think he didn't look happy to be there supporting them. I also thought he was repping team USA like I really didn't get into detail with the picture, I didn't think they were on one team together.
>
> After reading the article I realized that Norman was actually working with Smith and Carlos, not only supported them, but actually gave them ideas and had repercussions for the rest of his life, all represented in this simple picture.

Figure 3.3. The Architecture of a Lesson

PREPARING LEARNERS

• Activate prior relevant knowledge, build the field
• Focus attention to concepts to be developed
• Introduce vocabulary in context

INTERACTING WITH TEXT

TEXT

• Deconstruct text, focus on understanding of meaningful chunks
• Reconnect chunk to whole text
• Establish connections between ideas within text

EXTENDING UNDERSTANDING

• Connect ideas learned to other ideas outside the text
• Apply newly gained knowledge to novel situations or problem-solving
• Create or re-create based on new understandings

Task 1
↓
Task 2
↓
Task 3

↓

Task 4
↓
Task 5
↓
Task 6

↓

Task 7
↓
Task 8
↓
Task 9

Figure 3.3 outlines our discussion of the Three Moment Architecture of a lesson and the purposes each Moment accomplishes. An important note that needs to be made here is that each Moment does not necessarily contain three tasks, nor should each Moment take the same amount of time. In fact, a rule of thumb we offer teachers when we work with them is that a good proportion for Moments in a lesson is that about 20% of the time be spent in Preparing Learners, 50% Interacting with Text, and 30% in Extending Understanding (homework counts here, as in continuing the writing of an essay initiated in class). This is just a rule of thumb, one to be overruled by contingency—the need to respond to student needs as they emerge.

FOCUS ON LANGUAGE

How do teachers help their students focus on language practices to guide their future use of English? Our proposal for lesson design includes opportunities to focus on language use as students are reading or listening to text. This focus centers students' attention on the larger elements of language:

the types of ideas discussed in a text, the specific terminology used to create diverse impressions in readers or listeners, and the claims and counterclaims presented in a text. The following three tasks designed by Ms. Glick take us to Lesson 3 of the unit *Youth, Protest, and Change*. This lesson invites students to learn about young people around the world who have taken a stand to protest injustices that surround them. One of these youngsters is Nobel Peace prize winner Malala Yousafzai. First, students are asked to read a speech Ms. Yousafzai gave to a youth group convened by the United Nations. As students read the text, working in dyads or in groups of four, they discuss the ideas presented and fill out the chart shown in Table 3.5. The activity invites students to reread the text with a purpose, not to look for words in isolation, but in order to make sense of key ideas in the speech and how they are presented and elaborated throughout.

The next task is designed so that students focus their attention on key aspects of language as they construct meaning from the text. Appropriately called Becoming a Language Detective (Table 3.6), this task involves precisely the stand English Learners need to adopt as they read text, namely determining what in the text is essential and how clues construct an explanation.

Table 3.5. Idea Hunt Matrix

Find three rights that Malala believes all people should have.
Find three challenges Malala and other young people have had to face.
Find three requests Malala makes in her speech.

Table 3.6. Becoming a Language Detective

Determining an Author's Tone

An author who supports the topic of his/her writing chooses language that has a positive connotation, meaning the words suggest approval. An author who is upset about the topic of his/her writing chooses language that has a negative connotation, meaning the words suggest disapproval or even outrage. When most of the language suggests approval, we say the tone is positive. When most of the language suggests disapproval, we say the tone is negative.

Directions

Read each of the sentences below and identify how words convey either a positive or negative tone. Write those words in the corresponding columns, and provide an explanation for your choice. Then complete the bottom portion of the chart, deciding whether the overall tone of the text is positive or negative. Provide evidence for your choice.

Language from Malala Yousafzai's Speech at the Youth Takeover of the United Nations	Examples of Language Used to Suggest a Positive Tone:	Examples of Language Used to Suggest a Negative Tone:	Explanation for Choice
1. I raise up my voice—not so that I can shout, but so that those without a voice can be heard.			
2. Today is the day of every woman, every boy and girl who have raised their voice for their rights.			
3. One child, one teacher, one pen, and one book can change the world.			
4. We call upon the world leaders that all the peace deals must protect women's rights. A deal that goes against the dignity of women and their rights is unacceptable.			
Decide whether the overall tone is positive or negative and provide an explanation. Overall the tone of the text is _____ because			

Not all clues are of equal importance for a detective. For a reader not all words are essential, and this activity guides them to what constitutes the core of the text.

A third activity from the same lesson invites students, this time as they read the speech that Malala gave to the United Nations Assembly—symbolically wearing the shawl Benazir Bhutto was wearing when she was assassinated—, to focus on the claims and counterclaims that she identifies to strengthen her position (see Table 3.7).

Having worked through the language of these two remarkable speeches written by a teenager, Ms. Glick decided that her students were now ready to build their own essay having explored in three consecutive lessons

Table 3.7. Claims and Counterclaims

One claim Malala makes in speech:	One counterclaim she identifies in speech (What do her enemies think or believe?):
Three pieces of evidence from speech she uses to support her claim:	One way Malala refutes the counterclaim ("But . . ."). If she doesn't refute it, write something she could have said to refute the counterclaim:
Evidence 1:	Rebuttal (How does Malala respond to the beliefs of her enemies?):
Evidence 2:	
Evidence 3:	

children's participation in the desegregation of schools in the South of the United States, the White "Black" hero's story with contemporary relevance, and youth protest in other parts of the world.

THE SPIRALED UNIT

Complexity, as we discussed earlier, emerges when increasing connections are drawn across components of a larger idea. That connecting activity provides students with depth of understanding and generativity, the possibility of extending those meaningful links and uses throughout their lives.

The lesson described in this chapter is the second in a larger unit (Figure 3.1) that Yael Glick designed to invite her students to explore the power of youth protest in creating change and the costs of protest. (We also discussed some tasks that focus on language in Lesson 3.)

The first lesson has the goal of engaging students in the exploration of the role children played in the desegregation of schools in the South. A wide variety of compelling texts (oral, visual, written, and multimodal) are used by students to make issues of segregation relevant and compelling. While written texts are not easy to read, students are provided with a wide variety of tools to work effectively through them. By the time they have to write an essay at the end of the second lesson, Ms. Glick's students write about the bravery of children who were willing to sacrifice their security in service of a larger ideal as they attended schools that did not want them. The third lesson has students explore similar issues in other parts of the world. When Ms. Glick's students read about Malala Yousafzai, they already have deep understandings about injustice and the power of being upstanders instead of bystanders (terms they have used time and time again in Lesson 1).

When is the time to focus on isolated ideas and the words that represent them? That comes after students have made sense of larger ideas, how they played in history and are still relevant today. Only then, the teacher checks that all students are clear about the meaning of pivotal words that have appeared throughout the lesson, and after students have used new terms time and time again with increasing understanding. An example of how to do this ludically, game-like, is using a Vocabulary Review Jigsaw that presents 12 terms and has students guess at them, reviewing clues that are presented by cards.

In this chapter, we have discussed how, with the destination in mind, well-designed lessons take students by the hand to lead them along a road where they increasingly take the responsibility for their journey. We have also illustrated how a classroom full of affordances provides students with opportunities to learn, revise their learning, extend it, amend it, and in the end, own it. We close the chapter by acknowledging some of the challenges that teachers may face in designing such learning opportunities, and how these challenges can be addressed.

CHALLENGES OF DESIGNING POWERFUL LESSONS

Multiple challenges face teachers engaging in the design or redesign of well-crafted lessons. For example, sometimes teachers say they lack subject matter knowledge to be able to locate good texts, or to decide what is more important and what is less so. Subject matter knowledge is deepened in the process of searching for materials, in listening to our own internal voices react to the reading of certain texts: "Do I find it compelling? Use it then! Do I find it boring? Then don't use it. The text is very complex? Engineer it and chunk it into its meaningful components, introducing subheadings that alert students but do not tell them what they are going to read. The text is too long? Chunk it and focus the lesson only on the most important parts." Each of these design dilemmas has a design answer, and teachers can, with guidance and over time, become more confident in their own assessment of the intellectual merit and potential challenges associated with focal texts, ideas, and problems.

A second and related concern is teachers' lack of knowledge about language, which in teachers' minds impedes their ability to design lessons for English Learners. Galguera (2011) introduced the concept Pedagogical Language Knowledge, which means that teachers need to be aware of the language they use to carry out disciplinary work (see also Bunch, 2013). We call this domain of teacher understanding Pedagogical Disciplinary Language Knowledge, to emphasize the situated nature of language use (e.g., the way in which mathematicians talk about problems is not the same way in which historians express them). Teachers do not need to be linguists, nor do they need to know how to describe verb conjugations, nominalization, and so on. Rather, they need to know how to use English to carry out activities in their discipline, and they need to gain awareness of what they say as they engage in the doing of their discipline. Once they are conscious of the way language is used in their disciplines, they can give their students options, using, for example, formulaic expressions, alerting them to the relationships connectors introduce, or working on how different types of texts are organized.

A third concern teachers express is the unavailability of time for designing lessons and collaborating in school. Ideally, school leaders understand the immense value of providing teachers who teach the same course with time to work together crafting lessons they will teach and then refine. This investment of time pays huge benefits, both in terms of student engagement and learning and in terms of strengthening and advancing teacher expertise. Even if the value of this investment is not acknowledged in a school, then teachers' personal investment of time to collaborate with peers will still render great results. Once a lesson or unit has been designed and then refined after implementation, it will be a good tool to use for many years.

A fourth and more intractable challenge includes the existence of mandated curricula in schools or districts where no adaptations are allowed by the administration. Similarly, mandated pacing guides that cannot be altered become prisons for students, with devastating consequences for student learning and the quality of schooling English Learners receive.

We believe that the answer lies in convincing educators that amplified, not simplified, lessons will engage all students, English Learners, and native speakers of English. Amplified lessons entail what we have discussed throughout the chapter: offering students rich semiotic budgets, multiple tools and opportunities to notice and use for the benefit of their own learning. Not all students will use the opportunities afforded in the same way, but they will all advance, learn, and reach in differential ways the goals of a well-crafted lesson. The following chapters illustrate, in more detail, how to design amplified curricula in specific disciplinary areas.

REFERENCES

Bruner, J. (1960). *The process of education.* Cambridge, MA: Harvard University Press.

Bruner, J. (1996). *The culture of education.* Cambridge, MA: Harvard University Press.

Bunch, G. C. (2013). Pedagogical language knowledge: Preparing mainstream teachers for English learners in the new standards era. *Review of Research in Education, 37,* 298–341.

Ellis, R. (2005). *Instructed second language acquisition. A literature review.* Wellington, New Zealand: NZ Ministry of Education.

Galguera, T. (2011). Participant structures as professional learning tasks and the development of pedagogical language knowledge among preservice teachers. *Teacher Education Quarterly, 38*(1), 85–106.

Montague, J. (2012, April 25). The third man: The forgotten Black Power hero. *CNN.* Retrieved from https://www.cnn.com/2012/04/24/sport/olympics-norman -black-power/index.html

Valdés, G. (2018, March). What's in a name? Paper presented at the 2018 annual meeting of the American Association for Applied Linguistics, Chicago, IL.

van Lier, L. (2000). From input to affordance: Social-interactive learning from an ecological perspective. In J. P. Lantolf (Ed.), *Sociocultural theory and second language learning* (pp. 155–177). Oxford, UK: Oxford University Press.

van Lier, L. (2004). *The ecology and semiotics of language learning: A sociocultural perspective.* Dordrecht, NL: Kluwer Academic.

Walqui, A. (2008). *Brain injury lesson.* San Francisco, CA: WestEd.

Walqui, A., & Heritage, M. (2018, Fall). *Meaningful classroom talk. Supporting English Learners' oral language development.* Washington, DC: The American Educator.

CHAPTER 4

Shakespeare's *Macbeth*

Making Powerful Texts Accessible and Engaging to English Learners

Mary Schmida

Because of its literary features and themes that prompt reflective analysis of human behavior, Shakespeare's *Macbeth* provides a wealth of opportunities for students to develop the 21st-century skills highlighted in Chapter 1 of this book. Focusing on a powerful text such as *Macbeth* provides opportunity for students simultaneously to develop deep understandings of literary themes, analyze components of literature (e.g., the arc of stories), and develop appropriate uses of language in the discipline. As the first chapters of this book explain, these three practices are critical for English Learners to succeed with high-challenge curriculum.

The lesson presented in this chapter provides an example of how teachers can support students' development of those disciplinary practices in literature. Using the tenets and frameworks presented in Chapters 2 and 3, it was designed by Yael Glick, a high school teacher, in collaboration with Aída Walqui and Mary Schmida as part of a portfolio of materials addressed for Intermediate levels of proficiency and above.

Why would teachers want to invite English Learners to engage in reading the original version of *Macbeth*? Many teachers might avoid working with a Shakespearean text because they consider the language to be too complex and the ideas too sophisticated for English Learners. The language is admittedly different from contemporary English since The Bard uses the everyday language of his time, an essential aspect of the play's artistry. English Learners, like all students, should be given the opportunity to read texts in their original, authentic forms. One of our goals, as the lesson in this chapter will demonstrate, is to demystify and amplify, not simplify, the dialect of the play to make it more accessible and enjoyable for English Learners.

Although *Macbeth* may present high challenges for English Learners (as it does for many students), the high level of support provided by the instructional design proposed in this book apprentices students and builds their future autonomy as readers of literature. In addition to the fact that English Learners deserve access to the canons of the field as much as any other student, there are other compelling reasons for teachers to choose *Macbeth* in particular, including:

- The timeless and engaging nature of the issues addressed in the play, such as the manifestation of human weakness, greed, manipulation, and deceit; the role of coincidence and how it accentuates human failings to trigger tragedy; and the inevitability of guilt and its consequences; and
- The expert construction of the play and artistic use of language, which, when recited by good actors, sounds almost like music.

PLANNING HIGH-SUPPORT PEDAGOGY
FOR HIGH-CHALLENGE TEXTS

Essential for quality learning for English Learners with quality texts such as *Macbeth* is the use of tools that enable students to access purposefully selected parts of the text as they work on carefully constructed tasks to enable them to engage with the central themes of the play. Before presenting the exemplar lesson on *Macbeth*, we begin with two key considerations for teachers to keep in mind as they plan instruction around literary texts for English Learners: addressing text complexity and constructing lessons for a lengthy complex text.

Addressing Text Complexity, Difficulty, and Accessibility

When gauging the difficulty of texts, it has been common practice to think about *complexity* as measured by lexile levels, as determined by word frequency and sentence length in a text. Confined to such quantitative measures as key considerations for text selection, teachers may rule out a particular book or select a book based on words and sentences in the text. Using this criterion alone, for example, Steinbeck's *Of Mice and Men* and *Grapes of Wrath* would qualify respectively as 3rd- and 4th-grade reading texts (Lexile Framework for Reading, lexile.com).

To account for other important elements in gauging the appropriateness of a text especially for English Learners, Bunch, Walqui, and Pearson (2014) problematize the term complexity and introduce two other important considerations: difficulty and accessibility.

Complexity, they note, relates to features of the text itself. It includes the notion that complex sentences, such as those compounded by two ideas that are connected by transitional words such as *however* and *meanwhile,* may in fact be easier for English Learners to understand than less "complex" texts, since the meaningful relationship between statements is clearly marked by transition words. Likewise, a longer sentence may be clearer precisely because it includes a parenthetical statement that elaborates an idea.

Difficulty, however, refers to the relationship between the reader and a specific text, particularly readers' familiarity with meanings, themes, and topics of a text. Texts can be difficult for students to understand because of the background knowledge needed to make sense of the content, regardless of the types of words and phrases used. In the lesson described in this chapter, we prepare learners for this challenge by "building the field," introducing students to indispensable knowledge required to make sense of text.

Accessibility, on the other hand, refers to the extent to which English Learners can enter into and understand complex or difficult texts. The *Macbeth* lesson exemplifies how teachers can design pedagogical supports that facilitate that accessibility.

Constructing Lessons in Sequence with a Purpose

In English Language Arts classrooms, the teaching of long complex texts has traditionally involved either proceeding from cover to cover, in the hope that students absorb key themes and the genre of the writing in passing, or using simplified text, in the belief that minimum exposure is better than none.

In contrast, we show in this chapter how teaching complex text such as Shakespeare's *Macbeth* needs to be purposefully structured around carefully selected portions of text that highlight specific themes and engage students in analyzing particular literary devices. A deep, meaningful, and enjoyable reading of purposefully selected sections of a literary work provides the basis for students' successful visitations to other sections of the text or re-visitations to the same text, because they then bring enhanced background and skills that enhance their ability to access that work.

The exemplar lesson presented in this chapter is part of a larger unit on *Macbeth*. It represents the first and longest lesson in the unit, introducing the overall work and launching students' exploration into the main themes of the drama (see Figure 4.1). The five lessons as a whole focus on the development of the two main characters, Macbeth and Lady Macbeth, with scenes from the play selected precisely to track their character transformations as depicted through rich and diverse literary means. The examples provided here explicitly address the teaching of *Macbeth*, but the same instructional design principles can be applied to any complex literary text, such as novels, that English Learners are invited to read.

With longer texts, learning objectives can help teachers select the particular scenes or chapters to address. In this unit, we select pivotal moments in *Macbeth* that serve to move the story forward while addressing a common

Figure 4.1. *Macbeth* **in Five Lessons**

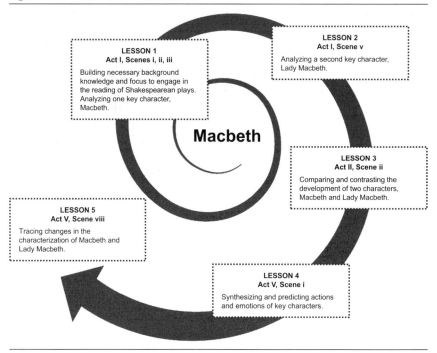

core learning standard focused on character analysis: *Analyze how complex characters with multiple or conflicting motivations develop over the course of a text, interact with other characters, and advance the plot or develop the theme* (CCSS, 2010). Other learning standards that influenced our text selection were those focusing on understanding the uses of language by the author and the use of two different mediums to analyze scenes in a literary work.

The lesson that follows illustrates this pedagogical stance and introduces tools that provide a high level of support to students, enabling them to read and understand this challenging text.

MACBETH ACT I: INTRODUCTORY LESSON IN THREE MOMENTS

Table 4.1 provides the lesson architecture for studying the introductory scenes of Act I of *Macbeth*, with activities for each of the Three Moments outlined. As with all of the lessons described in this book, the initial lesson on *Macbeth* (which comprises several days) is designed following the Three Moments framework introduced in Chapter 3. Subsequent lessons in the

Table 4.1. Architecture for Lesson 1 (Act I, Scenes i, ii, and iii): Students Are Introduced to the Play and to Macbeth

	Purpose	Description
Preparing Learners		
Jigsaw Project	Build the field of knowledge that prepares students to read and comprehend the text.	Students read different background texts on Shakespeare, his time, and literature; they discuss, summarize, and share their learning with others.
Shakespearean Phrase Play	Provide opportunity for students to interact with the colloquial language used in Shakespeare's time as it appears in the play.	Students collaborate to write a dialogue using both Shakespearean phrases as well as modern language.
Extended Anticipatory Guide	Activate students' prior knowledge about the themes they will encounter in the text.	Students work with a partner to make and justify initial judgments about themes that occur in *Macbeth*.
Interacting with Text		
Read Aloud Act I, scene i	Provide opportunity for students to experience and appreciate the language, tenor, and mood of a scene.	Students listen to the teacher read the first scene aloud, setting the stage for the rest of the play.
Viewing with a Purpose	Help students build their understanding by comparing their own ideas about characters to their portrayal in a film.	After imagining what the three witches might look and sound like, students watch two different versions of Act I, Scene i.
Double Entry Journal Act I, scene ii	Scaffold students' reading of a text by providing structure for them to document claims and evidence.	Students' reading of a scene is guided by focus questions; they work with a partner to find descriptions and quotes that help them construct an image of Macbeth at this point in the play.
Reading with a Focus, Act I, scene iii	Scaffold students' reading by providing specific foci to help them tolerate ambiguity and focus on pertinent details.	Students read the scene, focusing on two questions that help them better understand the role that the witches' prophecies play in the text, as well as the main characters' reactions to the prophecies.
Extending Understanding		
Mind Mirror #1: Macbeth	Structure opportunities for students to synthesize understanding of a character's thoughts, feelings, emotions, and motivations.	Students collaboratively create a visual representation of Macbeth thus far in the text before reading any further.

Macbeth unit also use the Three Moments architecture, as students explore other selections from the play.

The initial lesson in this unit focuses on the first three scenes of Act I. As shown in Figure 4.1, subsequent lessons involve reading additional pivotal scenes of the play focused on character development and the other standards being addressed. As explained earlier, when reading a difficult text such as *Macbeth* (or any lengthy literary text) with English Learners, it is acceptable—and advisable—to select three or four engaging and pivotal sections of text with which students can interact. Students do not need to read the entire play from beginning to end. Rather, they can engage deeply with selected portions of the text that represent pivotal or key scenes that are indispensable to understanding the characters or events. The teacher can summarize parts of the text they are not going to be reading in the class to clarify the course of events as needed. Building conceptual, analytic, and language practices around key portions of a long text gives students the opportunity to appropriate those disciplinary practices that they can then apply to other texts or other sections of the same literary work.

Preparing Learners

In this first Moment of the lesson, tasks are organized to support students' access to and understanding of the central text they are about to read.

Building the Field for English Learners. As noted earlier in this book, teachers today face new challenges in supporting all learners' development of analytic, conceptual, and language practices required in the 21st century. For English Learners studying literature, these learning goals pose unique literacy and literary demands. Interpreting the meaning of text requires students to be able to connect with and have some understanding of the genre, context, central themes, and uses of language in a text—as well as to express that understanding. The first Moment of a lesson, Preparing Learners, is thus a particularly critical phase of instruction for English Learners when the tasks support students' activating their prior knowledge and experience as well as their development of new knowledge needed to comprehend the text they are about to read.

When inviting English Learners to read texts that deal with topics or eras that are beyond the scope of their life experiences, it is critical to situate them within the context of the reading. One way to do this is by "Building the Field" (Derewianka, 1990; Hammond & Gibbons, 2005; Walqui & Heritage, 2012); that is, by engaging students in the reading of informational texts that provide the essential contextual background knowledge they need. For example, in order for students to engage deeply with a text that is situated in a particular time in history, that makes reference to a particular event, or that is a genre used for a specific purpose, they must first build their understanding about that time, the context of the event, or the purpose of that text.

In designing the Preparing Learners Moment of a lesson connected to a literary text, the teacher can begin by asking themselves two questions: (1) Are the themes and contexts ones that my English Learners can relate to from their prior experience and, if so, how can tasks help to activate that knowledge? and (2) Where my English Learners have little or no prior experience that enables them to relate to the themes, context, setting, or purpose of the text, how can tasks help to build the field of knowledge that will make it possible for them to connect more fully with the meaning of the text? When considering a text like *Macbeth*, students need first to engage in an activity that is designed to build new knowledge about a genre and historical context that is likely to be less familiar to most of them.

Jigsaw Project. In order to read and comprehend the play in its original form, students must first construct clusters of understanding to help them navigate and make sense of the text. In the case of *Macbeth*, students need background knowledge about the author and the context in which he wrote, the purpose for which the work was written, themes addressed in the play, and the language students are going to encounter. One way to accomplish this is to engage students in a Jigsaw Project. (For details, see the sidebar text.)

In the Jigsaw Project for this lesson, four readings are provided by the teacher, one each on Elizabethan drama, Elizabethan language, Shakespeare's life, and the relevance of the themes in Shakespeare's work today. For each background reading, students focus on the following three questions (see Table 4.2):

1. What are the main points of the article?
2. How are things different or similar today?
3. What else would you like to know? Write down two or three questions you have about the topic.

Students are invited to take notes in the right-hand column of the prepared reading assigned to their group. Once they discuss their responses in their Expert Groups, they must reach a consensus as to what specific information they will bring back to share in their respective Base Groups. Only after reaching a consensus—which has been checked with the teacher for content accuracy—may students write down their responses in the column of the Notetaker (Table 4.2) that corresponds with their reading. When ready, students return to their Base Groups and share their findings. As each student shares, others in the group fill out the Notetaker, jotting down important or pertinent information, as shared by the "Expert" in the group.

Creating Jigsaw Projects. Jigsaw Projects provide an abundance of scaffolding opportunities, as students work together to understand a text and

A Note on Jigsaw Projects

The term "Jigsaw" is used in many different ways by teachers. It was originally adapted in the United States to foster collaborative learning (Aronson & Patnoe, 1978) to ensure the success of school desegregation efforts.

In a Jigsaw Project such as the one described here, one of the essential elements is that there is an "information gap" (Ellis, 2003). Each student or group has information that the others do not have. Thus, in order for students to gather all of the information they need, every individual's or group's participation is necessary. Students first sit in heterogeneous groups of four (Figure 4.2). This is called the Base Group.

Students are then assigned letter A, B, C, or D and move to an Expert Group where they read one of four texts. While placing students heterogeneously in their Base Groups, teachers can also, if necessary, assign specific students to a particular text; thus, the grouping in the Expert Group can be homogeneous.

Figure 4.2. Jigsaw Project Diagram

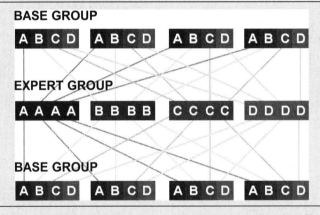

By assigning students a particular text to read in their Expert Group, teachers have the opportunity to select or create texts that meet the needs of a specific subset of students. For example, students who need the most support may be assigned to read a text that contains pictures, subheadings, short section summaries, guiding questions, and other amplifications to support their reading and discussion of the information.

Students who need the least support may be assigned to read a text that is longer, has more complex language, has few or no pictures, and has few or no headings and summaries. The structure also allows teachers to provide extra support to individual Expert Groups as needed. Note that, in contrast to other versions of "differentiated instruction" often used today in classrooms, what is not being differentiated (or simplified) here is access to the central ideas and goals of the text.

Table 4.2. Jigsaw Project Notetaker

JIGSAW PROJECT MATRIX:
ABOUT SHAKESPEARE AND HIS TIMES

	Elizabethan Theatre	Shakespeare's Language	Shakespeare's Life	Shakespeare's Relevance
What are some of the main points the article makes? What did you learn that you found interesting?				
How are things similar and different today?				
What else would you like to find out about the topic? Write down two or three questions.				

become an "expert" before they share their new knowledge with and learn from their peers. In order to create a Jigsaw Project, teachers must first decide what information students need to have in order to engage deeply with the main text or content. The components must each be valuable content-wise while, as mentioned, varying in length or difficulty. The other necessary component is a grid that guides both the students' reading and subsequent sharing in their Expert Group discussion, as well as their participation once they return to their Base Group to share and listen to others' summary of findings from the reading of their assigned text. Regardless of the topic, theme, or text the Jigsaw Project is designed to prepare students to study, the three or four questions posed in the Notetaker must be broad enough to pertain to and be relevant across all four texts (as can be seen in the example from *Macbeth* in Table 4.2).

Shakespearean Phrase Play. In order to prepare students for both the language and the themes of *Macbeth*, we give them an opportunity to interact with the colloquial language used in Shakespeare's time during this activity, even before they read the play. By engaging in the Shakespearean Phrase Play and using the language itself, students begin to examine the theme of manipulation, a theme that is woven throughout the text and that is central to the overall message of the play. For this task, students are given a list of 27 commonly used Shakespearean phrases that appear in *Macbeth*, along with their modern English translations.

To begin, the teacher reads each phrase aloud, and students practice saying the phrases and their English translation (see Figure 4.3). Next, students are assigned the task of working in groups of four to create a 30-line dialogue between a husband and a wife. The theme of the discussion is that the wife wants the husband to do something he does not want to do—thus, exposing students to both the language and one of the themes in Macbeth. Fifteen of the 30 lines in the dialogue must come from the list of Shakespearean phrases, and students are free to use modern English for the other 15 lines.

Once students have agreed on a conflict (for example, the wife wants her mother to come visit and the husband does not want her to), students work together in their groups of four to write the dialogue, including setting the scene and adding narrator comments or stage directions. It is important that all students keep a full copy of the script and have a role to play in the presentation, either by sharing roles or functioning as narrators. Once students have had a chance to practice, each group presents their dialogue to the class. In this way, students have an opportunity to hear the phrases multiple times, in context. Figure 4.4 contains the beginning of a dialogue written and performed by a group of 9th-grade students. As the script indicates, students incorporate modern English and Elizabethan phrases into their dialogues.

In the dialogue in Figure 4.4, it is important to note that students are using and engaging with the language in authentic ways, rather than memorizing a list of isolated vocabulary words. In this way, students are exposed to phrases that they will encounter in the play, begin to have a sense of how the language works, and learn how it is similar to and different from modern English.

Extended Anticipatory Guide. The next task in the Preparing Learners segment of the lesson is the Extended Anticipatory Guide (Table 4.3). Unlike

Figure 4.3. Shakespearean Phrases from *Macbeth*

cleave to my consent—support me
I shall be counseled—I will be willing to listen
beguile the time—deceive those around us
say sooth—speak truthfully
have not seen—have never seen before
give him tending—take care of him
jump the life to come—risk the fate of my soul
soundly invite him—invite him to sleep soundly
heavy summons—a demand
entreat an hour to serve—find a time that suits us
sensible to feeling—can be felt by touch
heat oppressed—extremely excited
left you unattended—abandoned you
giving him the lie—lying to him
slipped the hour—allowed time to fly by
nothing serious in mortality—nothing important in life
command upon me—invite me in a royal (aristocratic) way
attend those men our pleasure?—are those men waiting to see me?
champion me—oppose me
in restless ecstasy—in frantic sleeplessness
lave our honors—wash our reputations
leave this—stop talking and thinking this way
the subject of our watch—the person we are waiting for
give the cheer—entertain your guests properly
upon a thought—in a moment
very guise—usual behavior
gently rendered—surrendered without a fight

Figure 4.4. Student Sample of Shakespearean Phrase Play

Conflict: A wife wants her husband to make dinner instead of watching soccer on TV.

Wife: **Say sooth,** husband. What's for dinner tonight? I'm hungry.
Husband: Wife, I don't want to make dinner because that is a **heavy summons!** I want to watch my favorite team play soccer.
Wife: But you promised! It's your turn. I don't want to watch soccer!
Husband: **Leave this!** I just want to watch the game. Let's order pizza. Then I can watch Ronaldo and eat pizza.
Wife: Why do you **champion me?** It's your turn to make dinner.
Husband: Wife, you are very **heat oppressed.**
Wife: You said you would cook dinner tonight. **Upon a thought,** I am leaving. So there.
Husband: Wait? Hold up! I will be **gently rendered.** You win.
Wife: Thank you! I knew you would not **champion me!**

Table 4.3. Extended Anticipatory Guide

EXTENDED ANTICIPATORY GUIDE: MACBETH

	Opinion		Finding		Evidence: Explain Using Your Own Words
	Agree	Disagree	Agree	Disagree	
1. Some people do not feel guilt; that is, they do not feel bad when they do something wrong.					
2. Keeping secrets can hurt you because it is not good to keep things inside.					
3. There is no such thing as fate; in other words, we CAN change our destiny.					
4. Committing one crime leads to committing more crimes.					
5. Ambition is a positive trait or characteristic.					

the previous two activities, which build the field for students by developing new knowledge, the Extended Anticipatory Guide prepares the learner by activating prior knowledge. This task is used at the beginning of the unit, to introduce students to overarching themes in *Macbeth*, and also at the end, when students are invited to return to their original responses to the statements and consider whether they have altered their thinking. Students are also asked to provide evidence from the text in their own words that either validates or challenges their original opinions.

To begin this task, students work in dyads, taking turns reading each statement aloud and responding to it using the formulaic expressions (Ellis, 1994) shown in Figure 4.5. Note that students are provided two options of formulaic expressions, giving them a choice in how they can respond, while still providing them the initial language and structure to use in discussing their opinions with their partner.

After each response, the listening partner then responds to what the first partner has said and continues to read the next statement and respond. Students continue taking turns reading and responding until all statements have been read.

The statements in the Anticipatory Guide activate students' prior knowledge regarding the themes of the play, in this case, ambition, power, guilt, and deceit. When students interact with each other about these statements using the formulaic expressions as a guide, it is critical that they not only explain their opinion about the statement but also follow up with a question about what their partner thinks, with the partner responding to that question and then giving their own rationale for their answer. Contrary to some formulas that involve students' reciting and sharing their ideas without any

Figure 4.5. Formulaic Expressions

Formulaic Expressions I

S1: I will read statement 1. It says _____. I agree/disagree with it because _____.
So, I am going to mark it agree/disagree. What do you think?
S2: I agree/disagree with you because _____. So, for statement 1, I will mark agree/disagree. Now let me read statement 2. It says _____.
I agree/disagree . . .

Formulaic Expressions II

S1: OK, I will begin by reading statement 1: ". . . ." Based on what I know, I would say this statement is true/not true, so I will agree/disagree. One reason for my opinion is that . . .
S2: I agree/disagree with you. The reason for my agreement/disagreement is that I know that _____. Now I will read statement 2: ". . ." Based on what I know I would say this statement is true/not true, so I will agree/disagree.

semblance of dialogue, the formulaic expression requires students to engage in listening and responding to one another's ideas and rationales for those ideas. Also, note that the formulaic expressions allow students to construct complete thoughts in the blanks provided, rather than "sentence frames" that force students to "fill in the blanks" of already-mandated constructions.

Once students have finished the entire unit, they return to their original opinions that they logged in the Extended Anticipatory Guide, and check them against their new understandings in the second column. In the third column, they will indicate the evidence from the text that they used to either validate their original thoughts or to support their new ideas.

An Extended Anticipatory Guide can additionally be used to familiarize students with thematically related vocabulary in context. While students were introduced to and engaged with colloquial Elizabethan English in the Shakespearean Phrase Play activity, in the Extended Anticipatory Guide, students are exposed to thematic vocabulary in context. For example, students read and respond to statements that refer to fate, destiny, guilt, and ambition, all themes that are woven throughout the play. Each concept is defined in the body of the statement, and students read and interact with these ideas as they simultaneously learn new vocabulary.

The formulaic expressions scaffold the language students need to use in responding metacognitively to both the statements and to others' ideas. The goal, of course, is student autonomy, but until students have appropriated the language and are able to share and expand on each other's ideas on their own, formulaic expressions help to scaffold both the interactions of the students as well as the language they use. Over time, then, formulaic expressions become unnecessary.

INTERACTING WITH TEXT

In this second, and central, Moment of the lesson, students engage in tasks that support their exploration and analysis of the text, understanding of its key themes, and development of the language needed to discuss their ideas and analyses. It should be noted that, although we spend less space here discussing Interacting with the Text, in implementing the actual lesson, the majority of instructional time would be spent here.

Read Aloud. Before students engage in the reading of the first scene in Act I, the teacher sets the stage by explaining key information, such as the role of witches in Elizabethan times. It is important for students to understand that it is the prediction of the three witches that sets the tragedy of *Macbeth* in motion. The first scene of Act I is short and can be read aloud by students, then viewed online via sources such as the Globe Theatre production available through YouTube.

In any given scene, students may not understand every word, but the teacher can invite students to participate in brief dyad discussions to come up with statements that describe what is happening in the scene, drawing on words in the text, visuals, and action of the witches. Students can then share these descriptions with the entire group. By guiding the conversation and drawing on all the descriptions, the teacher can help students understand that there is confusion (*hurlyburly*) and also invite them to notice the abundance of imagery involving weather (*rain, fog, thunder, lightning, filthy air*), all of which help the reader create a vision of the three witches' seemingly casting a spell. It is not necessary for students to understand every word, such as that *Graymalkin* is the name of the witch's cat. Indeed, students need to understand the main ideas and the important motivations and actions of key characters that serve to move the plot forward, rather than focusing on every word and defining it before discussing or moving on to the next scene.

Viewing with a Purpose. In order to support students' construction of their understanding throughout their reading of the play, video clips can be used to contextualize particular scenes. There are many versions of *Macbeth* available, and we suggest choosing two very different depictions. The story remains the same, but the actors, scenery, costumes, and setting may change. By viewing more than one version, students can see how the same text is interpreted in different ways.

Accompanying their initial reading of the text, students write and share with each other how they imagine the three witches. They are then provided with various viewings, which as affordances help them compare these perceptions with what they had imagined on their initial reading of Act I, Scene i. Using a triple entry journal (a three-column organizer focused on a particular question), they compare their images with the portrayals of the witches in two video versions. By engaging students in both the reading of the text, and of how people have chosen to portray the scenes, students deepen their understanding of the text and realize more deeply the performance aspects of the genre.

Double Entry Journal. As students move on to Scene ii, the teacher introduces the description of Macbeth's brave acts of war, which establish him as a hero. Students may need to be reassured that, though it might be difficult for them to get through the text, they should not worry about trying to understand everything. Rather, as they read, they will do so with a particular focus that corresponds to the prompts in a Double Entry Journal on how Macbeth is described by other characters.

After independently reading Act I, Scene ii, students work in pairs to review the text and decide what characteristics of Macbeth to enter in the left column of a Double Entry Journal. In the right column, partners write the phrases or sentences that support their statements. After reading Scene ii, even if students do not understand many of the words, they do understand that others see Macbeth as a brave and fearless leader and soldier, and the king himself speaks of him in glowing terms. This is a key element of the overall play. After students complete their journals, they may share and check ideas as a whole class, taking the opportunity to reinforce understandings and clarify misunderstandings before moving on.

Using a Double Entry Journal supports students' reading of difficult texts because it alerts them to exactly what to focus on. Teachers may choose to have students read either one or two paragraphs of a text using a Double Entry Journal or a whole section or chapter of a text. In either case, the focus of students' reading is based on the question in the Double Entry Journal, and their responses include their own thoughts as well as quotes from the text that support their ideas. In the case of *Macbeth*, students may struggle, but their confidence grows as they are able to jot down their ideas and the quotes from the text that support their ideas. They also co-construct ideas by adding new thoughts shared by their peers within dyads, small groups, or the whole class.

Reading with a Focus. Similar to a Double Entry Journal, the next task, Reading with a Focus, signals for students what is pertinent versus extraneous information. Students begin by either reading Act I, Scene iii silently to themselves or watching the scene as it is dramatized by the Globe Theatre. Then students read the text aloud together in small groups, sharing the five parts. As students read (and watch) the scene, the teacher encourages them to focus on the following two questions:

1. What do the three witches predict for Macbeth and Banquo?
2. How do Macbeth and Banquo react to these prophecies?

Students individually take notes on the two questions. After they have come up with answers to the questions, they can discuss their answers as a class, with the teacher focusing the discussion on clarifying the prophecy. It is important here to point students' attention to the idea that Macbeth and Banquo are friends at the beginning of the scene, and by the end, the witches' prophecies set up the two men as rivals.

This series of tasks (Read Aloud, Viewing with a Purpose, Double Entry Journal, and Reading with a Focus) works together and serves to guide students' reading of a text that may, in fact, be beyond their current ability to read on their own. English Learners may struggle in reading difficult, complex texts, but the tasks and their structures provide students several entry points, including working on their own, sharing with a partner or in a small group, sharing out with the class, and whole class discussions. As with any difficult text with which students engage, it is important to consider how the combination of selected tasks works together to scaffold students' understanding. The tasks also support students' engagement with texts that they would otherwise not be able to experience, as they are typically given only a simplified version of the original, authentic text.

Extending Understanding

As the design of the *Macbeth* Unit (Figure 4.1) indicates, studying the drama requires a series of lessons, each of which ends with this synthesizing moment. Lesson 1 thus ends at the end of the first three scenes of Act I—an appropriate moment for students to articulate and extend their understanding of the themes and character development thus far through a task known as a Mind Mirror, to which we now turn.

Mind Mirror. Having been introduced to the story and the main character, students are invited to synthesize what they have learned about Macbeth by creating a Mind Mirror. By developing this portrait of the character as portrayed thus far, students will be establishing a baseline for tracking changes in the character as events unfold in the drama—and representing those changes in subsequent Mind Mirrors as each lesson concludes.

In a Mind Mirror, students review a rubric provided by the teacher to establish a clear understanding of the goals of the task and how to self-assess the products they create. Students work in groups of four (because that number supports dialogue and co-construction of ideas in dyads and across dyads) to synthesize their understandings of a specific character (in this case, Macbeth). To illustrate graphically the state of mind and internal perspective of a character at a point in time, students use the outline of a head to depict what this character is feeling and thinking, including what questions, dilemmas, or conflicts the character may be experiencing. To illustrate these ideas and emotions, students use relevant quotes and symbols. Students also include original phrases and drawings that elucidate the character's perspective. The task engages students in textual analysis as they discuss which quotes and symbols to select, and it invites them to produce artistic renditions or "internal mirrors" of the character selected. Furthermore, students begin to assume a critical stance as they craft original phrases that represent their analysis of the character's perspective.

In brief, students discuss Macbeth's state of mind at this point in the drama (at the end of Scene iii) to co-construct a Mind Mirror that contains the following:

- quotes that explain Macbeth's feelings;
- original phrases that synthesize his state of mind;
- symbols that represent the turmoil he is going through; and
- pictures that represent his mental state.

The Mind Mirror task is a useful artifact for tracking character development because it provides students with a visual representation of their character analysis. Furthermore, it allows students to visually compare changes in characters over time, if done more than once during the course of reading a longer text. These artifacts can ultimately support students' writing as well, as each Mind Mirror contains both original text and readers' reflections on that text.

FOLLOW-UP LESSONS: ENGAGING WITH ADDITIONAL SELECTED SCENES USING THE THREE-MOMENT ARCHITECTURE

Once students have been introduced to a major text and begun to explore its themes through carefully constructed tasks that scaffold their learning, as this Introductory Lesson to *Macbeth* has shown, they are ready to read additional purposefully selected sections and engage in tasks that support their continued access to and analysis of those themes in collaboration with their peers. Those selections, as shown in Figure 4.1, each become the focus of a 4–5-day lesson that the teacher designs using the Three Moment Architecture.

In the case of the *Macbeth* unit, Lessons 2–5 provide an opportunity for students to read and engage with additional pivotal scenes that illustrate the development of the two lead characters, Macbeth and Lady Macbeth. Similar to students' introduction to the character of Macbeth in Lesson 1, in Lesson 2 (see Table 4.4) students read a scene in which they meet Lady Macbeth and in the third Moment of that lesson pause again to capture their understanding of her character in a Mind Mirror. In later scenes in the play, students continue to trace the development of both Macbeth and Lady Macbeth through Mind Mirrors during the Extending Understanding Moments of those lessons. The visual and textual representations of ideas in each new Mind Mirror help students articulate the changes of these key characters over time as the dramatic events unfold.

The Three Moment Framework provides the architecture for each lesson (see Tables 4.4 and 4.5 for Lessons 2 and 5 of the *Macbeth* Unit). Purposefully selected interactive tasks support students' continued deepening exploration and articulation of the key themes. During the Preparing Learners Moment of Lesson 2, for example, a Think-Pair-Share task leads students through a discussion of their current conceptions of power because it begins to be manifested in the portrayal of the characters during the scene addressed during that lesson. Similarly, in the Preparing Learners Moment of Lesson 3, a peer interview task allows students to explore their understanding of the concept of guilt and how it influences human behavior, a theme that surfaces during the scenes selected for that lesson.

Table 4.4. Architecture for Lesson 2 (Act I, Scene v): Students Encounter Lady Macbeth

	Purpose	Description
Preparing Learners		
Think Pair Share	Activate students' background knowledge about the concept of power and what characteristics they associate with people who have it.	In dyads, students respond to a prompt about the role of power in their own lives.
Interacting with the Text		
Listening with a Focus	Support students' understanding a text by providing them a focus for listening as the text is read aloud.	Students listen to the teacher read the scene aloud, where they first meet Lady Macbeth. As they listen, students jot down ideas about how Lady Macbeth responds to the prophecy, and what actions she wants to take.
Double Entry Journal	Scaffold the reading of a text by providing students a graphic organizer to document specific information or opinions, and evidence from the text.	Having heard the scene read aloud, students' read Act I, Scene v on their own, and respond to the prompts in a Double Entry Journal, noting what Lady Macbeth thinks, what she wants, and evidence from the text.
Extending Understanding		
Mind Mirror: Lady Macbeth	Support students' synthesizing their understanding of a character's thoughts, feelings, emotions, and motivations.	Students pause and synthesize what they know about Lady Macbeth thus far in the play by developing a Mind Mirror.

Other Preparing Learners Moments in later lessons involve making predictions about the story and imagining scenes in advance of reading the texts for those lessons. By predicting, students use the information they have gathered from the reading so far, as well as their own personal experiences, to anticipate what characters (in this case, Macbeth and Lady Macbeth) will do next. Predicting is a useful and powerful reading strategy that provides students the opportunity to consider their understanding of the text thus far, think ahead, and ultimately verify or revise their predictions as they continue reading (Duke & Pearson, 2009; Goodman, 1988).

While the tasks in the Preparing Learners Moments continue to engage students in exploring the meaning of key themes, the tasks during the

Table 4.5. Architecture for Lesson 5 (Act V, Scene viii): Students Analyze Key Themes and Character Development Using Text as Evidence

	Purpose	Description
Preparing Learners		
Imaging a Scene	Activate students' prior knowledge about battles and war to predict an outcome to a scene.	Students imagine how the fight scene between Macbeth and Macduff might be described and predict the outcome of the battle, choosing a victor and giving a justification for their choice.
Interacting with the Text		
Reading with a Focus	Scaffold the reading of a text by providing focus questions.	Students read the scene, focusing on the emotions of the characters.
Selected Quotes	Provide a structure for students to analyze specific quotes from a text.	Students work together as a whole class to discuss and reach a consensus about specific quotes and their meaning.
Extending Understanding		
Mind Mirrors	Help students synthesize their understanding of a character's thoughts, feelings, emotions, and motivations.	Dyads work on one of two Mind Mirrors, either Macbeth or Lady Macbeth, documenting how the character has changed over time.
Extended Anticipatory Guide	Engage students in identifying evidence from the text that supports or challenges students' ideas about key themes in the text.	Students revisit their original responses to the statements and consider if their opinions have changed, using evidence from the text to justify their reasoning.

Interacting with Text Moments in each lesson continue to support students' collaborative focusing on particular questions or ideas as they read, listen to others read, view the play, organize their thoughts in journals, and discuss the unfolding events. Some interactive tasks also focus on specific quotes that explicate important ideas about the characters or events; with support and modeling from the teacher, students engage in translating that text into their own words, as seen in Lesson 5 (Table 4.5). While they will not understand everything, these focusing tasks support students' zeroing in on pertinent information and strengthen their capacity to tolerate ambiguity with parts of the text they do not understand or find confusing.

The Unit culminates with an Extending Learning Moment built on two tasks. One task supports students' final analysis of the two main characters in relation to the dramatic course of events. The other invites students to revisit their thinking about the central themes of the play that they articulated during the Anticipatory Guide task, now using evidence from the text to validate their arguments and opinions.

CONCLUSION

This chapter has provided an example of a Three Moment instructional design that supports English Learners' engagement with a particularly complex literary text that is difficult for many students regardless of their English proficiency. The model emphasizes the importance of providing multiple opportunities for English Learners to engage with a challenging text, first by connecting with their prior experiences and ideas and building the field of new knowledge needed to comprehend unfamiliar text genres, contexts, settings, and language. Asking students to read background texts serves to construct their understanding of the time and place of Shakespeare and prepares them to read and engage in the original version of the play, rather than a simplified version.

This chapter also illustrates how to design a series of lessons, each following the Three Moment Architecture, around purposefully selected portions of a longer text, pausing periodically to give students an opportunity to reflect and synthesize their understanding before moving on. This helps to address the concern that teachers often face with longer texts—that they take a significant amount of time to read—and illustrates our recommendation of selecting only a few pivotal and key episodes throughout the play, while providing summaries of what occurs in the scenes that students will not read. Ultimately, by experiencing deeper engagement with a portion of a complex and long text, students develop conceptual, analytic, and linguistic practices that they can apply with increasing power and autonomy as learners to other parts of the same text or to new texts that they will encounter in the future.

REFERENCES

Aronson, E., & Patnoe, S. (1978). *Cooperation in the classroom: The jigsaw method*. London, England: Pinter & Martin Ltd.

Bunch, G. C., Walqui, A., & Pearson, P. D. (2014). Complex text and new common standards in the United States: Pedagogical implications for English learners. *TESOL Quarterly, 48*(3), 533–559.

Common Core State Standards. (2010). CCSS.ELA-Literacy.RL.9-10.3. Retrieved from http://www.corestandards.org/wp-content/uploads/ELA_Standards1.pdf

Derewianka, B. (1990). *Exploring how texts work*. Portsmouth, NH: Heinemann Educational Books.

Duke, N., & Pearson, P. (2009). Effective practices for developing reading comprehension. *Journal of Education, 189*(1–2), 107–122.

Ellis, R. (1994). *The study of second language acquisition.* Oxford, UK: Oxford University Press.

Ellis, R. (2003). *Task-based language learning and teaching.* Oxford, UK: Oxford University Press.

Goodman, K. (1988). The reading process. In P. L. Carrell, J. Devine, & D. Eskey (Eds.), *Interactive approaches to second language reading* (pp. 11–21). Cambridge, UK: Cambridge University Press.

Hammond, J., & Gibbons, P. (2005). Putting scaffolding to work: The contribution of scaffolding in articulating ESL education. *Prospect, 20*(1), 6–30.

Lexile Framework for Reading. Retrieved from https://lexile.com/educators/measuring-growth-with-lexile/lexile-measures-grade-equivalents

Walqui, A., & Heritage, M. (2012, January). Instruction for diverse groups of English Language Learners. Understanding Language: Language, literacy, and learning in the content areas. Paper presented at Understanding Language Conference, Stanford University, CA.

CHAPTER 5

Investigating Disease Transmission

Engaging English Learners in a Phenomenon-Based Science Lesson

Tomás Galguera, Catherine Lemmi, and Paolo C. Martin

As former K–12 science teachers and current preservice teacher educators and researchers, we embrace the vision of amplified instruction for language development and knowledge growth described in previous chapters. Amplifying science instruction with a focus on relevant scientific phenomena provides English Learners with multiple entry points and opportunities for knowledge building, analysis, and the development of new scientific practices. Well-supported invitations for students to meaningfully investigate scientific phenomena are not just motivating, they develop students' ability to participate in science discourse (Gutierrez & Rogoff, 2003; McNeill, 2009; Warren, Ballenger, Ogonowski, Rosebery, & Hudicourt-Barnes, 2001).

Imagine a classroom full of learners with diverse language backgrounds during a simulation on the spread of communicative diseases. They wait with high expectation to observe whether the liquid in their test tubes turns bright magenta, indicating they have been "infected." A small group of students runs to computers to look up information, while others move through the room, clipboards in hand, recording results. Afterward, the students and their teacher engage in a robust discussion about how infectious diseases spread through a population, about the probability of contagion, the efficacy of vaccines, and ideas for educating the public about risks for and prevention of infections.

How can teachers design such learning experiences and engage English Learners in considering and discussing fascinating scientific concepts with real-life implications? How can they challenge and support students in carrying out tasks that are connected to their worlds and expand their skills, while processing and creating meaning?

With new science standards representing the new educational imperatives of the 21st century, all students, including English Learners, are expected to engage in language-rich, sophisticated science and engineering practices

(Lee, Quinn, & Valdés, 2013; National Research Council, 2012; NGSS Lead States, 2013). The work we describe in this chapter emerges from this timely opportunity to reconsider teachers' approaches to designing and refining quality learning experiences. A new consensus stresses the importance of engaging students in authentic science experiences to investigate phenomena, build models, and construct explanations. This emphasis marks a departure from traditional science instruction that stressed discrete content knowledge and vocabulary development, even in classrooms without English Learners.

Teachers must provide rich opportunities for students to engage in science discourse because, as students talk, they learn; explorations through talk are indispensable in doing science (Lemke, 1990; van Lier & Walqui, 2012). Learning opportunities for science and language emerge by asking questions, defining problems, developing and using models, designing investigations, analyzing and interpreting data, using mathematical and computational thinking, constructing explanations, arguing from evidence, and obtaining, evaluating, and communicating information—practices consistent with scientific discourses and current reforms in science education (NGSS Lead States, 2013). These behaviors also help foster the 21st-century skills necessary to succeed as adults in personal, professional, and civic realms by, for example, adjusting to uncertain conditions and complex problems, collaborating, and dialoguing to find advantageous compromises (Mehta & Fine, 2017).

We begin by considering advantages and challenges associated with the language and discourse of science. Next, we discuss the Pedagogical Language Knowledge (PLK) that teachers need to envision and enact quality instruction for English Learners (Galguera, 2011). We then propose three guidelines that teachers can use to design learning activities and lessons. In the remainder of the chapter, we present a science lesson that illustrates challenging and supportive approaches to create and refine science curriculum.

LANGUAGE AND DISCOURSE IN SCIENCE: AFFORDANCES AND CHALLENGES

Rather than a rigid set of rules, conventions, or structures needing to be taught didactically, language in science can be thought of as a "linguistic register" (Halliday & Martin, as quoted in Lee, Quinn, & Valdés, 2013, p. 226) that is learned as students engage in the action of science tasks (van Lier & Walqui, 2012). The three dimensions articulated by the Next Generation Science Standards (NGSS)—scientific and engineering practices, cross-cutting concepts, and disciplinary core ideas—provide both affordances and challenges for students engaging in the discourse of science.

Scientific Practices

Students' diverse linguistic, cultural, and experiential backgrounds can be used to explore, understand, and benefit from the overlaps and gaps that naturally emerge when studying scientific phenomena (Mehta & Fine, 2017). In authentic spaces and moments of wondering, language becomes the activity, rather than solely the medium or tool for completing tasks (van Lier & Walqui, 2012). Yet, scientific or engineering jargon and related lexicon can still become a powerful means of exclusion for students not yet familiar with such terms. To help students access high-level science content, lessons can encourage language development by engaging students in exploring scientific phenomena and co-constructing conceptual understandings as they participate in meaningful dialogue, generating scientific arguments from evidence. This approach stands in contrast to both "pre-teaching" vocabulary lists before students engage the content of the lesson, or teaching rules associated with native-like uses of English before inviting learners to make meaning in science.

Cross-Cutting Concepts

The learning of cross-cutting scientific concepts—patterns, cause and effect, stability and change, systems, and models—also presents teachers with unique affordances and challenges, especially when considering English Learners. The universal aspects of these concepts make it possible for students to discuss and analyze their meaning in relation to their background knowledge. Such concepts present teachers with excellent opportunities to scaffold the development of language and to contextualize the study of phenomena. At the same time, scientific contexts present very particular uses of language that sometimes do not overlap with vernacular or popular use. Thus, designing science curricula with cross-cutting concepts and language use requires careful consideration of context as well as students' background and interests (Lyon, Tolbert, Solís, Stoddart, & Bunch, 2016).

Disciplinary Core Ideas

The NGSS privilege learning disciplinary core ideas in four domains: physical sciences; earth and space sciences; life sciences; and engineering, technology, and applied science. These ideas, such as heredity, Earth's place in the universe, energy, and engineering design, can build on learners' experiences, provoke their curiosity, and invite them to consider addressing societal problems. Furthermore, they lend themselves to spiraling throughout multiple grade levels' curricula, offering multiple opportunities to deepen students' knowledge.

Linguistic ideologies, or moral and political interests that shape our beliefs about the role of language in society (Irvine, 1989), influence consideration of the discourse of science in classrooms. The challenge for teachers is becoming aware of ideologies that influence decisions about when, how, and for what purposes students use languages as behavior in a science classroom (Lemmi et al., 2019). Ideologies also shape views of science discourse as product or process. Translanguaging, either as theory or pedagogical practice (Wei, 2017), is common in research about science in multilingual classrooms (e.g., Poza, 2018). Wei (2017, p. 15) explains that translanguaging is "a practice and a process—a practice that involves dynamic and functionally integrated use of different languages and language varieties, but more importantly *a process of knowledge construction* that goes beyond language(s). It takes us beyond the linguistics of systems and speakers to a linguistics of participation." Thus, translanguaging advances a view of language as action for addressing social inequities, focusing on the learner, not language structure (García & Leiva, 2014). Desirable ideologies inspire teachers to design learning experiences that help students build knowledge and carry out analyses, while engaging in scientific and linguistic practices across contexts, languages, and modes. Still, as such ideologies are difficult to translate into teaching practices, an unfortunate outcome can be laissez-faire learning and discourse (Poza, 2018).

PEDAGOGICAL LANGUAGE KNOWLEDGE

Designing science curricula for English Learners requires a particular approach to pedagogy, one that builds on understanding of science as disciplinary activity, language as action (van Lier & Walqui, 2012), and students as active explorers of scientific phenomena and language. Designing curriculum requires that students be invited to multiple and recursive opportunities to interact with each other, while engaged in collaborative analysis and co-construction of conceptual understandings. Building on Shulman's (1987) teacher knowledge model, Galguera (2011) proposes five domains of Pedagogical Language Knowledge (PLK) related to curriculum design.

1. Language Ideology

The role of language in science curricula emerges from teachers' language ideology. Do teachers think that students should only use "correct" or "standard" English in their discussions of science problems (Lemmi et al., 2019)? Do they accept minor grammatical errors when the message is clear? These decisions depend on whether teachers think of language as a structure, communication tool, subject with discrete content (Kibler & Valdés, 2016), or dynamic action and behavior for "making meaning and shaping knowledge" (Swain, 2009, p. 98), clearly signaling how ideology influences decisions teachers make regarding what and how to teach.

2. Language as Local Practice

To teach science in the manner we propose, it is necessary to consider time, space, history, and location associated with language (Pennycook, 2010)—rather than structure alone. As an alternative to asking students to memorize vocabulary and corresponding definitions, or simply to complete sentence starters, we envision teachers who see students being regularly engaged in utilizing language that is defined and stimulated by relevant experiential content associated with phenomena. This second PLK domain assumes teachers' nuanced and individualized knowledge of language alone and in relation to content. While choosing content and designing tasks, teachers must reflect on current and historical factors that shape the learning conditions in the classroom, school, community, and the world from the students' perspective.

3. Language as Action

A third domain concerns communicative tasks that invite and reward metalinguistic and metacognitive analysis by students and teachers. A central element of teachers' pedagogical strategies is that of language as action (van Lier & Walqui, 2012), not as a prerequisite for learning science content or a collection of words and grammar rules required to demonstrate knowledge correctly, but as an integral component of what students do while exploring and learning about scientific phenomena, and as a way to create powerful scientific meaning (see also Lee, Quinn, & Valdés, 2013).

4. Language Development Curriculum

The fourth PLK domain calls for teachers to reexamine their views and ideas about how students' engagement with units, lessons, and tasks can create opportunities for language to emerge and develop. Teachers' beliefs about and decisions regarding content that is inviting, challenging, and supportive have powerful implications for the scope and sequence of tasks and activities. Following the Lesson Architecture described in Chapter 3, we recommend organizing learning experiences that (1) prepare the field for students' learning, (2) have students interact with the phenomenon and text(s), and (3) extend students' understanding. This sequence spirals upward, building on previous knowledge and enhancing students' language proficiency.

5. Assessment of Students' Language Use and Development

We argue for teachers' facilitating students' use of language-rich scientific practices, making assessment synonymous with authentic data collection and analysis, rather than points or percentiles on tests of discrete skills. Designing tasks that require students to perform actions and create products that demonstrate conceptual understandings, analysis, and language use for academic purposes (Valdés, Kibler, & Walqui, 2014) is but one component of assessment. Another is understanding how students learn content and develop language competencies by analyzing data from students' performances and products. While assessing students' learning and development in both science and language use, it is essential that teachers avoid a deficit view (MacSwan, 2000). Rather, we favor a view of English Learners as multilingual individuals capable of reading the world and creating rich meaning in it (Freire & Macedo, 1987). Teachers must design pedagogy and content that support and guide students through discourse that includes their multilingual assets, while fostering and assessing critical awareness toward academic language norms and conventions.

GUIDELINES FOR DESIGNING PHENOMENON-BASED INSTRUCTION FOR ENGLISH LEARNERS

Humans are naturally interested in phenomena—facts or situations that we can perceive through our senses and that are puzzling—and we see this as the germ of scientific endeavor. Yet, choosing phenomena to design language-rich learning opportunities must be strategic and informed by teachers' understanding of language as something we *do* while doing science, of the pedagogical structures necessary to facilitate rich, multimodal meaning-making, of appropriate and relevant texts and materials, and of evidence regarding students' learning and development. Our overarching concern is to engage and guide students as they conduct investigations to understand, explain, and analyze problems and possible solutions, and elaborate on concepts, all while processing and producing meaning. We offer three guidelines to develop opportunities for English Learners' science learning and language development:

1. Create space for students' discussions of scientific phenomena that build on their linguistic resources; provide space for students to elaborate on their thinking, to confer, resonate, or disagree with peers about their sense-making.
2. Remain open to an array of modalities that students might use to understand content and express ideas, a disposition that in turn requires that teachers reflect on their role and discursive moves

    as facilitators relative to students' role as resources of valued
    knowledge.
3. Choose resources that pique students' interest, raise questions,
    and spark debate. Careful text selection is paramount in designing
    quality language development lessons. Experiences, phenomena,
    and artifacts selected to engage student sense-making are equally
    important in designing quality science curricula.

We designed the lesson we present in this chapter to serve as an example
of how to amplify phenomenon-based science instruction to allow access for
all students, especially English Learners. Working iteratively with each other
and with the editors of this volume, we designed the lesson based on our
collective experience of over 60 years teaching, engaging in research, and
preparing teachers for English Learners in science classrooms. The lesson is
based on tasks similar to those we have taught to teachers and implemented
ourselves. We offer the lesson as an illustration of the guidelines discussed
above, not as a rigid lesson plan; hence, it should be viewed with teachers' particular classroom contexts in mind and adapted to serve students in
those classrooms.

We chose disease transmission as the lesson's topic because of its potential to engage the interests of students, especially students in middle or high
school, who are often fascinated by morbid facets of human life. The outline
and details we present are examples of opportunities for content learning
and language development in science, aligned with Pedagogical Language
Knowledge (Galguera, 2011) and the three design principles discussed
above. We ask readers to pay close attention to the parts of the lesson that
position students as scientists, the ways in which text is treated in different
modalities, and opportunities to engage students in formal and informal
scientific discourse developing their language repertoire.

Our choice of materials and tasks provides students with frequent and
purposeful opportunities to discuss the phenomena in question, encouraging and supporting *languaging*—the use of language that is always in evolution and that privileges communication, not correctness (Swain, 2009). This
stance is inclusive of languages, dialects, registers, and modes.

THE SCIENCE LESSON: INVESTIGATING THE
TRANSMISSION OF DISEASE

In exploring disease transmission, the central driving question that students
will seek to answer in this lesson is, "How do we get sick?" Through a
series of experiences, students develop their understanding of how communicable diseases can spread and how to prevent disease transmission. To
accomplish these goals, students engage in the scientific practices of asking

questions; using models; analyzing data; constructing explanations; and obtaining, evaluating, and communicating information (National Research Council, 2012). The lesson ends with a mock World Health Assembly meeting in which students propose strategies for limiting the global spread of antibiotic-resistant tuberculosis, one of the United States' top drug-resistant threats (Center for Disease Control, 2013).

The tasks we developed utilizes students' natural curiosity about germs and diseases. For example, students are invited to make sense of an article about antibiotic-resistant tuberculosis as a real concern for increasing numbers of urban communities and to apply their understanding to the creation of multimodal texts to promote infection-prevention initiatives. The lesson extends the understanding of students and spirals upward, providing students opportunities to further their conceptual and linguistic understandings, practice analysis skills on data from a simulation that models infection, and role play as members of the World Health Organization. The tasks throughout the lesson follow views of multiple languages and registers in contact, as local practice and as action, interacting with content, and as multiple opportunities for formal and informal assessment of students' understanding of disease transmission and of their ability to decode and encode relevant meaning.

Choosing a Focal Phenomenon

We focus on disease transmission because it affords opportunities for students to discuss a relevant topic with contemporary local and global significance. The selection of tuberculosis (TB) as a focal point provides students opportunities to discuss what differentiates bacterial from viral diseases, drug resistance, and the modern resurgence of diseases we thought were extinct. Until recently, TB was considered to be under control in more economically developed nations, like the United States. However, in 2013, the Centers for Disease Control published a report citing TB as one of the top 18 drug-resistant threats in the United States (Centers for Disease Control, 2013). News reports beginning in 2006 detailed the rising threat of drug-resistant TB in California (Allday, 2006) and the occurrence of TB in a number of other states (e.g., Freeman & Hipolit, 2017; Lindquist, 2018). Studying TB offers students an opportunity to discuss the microbial causes of the disease and, later, to compare bacterial and viral illness. Additionally, antibiotic resistance can be discussed in relation to a broader set of emergent resistant strains of disease (Centers for Disease Control, 2013).

This opportunity for students to make sense of, debate, and discuss the phenomenon of disease transmission occasions teachers' use of Pedagogical Language Knowledge discussed earlier. Activities provide students opportunities to interact with each other in ways that are meaningful in a science classroom and involve use of language that is local, meaningful, and relevant. Possibilities exist and are encouraged for multimodal language use, that is, representing ideas via various appropriate media, illustrating at the same time how classrooms can promote language as dynamic action. The lesson is organized around the three Moments described in Chapter 3: Preparing Learners, Interacting with Phenomena, and Extending Understanding.

Preparing Learners

The lesson begins with activities that prepare learners and help them build the field, developing understanding of diseases and disease transmission. Building on students' prior knowledge and experience, as well as developing new basic understandings, prepares learners to interact with the complex ideas and texts they are about to encounter and to develop conceptual understandings, skills, and language practices to access future texts, ideas, and problems. Such opportunities are especially important for English Learners, given their developing language proficiency and the rich experiences they possess that might be especially relevant.

The Preparing Learners segment of the lesson activates students' prior knowledge about the symptoms of communicable diseases and ways that diseases can be transmitted. It focuses students' attention specifically on coughing and sneezing and introduces the key terms "tuberculosis," "bacteria," and "outbreak." Three learning tasks are designed to accomplish the goal of preparing learners.

Describe a Time You Were Sick. The first activity is an opportunity for students to reflect on a time that they were sick and the symptoms they experienced. The teacher begins by posing a prompt like, "Think back to a time you were sick. How did you feel? Do you know what kind of sickness you had?"

In pairs, students interview each other—they ask for information and offer information in response to their partner's questions—and report their findings to the class, producing a composite list of symptoms and illnesses. The conversation does not delve into disease causes, but focuses on observations of symptoms and guesses or conjectures, expressed in students' own words, relating what they think might have made them sick (e.g., flu, cold, food poisoning). At this stage, the teacher refrains from correcting misinformation, collecting instead a list of students' ideas, leaving open the possibility to return and build on initial understandings. Further into the lesson, students will delve deeper into the different categories of disease and their causes. The purpose of this first activity is to help students tap into and build upon prior knowledge about symptoms such as fevers, body aches, coughing, and sneezing, and for teachers to assess students' knowledge and bridge relevant experiences to the practices intended by the lesson goals.

How to Sneeze. For the second activity, we chose a short video (https://www.youtube.com/watch?v=cQOSh6GLa_w_) that challenges students to think about how diseases are transmitted, builds their knowledge regarding Germ Theory (the notion that illness is caused by tiny living or nonliving things invisible to the naked eye), and introduces experimental design. The 2-minute video poses the question, "What is the safest way to sneeze?" In the video, investigators test sneezing without any coverage, sneezing into one's hands, sneezing into the elbow, and sneezing into a tissue to see which one is safest. Their method for measuring the effects of each technique involves inserting dye into the mouth of the sneezer and covering the floor with white paper. Next, investigators measure the length from the sneezer to the most distant spot of dye on the paper. Ultimately, the conclusion is that sneezing into a tissue is safest because nothing gets through.

After the class watches this video, the teacher asks students to evaluate and discuss the claim that using a tissue is the safest way to sneeze. What may arise in this debate is a discussion of scale: some things are too small to be seen with the naked eye. The tissue has tiny holes in it that are too small for us to see, and so it is possible that tiny objects could get through. However, sneezing through a tissue is one of the best medically accepted ways to prevent disease transmission. Students may also begin to discuss specifics of bacteria, viruses, and other pathogens here, if they have not already done so in the previous introductory activity.

Some students, especially English Learners, may be unfamiliar with terminology related to disease transmission in advance of such discussions. Teachers should, therefore, do their best to incorporate students' own words and encourage the expression of their ideas, although they may not be totally correct. The goal in this discussion is co-constructing understanding and meaning, rather than utilizing standard terminology. One possibility is to have students play "Language Detective" (see Chapter 3), viewing a short video on microorganisms with the task of identifying specific words used to describe size and shape, structural components, and life cycles. After the class has come to an adequate understanding of the topic, the teacher can introduce key words strategically. This may happen immediately in the lesson or later, depending on the class, the direction of discussion, and students' knowledge.

Case Studies of Pathogens. For the third and final Preparing Learners activity, students work toward building an understanding that there are different types of pathogens causing diseases of varying severity. Following a Jigsaw structure (see Chapters 2 and 4), the teacher assigns students to Base Groups, each representing a World Health Organization's response team. The teacher also sets up four stations, each representing infection hot spots around the world, and assigns students to corresponding Expert

Groups. One student from each Base Group travels to a specific hot spot to become an expert on one case and diagnose the disease it represents, relying on sources on resource cards (see Figures 5.1, 5.2, and 5.3). Students then go back to their Base Groups and report their findings. Jointly, the Base Group reaches a consensus on team recommendations for action. This portion of the lesson builds the field by introducing students to the notion of a pathogen and centering their attention on several pathogens of contemporary significance, including tuberculosis, the lesson's disease of interest.

The Jigsaw structure provides students with opportunities to develop an understanding of one particular pathogen and its local geographic context through interactions with peers and teacher in Expert Groups. The teacher reminds students that their goal is to use language, media, or other means available to understand their respective cases. Also, students practice reporting conclusions before going back to their Base Groups. To assess students' understanding and prevent the spread of erroneous information, the teacher reviews students' clinical notes before returning to their Base Groups. When reporting, students are invited to be creative when speaking, writing, drawing, or acting out what they learned about their particular disease.

Students complete all quadrants of the graphic organizer (Figure 5.1) in collaboration with Base Group peers, again using words, symbols, or pictures creatively to describe each hotspot's location and relevant information about the disease. Requiring students to present a recommendation for action in response to the hot spots creates authentic information gaps and opportunities for students to co-construct understandings about disease. Along the process, students are languaging; that is, they are developing their ability to express their ideas in increasingly more precise ways. Furthermore, the Jigsaw structure presents multiple entry points to understand disease transmission, enabling all students to participate and grow in their ability to engage in scientific practices. It also holds students accountable for communicating specific information to their Base Group because they have been supported through deliberately crafted interactions.

Pedagogically, the activities and materials described thus far represent curriculum that promotes language development, with students engaged in activities and language as local practice (Pennycook, 2010), relying on multimodal content. Further, the multiple communicative tasks that make up the lesson offer opportunities for authentic assessment, which in turn provide opportunities for teachers to gather data about students as learners and users of content and language.

The Disease Hotspots activity (Figures 5.2 and 5.3) offers students opportunities to rely on each other, to build on their experiences, and to develop linguistic resources to discuss a disease, its symptoms, and its geographic context. The task requires students to understand, then communicate with

Figure 5.1. Disease Hotspots: Case Studies in Pathogens

Disease Hotspots!

Today, you will travel around the world to four different countries. These countries are having outbreaks of certain diseases, so we call them "disease hotspots." You will play the role of a doctor who studies diseases (Epidemiologist), and you will meet with one patient in each country. Use clues in the patient's history to figure out what diseases they have.

Please use the resources provided on your resource card to help you make your diagnoses.

Clinical Case Study #1

Clinical Notes:

Diagnosis:

Why I gave this diagnosis:

Clinical Case Study #2

Clinical Notes:

Diagnosis:

Why I gave this diagnosis:

Clinical Case Study #3

Clinical Notes:

Diagnosis:

Why I gave this diagnosis:

Clinical Case Study #4

Clinical Notes:

Diagnosis:

Why I gave this diagnosis:

Teacher notes: Case # 1: Hanta virus (virus), Case # 2: Drug-resistant tuberculosis (bacteria), Case # 3: Histoplasmosis (fungus), Case # 4: Malaria (parasite)

words, pictures, gestures, or media what they learn to a different group. Teachers can assess students' understanding at specific points, such as the transition between Expert and Home Groups. Informally, teachers can observe students communicating, while posing open-ended questions that encourage students to elaborate on their understandings about disease transmission, pathogens, and disease symptoms.

Figure 5.2. Clinical Case Study Cards for Disease Hotspots Activity

Clinical Case Study #1

Location: San Jose, California, USA

Patient: A 16-year-old boy comes into his pediatrician's office reporting muscle aches in his back and legs. He has a headache, and he's coughing so hard that he sometimes vomits. You take his temperature, and it is 102°F. When you ask about his recent activities, he mentions that he has been working for the past 2 weeks to help clean out an old attic in his grandmother's house that was infested by mice.

Clinical Case Study #2

Location: Dushanbe, Tajikistan

Patient: A 45-year-old man comes into a clinic reporting that he has had a bad cough for 4 weeks. He has started coughing up some blood and he has a lot of sweating and a fever every night. You take his weight, and he notices that he is 10 lbs lighter than normal. He has lost weight! He also mentions that a few weeks ago he was diagnosed with bacterial bronchitis. At that time, he took some antibiotics, but they did not seem to help.

Clinical Case Study #3

Location: Memphis, TN, USA

Patient: A 14-year-old girl comes into her primary care physician's office saying that her knees and hips are aching and she has a dry cough. You notice that she has a rash on her torso, and also a fever of 101°F. The girl adds that she has recently come back from a school trip in Chattanooga where her class went spelunking in a cave.

Clinical Case Study #4

Location: Bogotá, Colombia

Patient: A 29-year-old woman comes to a public health clinic reporting that she has the chills and a high fever of 105°F. She feels very sick and has recently started vomiting and having diarrhea. When you do a physical examination, you notice several mosquito bites on her legs. She tells you that she has trouble with mosquitoes biting her often at night while she sleeps.

Figure 5.3. Resource Card for Disease Hotspots Activity

You may use the following resources as you try to diagnose each of your patients:

The Mayo Clinic Website: https://www.mayoclinic.org/
The Centers for Disease Control Website: https://www.cdc.gov/
The Kids' Health Website: https://kidshealth.org/

Interacting with the Phenomenon

The second Moment in this lesson involves grappling with the phenomenon of disease transmission. Recall that the big idea for the lesson is that infectious diseases are caused by tiny living or nonliving things that we cannot see with the naked eye and are transmitted through bodily fluids.

Living and Nonliving Things. In this segment, students begin by engaging with the notion of living and nonliving things, exploring what it means to be alive by examining and discussing whether particular objects are alive. Students then participate in similar discussions and classification of other types of pathogens, including viruses, protozoa, fungi, and worms. They then grapple with the notion that something can exist, yet be too small to be seen.

Reading about a TB Outbreak. The second activity in Moment Two asks students to engage in the focal phenomenon by reading one short article that is relevant to the topic and has the potential to engage students' interest: a *New York Times* (1994) article about a California high school that became notorious for a TB outbreak. This reading activity asks students to practice making sense of written text as they summarize key ideas, discuss parts that either coincide or run in conflict with their experiences, and jot down their reactions to organize their thoughts. This reading activity should be adapted with students' strengths in mind and with existing practices and norms teachers use to support students' sense-making and literacy development. For example, teachers might choose to have students read certain sections of the article silently or interactively and aloud. Teachers might also choose to focus on certain textual structures before, during, or after reading the text.

Before reading, the teacher hands out the Anticipatory Guide (Table 5.1) and students select their reactions to each statement, subsequently explaining their responses. The teacher begins by reading the first three paragraphs aloud to the class in an animated fashion. Then the teacher asks the students to think-pair-share about the questions: "What happened at the high school?" and "What do you want to know more about?" The first three paragraphs introduce the terms *tuberculosis, drug-resistance*, and *outbreak*. The teacher leads the class, discussing briefly related background knowledge before handing out the text of the sixth paragraph. Students spend about 5 minutes reading and making sense of the text individually first and then with a partner, asking "What did I understand?" and "What questions do I have?" Finally, the teacher leads the class in reading aloud the entire paragraph, making sense of its meaning.

The Anticipatory Guide and *New York Times* article support English Learners by engaging their interest in something fascinating, a disease outbreak affecting students their own age, and inviting then to predict possible outcomes. By making predictions before reading and adjusting them

Table 5.1. Anticipatory Guide for Readings

Statement	BEFORE READING: Do you agree or disagree? Circle one.	BEFORE READING: Why? Explain your thinking.	DURING READING: Is there evidence in support? Circle one and write page number.	AFTER READING: What is your conclusion? Explain your thinking.
It is possible for some diseases to become stronger than medicines.	Agree / Disagree		Agree / Disagree / Not sure Page: ___	
There are disease outbreaks happening in California.	Agree / Disagree		Agree / Disagree / Not sure Page: ___	
An outbreak is when diseases go away completely.	Agree / Disagree		Agree / Disagree / Not sure Page: ___	
You should never touch someone who is sick.	Agree / Disagree		Agree / Disagree / Not sure Page: ___	
Learning about diseases can help you stay healthy.	Agree / Disagree		Agree / Disagree / Not sure Page: ___	

afterward, students are given multiple opportunities to engage with the content, formulate ideas, and co-construct understandings, eventually becoming able to revise their original responses. Additionally, reading strategies described above—such as producing short summaries, jotting notes, or reading alone and then speaking with a partner—provide English Learners with abundant opportunities for social learning and nonthreatening steps toward understanding the article.

Experimenting with Bacteria Growth. The third activity in the Interacting Moment involves students designing an experiment to test a question about bacterial growth (see Figure 5.4). The teacher poses the question: "Can you develop an experiment that demonstrates the best conditions for preventing bacterial growth?" All groups receive a number of petri dishes filled with agar, selecting from among the following materials: a microwave, a refrigerator, hand sanitizer, diluted bleach solution, vinegar, water, salt, and sugar. Groups brainstorm together and come up with two or three different experimental designs with which to test materials they chose. Students should be familiar with treatment and control variables, and general procedures for setting up an experiment, but teachers may provide examples of

Figure 5.4. Experimental Design: Bacterial Growth

Battle of the Bacteria

Bacteria are all over the place! They are on our skin, inside our bodies, and on every surface in the room. They are so tiny that we can't see them, but they are there. Many bacteria are good for us and they help us to live. However, some bacteria are harmful and can make us sick. We need to learn how to stop the growth of these harmful bacteria!!

Your challenge: Design an experiment to show the best conditions for preventing bacterial growth.

Materials available: Petri dishes, agar, q-tips, a refrigerator or cooler with ice, a microwave or container of boiling water, vinegar, diluted bleach solution (½ cup bleach in one gallon of water), baking soda.

Hints: You don't need to use ALL of the materials for your experiment, but you do need to use the one your teacher assigns you. Each group will design a different experiment, so don't worry about what the group next to you is doing. You will get a chance to plan your experiment and share your plans with your teacher and the class to get feedback. After you get feedback, you'll have a chance to modify and improve your design before you run a second experiment.

Note: Instead of bacteria, it is possible to use mold growing on bread, which may be more accessible in some locations. If mold is used, the teacher can lead a discussion about the similarities and differences between mold and bacteria.

experimental designs that might be used, as needed. Also, to ensure that all variables are tested, the teacher assigns one to each of the teams.

The next step of the lesson involves groups comparing experiment plans and offering critiques and feedback to each other. The teacher circulates around the groups, answering and posing questions to them, thus helping them refine their experimental designs. It is important to note that the teacher does NOT lead with a lecture about the proper ways to design an experiment. By interacting with other group members, students further their understanding of principles like testing one variable at a time. After the peer-review and teacher review session is complete, groups set up their respective experiments.

The class must agree on the duration of the experiment, although students collect data about changes they observe throughout. The data collected can be qualitative (draw and describe what you see) or quantitative (measure the size and count the number of colonies you see). Again, these methods of data collection should be primarily developed by the groups prior to the experiment and in consultation with each other first, and with the teacher only when necessary. Ideally, the class has designed a set of six to eight different experiments, each one unique yet also addressing the same central question: What influences bacterial growth?

After collecting data, each group reports to the class on their initial question, how they tested it, and what they found. In preparation for this, the teacher makes clear the requirements and expectations for this report both for content (i.e., conclusion and supporting evidence) and form (i.e., clear, sufficiently loud, and involving all team members). Each group also comments on ways to improve their design if they were to repeat the experiment.

Simulating Disease Transmission. The final activity in the Interacting Moment is a simulation of how diseases are transmitted. This experience allows students to analyze data about how diseases are spread throughout a population and on the probabilities of being infected. Students each represent one individual in a population, and they each hold a plastic cup or test tube filled with clear liquid. The teacher tells the class that only one or two of their classmates are infected with a disease, represented by sodium carbonate, an invisible salt when dissolved in water. Next, students use eye droppers or q-tips to place a small amount of their liquid into the cups of five classmates. Here, the teacher explains that the exchange of liquids represents the exchange of bodily fluids, and that various pathogens are transmitted through different types of bodily fluids (e.g., a cold can be transmitted through saliva and mucus, but HIV is only transmitted through blood, breastmilk, or semen). After the fluid exchange, the teacher comes around to perform a test in which a drop of phenolphthalein or similar chemical indicator is placed into each cup; a change of color indicates infection. Aided by the teacher, students devise a method to record the class data and calculate the probability of becoming infected with the pathogen. For comparison, the teacher may choose to discuss the infection rates for TB in the local area. As an extension, the teacher may ask students to come up with strategies and methods to find out which classmates originated the "infection." The class can then discuss reasons for finding infection sources, which include discovering how diseases originate and spread through a population, as well as rates of infection, which can inform control and eradication programs.

For English Learners, this task offers opportunities for physical engagement in modeling the way that diseases are spread. The visual cue provided by the color change in each container of liquid provides a clear and powerful representation of percentages of infection, which can be generally understood even without much verbal or written explanation at all. Furthermore, carrying out the various steps in this activity provides students with rich and multiple opportunities for learning and languaging (Swain, 2009), and for the teacher to assess related knowledge and skills.

Again, rather than prescribing specific vocabulary use, or asking students to complete sentence frames, the tasks in this section of the lesson encourage students to rely on their linguistic resources to understand the simulation and demonstrate knowledge. Both in the discussion of experimental designs and in the analysis of rates of infection as indicated by phenolphthalein changing color, students are encouraged to rely on words, diagrams, or other forms of representation to explain their reasoning, both in small groups and to the entire class. These representations, depending on context and the linguistic composition of the group as well as purposes, may include various languages and spoken as well as written words, diagrams, and recordings. The language ideology behind such an inclusive view of meaning-making is likely to suggest other creative options for pedagogy and content that encourage students to combine modes and languages.

Extending Understanding

For the Extending Understanding moment, students participate in a mock World Health Organization (WHO) meeting called the World Health Assembly in order to develop a plan for addressing drug-resistant tuberculosis outbreaks. The activity extends students' understanding of disease transmission by addressing the issues of antibiotic resistance and public health.

In this simulation (see Figure 5.5 and Table 5.2), the teacher arranges the class into groups of three or four students and assigns each group a nation that they will represent. Students first meet with their country group to research general information about their assigned country, including TB infection rates and the drug-resistant TB strains. One representative from each country group gives a brief presentation to the class about the problems of

Figure 5.5. World Health Organization Assembly Task

**World Health
Organization**

World Health Organization Assembly on Multidrug-Resistant Tuberculosis

Today, you will participate in a World Health Organization (WHO) Assembly. The WHO is a group in the UN that works together to solve health problems all over the world. You will meet to discuss the problem of multidrug-resistant tuberculosis (MDR TB) strains.

Meeting #1: Meet with your group to obtain relevant information about your assigned country, such as population size, poverty level, and health services. Summarize MDR TB as a problem in your country. How many people have MDR TB? What do you think the WHO could do about this problem in your country?

Meeting #2: Meet with your international small group. Introduce the problem from your perspective. As a group, come up with a list of at least five actions that could help solve the problem.

Finally, the entire WHO will come together (the whole class) and create a plan for controlling MDR TB.

Table 5.2. World Health Organization Assembly Handout

WHO Assembly Notes	
Meeting #1: Country Group	Meeting #2: International Small Group
Meeting #3: The entire WHO	**My notes or questions:**

TB infection in their nation, and the class brainstorms a list of proposed ways the nations can work together to address the problem. The class generates a list of top strategies they believe should be used to address the problem, and the teacher breaks students into groups to create a poster explaining and illustrating their strategies. The teacher works to ensure that the students' lists address the areas of prevention and treatment of TB itself and also prevention of drug resistance.

A final activity serves as a summative assessment of students' learning. In this segment, students record an educational radio or TV public service announcement to help raise awareness about antibiotic resistant TB. The audience for the announcement should be the general public in the town or city where the students live, including radio listeners of all ages and languages. Students develop a short 1–2-minute announcement that addresses the issues of prevention, treatment, and drug resistance, writing at least one draft for peer review with a partner before they complete the final version. Teachers encourage students to creatively mesh spoken and written language as well as images and sound to maximize the power of their message. At the end of the lesson, students may share their digital recordings with the class or small groups.

This activity provides English Learners with an opportunity to communicate what they have learned to a broader audience. The task provides the chance for them to distill what they now know and select the most compelling content through which to communicate their message to a local audience. This final task also provides students with opportunities to examine the value of content and mode in communication, as well as to gain metalinguistic awareness of genres and registers.

CONCLUSION

The language students use to engage in all of the above tasks can take many forms and modalities (e.g., speech, writing, representations, or performances), and students' development of scientific practices (conceptual, analytic, and language) is not reduced to prescribing a language focus on functions, structures, or specific forms. Nevertheless, teachers can be explicit with students about potential linguistic challenges as well as the linguistic performance expectations associated with each task. Scaffolds used throughout the lesson—such as asking students about their experiences with illness and disease, the use of learning centers, an extended Anticipatory Guide, questions and variables for their investigation, and a graphic organizer with prompts to help them plan and carry out the bacteria growth inhibitor experiment—all present "information gaps" that promote students' use of language for meaning-making within communicative tasks.

The sequence of tasks promotes an understanding of science practices as comprised of conceptual engagement, analysis, and language development and use for academic purposes. In the Preparing Learners Moment, tasks and content activate students' prior knowledge and interest, with personal narratives as an attainable product. In the Interacting with Text and Phenomena Moment, reading a text and designing an experiment require students to analyze and summarize information. Finally, in the Extending Understanding Moment, the tasks require students to extend their understanding by translating their knowledge across modalities and genres. The sequence of content and tasks represents a developmental perspective for both content and language learning, with tasks becoming increasingly complex and demanding, while remaining interesting and engaging for students. Similarly, each of the three Moments in the lesson contains points at which teachers may record students' behaviors or collect products to analyze as data in order to answer the questions, "What did students learn?", "In what ways did their language develop?", and "How can I provide further opportunities and supports for science learning and language development?"

REFERENCES

Allday, E. (2006, March 24). CDC concerned about drug-resistant TB/San Francisco has highest rate of disease in country. *San Francisco Chronicle*. Retrieved from https://www.sfgate.com/health/article/SAN-FRANCISCO-CD-concerned-about-2501152.php

Centers for Disease Control. (2013). Antibiotic/antimicrobial resistance: Biggest threats and data. Retrieved from https://www.cdc.gov/drugresistance/biggest_threats.html

Freeman, V., & Hipolit, M. (2017, April 24). Close to 200 Henrico students may have been exposed to tuberculosis. *CBS News*. Retrieved from https://wtvr.com/2017/04/24/henrico-students-may-have-been-exposed-to-tuberculosis/

Freire, P., & Macedo, D. P. (1987). *Literacy: Reading the word & the world*. London, UK: Routledge.

Galguera, T. (2011). Participant structures as professional learning tasks and the development of pedagogical language knowledge among preservice teachers. *Teacher Education Quarterly, 38*(1), 85–106.

García, O., & Leiva, C. (2014). Theorizing and enacting translanguaging for social justice. In A. Blackledge & A. Creese (Eds.), *Heteroglossia as practice and pedagogy* (pp. 199–216). Dordrecht, Netherlands: Springer.

Gutiérrez, K. D., & Rogoff, B. (2003). Cultural ways of learning: Individual traits or repertoires of practice. *Educational Researcher, 32*(5), 19–25.

Irivine, J. T. (1989). When talk isn't cheap: Language and political economy. *American Ethnologist, 16*(2), 248–267.

Kibler, A. K., & Valdés, G. (2016). Conceptualizing language learners: Socioinstitutional mechanisms and their consequences. *The Modern Language Journal, 100*(S1), 96–116.

Lee, O., Quinn, H., & Valdés, G. (2013). Science and language for English Language Learners in relation to Next Generation Science Standards and with implications for Common Core State Standards for English language arts and mathematics. *Educational Researcher, 42*, 234–249.

Lemmi, C., Brown, B. A., Wild, A., Zummo, L., & Sedlacek, Q. (2019) Language ideologies in science education. *Science Education*, 1–21.

Lindquist, S. (2018, August 21). Is tuberculosis making a comeback? *US News & World Report*. Retrieved from https://www.usnews.com/news/healthiest-com munities/articles/2018-08-21/is-tuberculosis-making-a-comeback

Lyon, E. G., Tolbert, S., Solís, J., Stoddart, T., & Bunch, G. C. (Eds.). (2016). *Secondary science teaching for English learners: Developing supportive and responsive learning contexts for sense-making and language development*. Lanham, MD: Rowman & Littlefield.

MacSwan, J. (2000). The threshold hypothesis, semilingualism, and other contributions to a deficit view of linguistic minorities. *Hispanic Journal of Behavioral Sciences, 22*(1), 3–45.

McNeill, K. L. (2009). Teachers' use of curriculum to support students in writing scientific arguments to explain phenomena. *Science Education, 93*(2), 233–268.

Mehta, J., & Fine, S. (2017). How we got here: The imperative for deeper learning. In R. Heller, R. E. Wolfe, & A. Steinberg (Eds.), *Rethinking readiness: Deeper learning for college, work, and life* (pp. 11–35). Cambridge, MA: Harvard Education Press.

National Research Council. (2012). *A framework for K–12 science education: Practices, crosscutting concepts, and core ideas*. Washington, DC: The National Academies Press. doi:10.17226/13165

NGSS Lead States. (2013). *Next generation science standards: For states, by states* (Appendix F). Washington, DC: The National Academies Press.

New York Times. (1994, July 18). California school becomes notorious for epidemic of TB. Retrieved from https://www.nytimes.com/1994/07/18/us/california-school -becomes-notorious-for-epidemic-of-tb.html

Pennycook, A. (2010). *Language as a local practice*. New York, NY: Routledge.

Poza, L. E. (2018). The language of ciencia: Translanguaging and learning in a bilingual science classroom. *International Journal of Bilingual Education and Bilingualism, 21*(1), 1–19.

Shulman, L. (1987). Knowledge and teaching: Foundations of the new reform. *Harvard Educational Review, 57*(1), 1–23.

Swain, M. (2009). Languaging, agency and collaboration in advanced second language proficiency. In H. Byrnes (Ed.), *Advanced language learning: The contribution of Halliday and Vygotsky* (pp. 95–108). London, UK: A&C Black.

Valdés, G., Kibler, A., & Walqui, A. (2014). *Changes in the expertise of ESL professionals: Knowledge and action in an era of new standards*. Alexandria, VA: TESOL International Association.

van Lier, L., & Walqui, A. (2012, January). How teachers and educators can most usefully and deliberately consider language. Paper presented at the Understanding Language Conference, Stanford, CA. Retrieved from http://ell.stanford.edu /papers/language

Warren, B., Ballenger, C., Ogonowski, M., Rosebery, A. S., & Hudicourt-Barnes, J. (2001). Rethinking diversity in learning science: The logic of everyday sensemaking. *Journal of Research in Science Teaching, 38*(5), 529–552. doi:10.1002/ tea.1017

Wei, L. (2017). Translanguaging as a practical theory of language. *Applied Linguistics, 39*(1), 9–30.

CHAPTER 6

Making Slope a Less Slippery Concept for English Learners

Redesigning Mathematics Instruction with Rich Interactions

Leslie Hamburger and Haiwen Chu

Imagine an algebra classroom buzzing as students talk in small groups about linear functions. Groups of four working together reflect the language diversity of students in the United States, including Chinese speakers who arrived in the late elementary grades, speakers of Spanish who have been recently reclassified as English language proficient, speakers of various languages other than English who were born in the United States, and students who have never been classified as English Learners.

Each student has a card with either a graph or a table corresponding to four points of a linear function. One key condition of the activity is that students are not allowed to show each other their cards (see Figure 6.1). As a result, students give each other information verbally to reconstruct either the graph or the table of a linear function. They then make the other representation together: if a graph is given, they make the table; if a table is given, they make the graph.

As they work together, each student talks, listens, and asks questions. Each student has a turn as the describer, and all students must contribute for the group to succeed. As students talk with each other, they build shared understandings of key mathematical representations and relationships. With their graphs and tables all complete, the students turn to describing changes in x and y from a selected starting point. Each student contributes by describing changes in x and changes in y for one of the other three points on the line, relative to the starting point. As they work, students explore generative mathematical concepts such as rates of change and mathematical practices such as attending to precision.

This kind of student activity illustrates opportunities that help all students learn mathematics deeply but are especially critical for English

Figure 6.1. Read and Do Table and Graph Cards

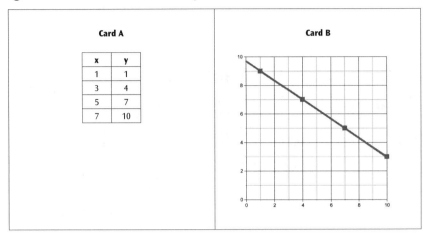

Learners. Structured, quality interactions with peers help to balance the high challenge of academic standards with high levels of support. If teachers of English Learners offer them abundant opportunities to connect their own experiences to new ideas, to participate in activities with their peers, and to engage in sustained talk that develops mathematical ideas, all students will benefit.

Unfortunately, typical mathematics instruction for English Learners does not yet consistently have all of these characteristics (e.g., Lampert, 2017). For their English Learners to meet the ambitious demands of new mathematics standards such as those in the Common Core, teachers will need to shift instruction from current practice. Specifically, shifts in practice are needed to ensure that students have greater access to important mathematical ideas and enhanced opportunities to participate in mathematical practices. These shifts connect three key areas: conceptual understanding, opportunities to participate and interact with peers, and abundant language practices (Heritage, Walqui, & Linquanti, 2015). In this chapter, we explore how shifts in these three areas provide explicit guidance for the design of learning opportunities in mathematics that benefit all learners, particularly English Learners.

As former secondary mathematics teachers who together have more than three decades of experience designing and enacting professional development for teachers of English Learners, we share in this chapter a lesson we created to help students understand the concept of slope in linear functions. We provide this example to illustrate three key characteristics of effective instructional design: a clear conceptual focus, rich opportunities for peer dialogue, and a focus on language that enables English Learners to connect ideas and engage in practices.

These three characteristics of instructional design are related to three shifts that extend the progress already being addressed in reform-oriented approaches to mathematics education, but that have an explicit focus on challenging and supporting English Learners:

- Because traditional instruction has been procedure-bound, rich problems involving important mathematics have been suggested as more challenging. For English Learners, it is critical that lessons be driven by clear, explicit conceptual goals that are well articulated.
- In making discussion less teacher-dominated, instruction needs to move beyond teacher-facilitated conversations to include carefully designed and structured opportunities where English Learners can control what they say and participate in rich *peer* dialogue.
- In moving past the meanings of individual words, English Learners need to attend explicitly to the language that enables them to develop deep conceptual understandings and engage in mathematical practices.

To enact these three shifts in designing mathematical lessons for English Learners, teachers can undertake three corresponding actions:

1. Center lessons for English Learners on concepts.
2. Foster quality peer interactions for English Learners to co-construct understanding.
3. Offer language supports that assist English Learners to develop understanding and engage in disciplinary practices.

SHIFTS IN MATHEMATICS INSTRUCTION FOR ENGLISH LEARNERS

Enacting these shifts requires transforming how teachers design and implement lessons. In this chapter, we illustrate how to enact these shifts by examining an exemplar lesson on the concept of slope, a central and generative idea of algebra. The focal lesson's conception of slope extends beyond the formulaic and algorithmic understandings usually featured in mathematics classrooms and instead develops the concept of slope as the rate of change connecting two variables or quantities (Lobato & Thanheiser, 2002; Stump, 1999). Without well-structured invitations to participate, English Learners may be excluded from this type of ambitious, conceptually oriented understanding of slope (Zahner, 2015). In the next section, details regarding each of the three shifts, discussed next, provide an explanation of their importance in supporting English Learners' access to high-challenge mathematics.

From Procedure-Bound to Concept-Driven

Mathematics instruction in the United States has typically been centered on teachers' modeling procedures without providing mathematical or practical motivation for what those procedures mean and why they work (Stigler & Hiebert, 1999). This teaching of procedures without connections to meaning results in low cognitive demand and leaves students unable to independently select and apply mathematical procedures in novel situations (Stein, Smith, Henningsen, & Silver, 2000).

As a response to this persistent and pervasive pattern, standards-based mathematics reform has sought to center instruction on rich problems (Stein et al., 2000). Solving these problems enables students to experience more contextualized mathematics, understand multiple solution approaches, and engage in developing important mathematical ideas. To make this happen, teachers need to enact pedagogical practices to orchestrate whole-class discussions that support students as they compare and connect solution methods, rather than just engage in "show and tell" of solution methods (e.g., Stein, Engle, Smith, & Hughes, 2008). Real-world contexts often serve as the setting for these problems. Instruction that relies on rich problems must ensure that English Learners have full, equitable access and opportunities to participate.

We acknowledge the importance of the problem-centered approach as we further claim that English Learners will benefit from mathematics lessons with designs other than those centered on a single, rich problem. By occasionally and strategically changing the focus to a carefully selected *concept*, teachers can ensure that English Learners do not lose the "mathematical point" of the lesson (Sleep, 2012). By focusing on the conceptual goal, teachers can prevent solving problems from declining into unsystematic exploration that does not work toward a clear conceptual goal (Stein et al., 2000).

From Interactions Led by Teachers to Rich Peer Dialogue

Teachers have traditionally controlled the discourse in mathematics classes, often with the Initiation-Response-Feedback pattern in which a teacher asks a question, a student responds, and the teacher provides feedback about whether the student is right or wrong (Herbel-Eisenmann & Breyfogle, 2005). As the teacher dominates interactions with students, key mathematical ideas often fade into the background (Stigler & Hiebert, 1999).

Alternatives to teacher domination have been centered primarily on teacher facilitation moves for students' sharing or presenting ideas to the whole class (Stein et al., 2008). In the same way, many of these approaches to mathematical discourse position students as presenting their finished solution methods, rather than negotiating meaning as it develops.

Opportunities for amplification, as conceptualized in Chapter 2, are more equitable for English Learners because they instead center on quality peer interactions that are characterized by sustained and reciprocal talk aimed at co-constructing mathematical understandings. Oral interactions are central to the development of understanding. Through sustained dialogue, students test out new ideas or conjectures, clarify understandings, rehearse explanations, and develop increasingly sophisticated ways to participate (Koelsch, Chu, & Bañuelos, 2014).

From Meanings of Words to Using Language for Developing and Connecting Ideas

Language is central to conceptual development and student participation, and its role in education needs to be radically reconsidered. In math, attention to language has typically focused on English Learners' acquiring vocabulary (Moschkovich, 2002). Often, definitions are introduced well before students need them (Lampert, 2017). We assert this approach is less productive than definitions that formalize a concept that students have already been exploring. We propose instead that a *working* definition is more inviting and provides greater access to the central idea of a lesson. A working definition captures the idea behind a concept in a way that is immediately accessible and which leads to a more formal definition. For example, rather than defining the arithmetic mean with the procedure for calculating it (i.e., the sum of the data values divided by the number of data points), the working definition is the *idea* that motivates a mathematical procedure (e.g., the amount if equally shared) (Chu & Rubel, 2013).

Other language opportunities for English Learners in mathematics instruction frequently include cloze activities in which students fill in the blanks in writing or complete oral scripts (such as, "The slope is . . ."). Such sentence starters, while intended to be supportive, place attention primarily on bits and pieces of language, grammatical correctness, and the substitution of specific words in isolated contexts. Furthermore, English Learners are often only offered simplified texts and story problems that are telegraphic in composition (assuming students already understand key relationships within the context and genre) or tailored to a cultural/linguistic frame of reference (such as making pancakes). These texts limit students' access and opportunities to make meaning about mathematical ideas.

In contrast, we propose a focus on purposes for language broader than individual words in isolation. To develop deep conceptual understanding, English Learners need ample opportunities to connect personal experiences, mathematical ideas, representations, and procedures. This grappling with ideas is only achieved with language, so participating in mathematical practices includes the development of conceptual, analytic, and language practices simultaneously (Heritage, Walqui, & Linquanti, 2015). Rich, complex texts that connect real-world experiences and contexts with mathematical ideas, such as the one at the center of the slope lesson, can enhance English Learners' access to important mathematical concepts (Chu & Rubel, 2013).

DEVELOPING CONCEPTUAL UNDERSTANDING OF SLOPE

Because the development of lessons is driven by conceptual goals, in this section we elaborate on why slope is a central and generative idea of algebra, how slope can serve as an anchor in a coherent unit of instruction, and how the lesson unfolds with these goals in mind.

Slope as a Central and Generative Idea of Algebra

Our conception of slope extends beyond usual formulaic and algorithmic understandings by developing the concept of slope as the rate of change connecting two variables or quantities (Lobato & Thanheiser, 2002; Stump, 1999). Focusing on the rate of change rather than graphical properties better aligns slope with the emphasis on *functions* as a unifying concept of algebra. This conception is richer than the static symbolic formula that students are often taught to recite:

$$m = \frac{y_2 - y_1}{x_2 - x_1}$$

For English Learners especially, familiar formulas such as "rise over run" are not only conceptually sparse but also linguistically opaque. That is, when recited as a formula, "rise over run" is purely procedural without explicit connections to the central idea of rates of change, while requiring highly specialized meanings of "rise" and "run" that do not continue to be useful in their later mathematical studies. While English Learners will need to understand and apply such formulas, we assert that such formulas are not pedagogically productive points of departure. Standard formulas better serve as "stops" on English Learners' journeys to developing conceptual understanding, or concise summaries of concepts they have explored in depth.

Slope as Anchor for an Instructional Unit

While this chapter focuses on the slope lesson, we do so understanding that it must connect to broader ideas and practices. "A Less Slippery Slope" is a lesson in a larger unit about linear functions, entitled *Straight at Any Rate,* developed in collaboration with secondary teachers at the International Newcomer Academy in Fort Worth, Texas. As part of a sustained, 3-year whole-school instructional coaching effort, we collaborated with teachers at the school to create, implement, and refine a number of lessons and activities. The curriculum that teachers were using addressed solving linear equations and linear inequalities as if they were completely disconnected topics. To better facilitate connections between equations and inequalities, our team designed a unit with linear functions as the central idea.

In this unit, students explore representations and concepts about linear functions in preparation for analyzing linear inequalities in one variable, and then systems of linear equations. Conceptual understandings are woven together with analytic and language practices to allow students to develop robust understandings of the concepts and procedures associated with linear functions in multiple representations. In the first lesson of the unit, students consider proportional relationships in which one variable is in direct variation with another, contrasting these with other linear or inverse variation relationships. Then, in lesson two, "A Less Slippery Slope," students analyze changes in x and y as direct variation to develop the notion of slope through the real-world contexts of stairs and ramps. In subsequent lessons, students connect two common forms for the equation of a line, that of slope-intercept and standard form, and analyze how x- and y-intercepts are related to these two forms. The unit culminates in investigating linear inequalities by comparing the graphs of two linear functions, as a preview of working with systems of linear equations. We present the overall trajectory of this unit in Figure 6.2.

Within the context of a broader unit of instruction, the slope lesson draws upon understandings of unit rates within contextualized story problems. These unit rates connect to different types of quantities that students explored in the first lesson (e.g., miles per gallon or dollar per hour). For the purpose of developing the slope formula in this lesson, however, units were intentionally omitted in order to focus instead on numerical relationships. In later lessons, as students connect the idea of linear functions to compare different rates and to develop the idea of systems of linear equations, rates and units are reintroduced as a means of grounding the meaning of slopes of different sizes and signs. These lessons illustrate not only how to make strategic choices about when to contextualize, maintaining an explicit focus on real-world contexts to draw upon prior knowledge or apply to new situations, but also when to decontextualize, focusing on the relationships between mathematical representations such as graphs, equations, and tables without referring to a real-world context. These moves connect to the need to "reason abstractly and quantitatively" in the Common Core Standards. Indeed, decontextualizing (i.e., not attending to real-world units) can facilitate other practices, such as "look for and make use of structure."

Figure 6.2. Design and Trajectory of a Unit on Linear Functions

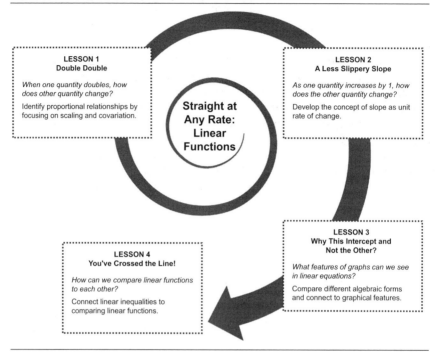

Slope as Developed in the Lesson

Using the Three Moments architecture introduced in Chapter 3, "A Less Slippery Slope" is comprised of six tasks that provide explicit structures for students to interact with one another in the exploration of mathematical ideas. These tasks are represented in Figure 6.3, with the conceptual objective of each task displayed on the left and specific type of scaffolding task named on the right side of the arrow. This diagram shows the "story" of the lesson, a scheme for making public both the conceptual trajectory of the lesson (the "what") and the specific pedagogical structures teachers will use to assist students in achieving those objectives (the "how") in ways that purposefully attend to language. The focus of this overview is on the conceptual trajectory of the lesson; in later sections, we will unpack the peer interactions that the scaffolding tasks enable and the language supports that further facilitate these interactions.

Preparing English Learners to Engage with Steepness and Slope. In order to maximize English Learners' access to the ideas underlying slope and to tap into the resources they bring to the learning experience, the lesson solicits

Figure 6.3. The "Story" of the Less Slippery Slope Lesson

Preparing	Focus on what facilitates climbing	Think-Pair-Share
	Compare and order staircases	Sort and Order
Interacting	Connect staircases to ramps	Read w/Clarifying Bookmark
	Calculate slope in graphs & tables	Read and Do
Extending	Extend to new situations with different given information	Collaborative Problem and Poster
	Make decisions and plans using slope	Collaborative Writing

- Calculate and identify slope in multiple representations, including equations, tables, and graphs.
- Identify real-world applications for slope involving stairs and ramps.
- Accurately describe and compare lines in terms of slope.

students' prior, but not prerequisite, knowledge through two interactive discussion tasks. The first draws upon students' experiences with climbing in general, inviting and allowing them to share all sorts of experiences that highlight how vertical motion and horizontal motion are related to each other. The role of the teacher in whole-class sharing is to highlight the horizontal and vertical components, as a way of narrowing the focus in subsequent tasks.

Pairs of students then take turns sorting and ordering staircases cut out of cardstock. Students sort these manipulatives in terms of how hard they would be to climb, and the term *steep* is introduced as a way of talking about how hard it might be to climb a staircase. The teacher provides explicit models that are particularly useful for English Learners, characterizing staircases as "steeper" or "less steep" in comparison to others. These initial experiences enable students to engage in attending to key features of staircases, in preparation for considering ramps or lines.

Interacting with Complex Texts and Mathematical Representations. The slope lesson is centered on two tasks that are focused on reading in two different senses: reading a complex informational text and reading mathematical representations (tables and graphs). First, students read a rich, complex text that names and connects familiar features of staircases with the real-world uses and rules for ramps. The text has been engineered to promote access with features that signal purposes and opportunities to make meaning. These text features include: subheadings, focus questions, and images. Students read this text in pairs, taking turns to apply the Clarifying Bookmark, which is designed to encourage students to make connections to prior experiences or knowledge in order to facilitate reading comprehension (see Chapter 3).

Students explicitly transition from stairs to ramps as they complete the second reading task. In the Read and Do task, students collaboratively co-ordinate tables with graphs of linear functions, as described in the opening to this chapter. The task also provides a specific formulaic expression for students to use as they explicitly describe the horizontal and vertical changes of points on a line with reference to a given starting point. This linguistic support is necessary for students to manage the cognitive load of connecting four parameters: a starting point, a second point, the horizontal change, and the vertical change.

From this analysis of the points on the line as paired horizontal and vertical changes, the teacher leads a whole-class discussion in which she de-velops with students the concept of slope as the *unit* rate of change. It is at this point in the lesson that students are able to understand slope as a way of measuring how two quantities co-vary, with a focus on numerical relation-ships found in tables and graphs.

Extending Understanding of Slope to Novel Situations. Students extend their understanding of slope as the lesson concludes with a number of col-laborative activities centered on real-world problems involving building ramps and modeling them mathematically with tables, graphs, or equations. In this portion of the lesson, teachers emphasize to students that they need to become strategic users of representations: while solving a problem, stu-dents may use different representations, but when they then re-present their solution in the format of a collaboratively constructed poster, they must select a single representation and provide a rationale for why that represen-tation is optimal for their purpose.

Students also jointly construct a business letter in which they apply their understandings of slope and federal regulations for wheelchair ramps to make decisions about the design of new construction projects. This task is also an invitation for students to engage in text representation, transferring their understandings into a new genre.

SHIFTS IN ACTION

In this section, we unpack how the slope lesson puts each of the three shifts described earlier into action. Quality learning opportunities for English Learners support students' engagement in rigorous disciplinary practices. This kind of instruction includes conceptual understandings along with the analytic and language practices valued by the community of mathematics and required for "doing mathematics." In well-constructed instructional ex-periences, these practices are woven together seamlessly, but for the purpose of understanding the design of such instruction and to unpack how lesson plans can be amplified for English learners, we will attend to different design elements one at a time. We introduce each redesign action with some generative questions that we have found useful for thinking through a lesson design. We then unpack how the slope lesson enacts actions related to each of the shifts, which are to:

1. Center lessons for English Learners on concepts to drive lesson activities.
2. Foster quality peer interactions with English Learners to co-construct understanding.
3. Offer language support that enables English Learners to develop understanding and engage in disciplinary practices.

Center Lessons on Concepts Driving Lesson Activities

For teachers to ensure that lessons are centered on concepts, three actions are helpful:

- Develop a clear conceptual focus;
- Tap into students' experiences and knowledge; and
- Enrich connection potential.

Develop a Clear Conceptual Focus. "A Less Slippery Slope" demonstrates a lesson design in which the concept is placed at the center of the lesson, with contextualized story problems serving as an opportunity for applying the concept in the Extending Understanding Moment of the lesson. We can retrace the design choices that went into the slope lesson from the middle out. That is, the starting point for the design of a lesson is anticipating the understandings and competencies that English Learners will need to develop in analyzing linear graphs in the coordinate plane. In order to see these linear graphs in terms of the constituent vertical and horizontal changes, it is helpful to connect the context of staircases with that of ramps (which resemble linear functions). Therefore, in order to complete the Read and Do task, students will need to have explicit ways to connect staircases to ramps, which determines the content and themes of the text they will engage with in the Read with Clarifying Bookmark task.

Tap Into Students' Experiences and Knowledge. Because we decided that students would need to understand the relationship between ramps and stairs, we created the sorting task to invite students to explore a variety of stair designs. This task also provides opportunities for English Learners to name what they see and sort the samples provided, even if their emerging schemata for sorting focus on the heights of individual steps or the whole staircase. This task then maps backward to the broader everyday practice of climbing in the Think-Pair-Share task, of which stairs are particular cases.

When we view the lesson as a whole, we see how the sequence of activities narrows to the highly specific details of describing vertical and horizontal changes within linear functions by taking as a point of departure climbing in general. The Think-Pair-Share and sorting tasks serve to activate prior knowledge and experiences that can help students contextualize the vertical and horizontal changes that will be the focus of this exploration of slope.

Enrich Connection Potential. Once English Learners have moved from general understandings of vertical and horizontal change as related to climbing stairs and focused in on how to measure the slope of lines contextualized as ramps, they can explore a variety of cases and apply their understanding of slope to represent in multiple ways (graphs, tables, equations) a variety of real-world situations. The focus of this extending moment of the lesson is for students to connect representations and determine which is the most appropriate given the context of the problem.

One notable feature of this approach is how it uses real-world contexts to analogically support conceptual development, rather than as the setting of a problem (Chu & Rubel, 2013). Specifically, the graph of a line is like a ramp. Just as with ramps and stairs, linear graphs can be seen in terms of vertical and horizontal changes of "steps." The conceptual analogy maps ideas from the real world (ramps, stairs, and steps) to mathematical representations (linear graphs and different representations of the vertical and horizontal changes).

The central Read and Do task, however, is actually decontextualized, as small groups focus on properties and changes of graphs and tables, but stairs and ramps remain as a supportive "fallback" context for thinking about what they are doing with the decontextualized graphs and tables. Providing this real-world anchor promotes students' flexibility in thinking about and with concepts, as it is an additional resource that they can choose to exercise: It is an optional heuristic, not a compulsory algorithm.

Foster Quality Peer Interactions That Co-Construct Understanding

This design consideration attends to a key tenet of sociocultural theory: the centrality of oral interaction in learning (Walqui & van Lier, 2010; Walqui & Heritage, 2018). Oracy is critical to the development of understanding and the construction of meaning. Students develop mathematical understandings through sustained oral interactions with peers and with the teacher as they question, explore, test hypotheses, articulate ideas, and clarify their thoughts. Given this centrality of oral interactions to learning, lessons must maximize students' opportunities to engage in sustained, rigorous interactions about disciplinary concepts. These opportunities are especially critical for English Learners who need abundant practice and support as they construct and articulate nascent understandings in a language they are simultaneously learning.

Given these considerations, we offer four guidelines to consider in redesigning the interactions offered English Learners in a math lesson:

- Structure activities to maximize participation;
- Offer different roles;
- Support co-constructing mathematics; and
- Ensure that opportunities to participate change over time.

Structure Activities to Maximize Participation. The tasks within the slope lesson illustrate multiple types of interactions between peers, which provide a range of opportunities for English Learners to engage in sustained and reciprocal talk through which they co-construct mathematical ideas and collaborate as they engage in mathematical practices (Chu, 2013). These interactions include sharing novel stories, providing necessary missing information, and negotiating meaning together. This section highlights three tasks that span these different purposes and formats of interactions.

The slope lesson opens with a Think-Pair-Share task, in which students engage in multiple interactions. First, they reflect individually on an experience of climbing, while thinking about what in that past experience made climbing easy or hard. Second, they pair with a partner and tell their story and reflection. Third, the teacher facilitates a whole-class discussion in which selected students share what their partners shared. In a time span of less than 10 minutes, English Learners will have had multiple opportunities to interact with a partner, the teacher, and the class as a whole.

Every student will have participated in oral interactions during this time and would have had to listen attentively, speak, and possibly paraphrase or summarize what they heard their partner say.

Offer Different Roles. The Read and Do task is an information gap task, which makes the contributions of each member indispensable for the success of the group. In each group of four, each student receives a different card that has either a table or a graph. As students take turns, they do not show their cards to their group members; instead, they must orally describe their representation in sufficient detail so that the others can record and reproduce the representation. Each student must strive to provide a clear description of the representation so that peers can complete the assignment. In the process of describing, students begin to use increasingly precise mathematical language to communicate their ideas. They may start with more colloquial or everyday uses of language, but by the nature of the task, they will begin to adopt more specific terms and efficient ways to convey mathematical information and relationships, not just a general description. The structure of the task requires students to practice different ways of conveying information for the understanding of their peers and ensures all learners must actively present ideas and listen to their partners (Chu & Hamburger, 2019). Each student has a piece of the information needed for all to complete the task successfully, so this structure holds students accountable to each other to participate in co-constructing a common pair of representations.

Support Co-Constructing Mathematics. How do these roles support the co-construction of mathematical knowledge? Students are given wide latitude in terms of how they provide information to their classmates in this task. For instance, in the table in Card A (see Figure 6.1), some students may orally list all the values of x, then link those to the values for y. Similarly, for describing the graph in Card B, students could give the coordinates as ordered pairs of each of the points, or they could describe the relative positions of points: e.g., "My first point is ((1,9)). The next point is three units to the right and two units down." The success of students' communication is determined only by whether there is adequate information provided for others to reconstruct the representation. The substance of their interactions is not prescribed and, instead, emerges in the moment-to-moment process of communicating and clarifying as requested by peers. Students exercise autonomy by choosing the ways of communicating that work for them and their peers, and they have a channel for "repairing" communications that are less than successful.

The Collaborative Problem task provides a somewhat different way of putting together information and ideas. Rather than focus on putting together pieces of a puzzle, the task is structured for students to put together ideas and interpretations in order to agree on an approach. The Collaborative Problem task opens with pairs of students reading the problem together and having a dialogue about their understanding of the problem. This discussion is the first step of Polyá's (1957) famous four-step heuristic for solving problems, which includes understanding the problem, making a plan, carrying out the plan, and checking the reasonableness of the solution.

Students read the story problem out loud and then take turns discussing the problem using the Math Clarifying Bookmark (see Table 6.1). Partner A signals a strategy from the left side of the Bookmark they can use to unpack the problem and make meaning. They then select one of the sample formulaic expressions to engage in dialogue with their partner to make sense of the problem, understand what is given, identify constraints, variables, conditions, and so on. Students then switch roles and Partner B repeats the process to continue the conversation about the problem to clarify what is being asked and what they might do to solve it. The structure of the task requires that both students participate fully in the dialogue as they listen, discuss, clarify, and make sense of the problem they have read. Discussion continues in this fashion until the two students have reached a consensus

Table 6.1. Mathematics Clarifying Bookmark, QTEL 2017

What You Can Do	What You Can Say
Identify what the problem is asking.	*The unknown in this problem is . . .*
	The units of the unknown are . . .
	Reasonable values for the unknown would be . . .
Identify the given data and constraints.	*The variables or quantities in this problem are . . .*
	The values given in the problem are . . .
	This problem assumes that . . .
Draw a picture or model to represent the problem in a different way.	*I can show this problem by . . .*
	A model that represents this problem is . . .
	I can represent this part of the problem with . . .

that they have understood the problem well enough to proceed to the next phase of the heuristic, which is to create a plan.

The interactions facilitated for English Learners by the Mathematics Clarifying Bookmark illustrate a key principle of sociocultural theory: that metacognitive and mathematical practices are first experienced in the social plane, in interactions with peers, before being appropriated into the individual plane (Koelsch, Chu, & Bañuelos, 2014). Autonomy is characterized by adaptive, as opposed to routine, expertise (Kilpatrick, Swafford, & Findell, 2001). Rather than relying on scripted utterances or rigid protocols for solving problems, English Learners need supported opportunities to develop strategic competence. The structure of the Clarifying Bookmark promotes students' metacognitive development by providing explicit labels for the constituent practices in which they can engage as part of an overarching practice. By signaling the strategies they use, students are developing metacognitive awareness of how to critically read and unpack word problems, a generative skill they will need in any mathematics course or content. The specific formulaic expressions further make possible students' entry by providing more specialized options in enacting that constituent practice (Koelsch, Chu, & Bañuelos, 2014).

Ensure That Participation Changes Over Time. Looking back at the slope lesson, Table 6.2 summarizes the different structured opportunities that students have to interact with their peers. These opportunities for participation change over time as students become more knowledgeable about the concept of slope.

Table 6.2. Types of Peer Interactions in the Lesson

Moment	Task	Conceptual Objective	Structured Interactions
Preparing	Think-Pair-Share	Identify what makes climbing easy/hard.	In pairs, students reflect, tell stories, listen, and retell to class.
	Sort and Order	Sort staircases in terms of difficulty to climb.	In pairs, students negotiate order, reach agreement, and identify criteria.
Interacting	Read w/ Clarifying Bookmark	Connect staircases to ramps in realistic contexts.	In pairs, students read, respond, interpret, connect, clarify, and elaborate.
	Read and Do	Coordinate vertical and horizontal changes in tables and graphs.	In a group of four, students supply and record missing information, and take turns to describe changes.
Extending	Collaborative Problem & Collaborative Poster	Apply the concept of slope to solving realistic problems.	In groups of four, students negotiate contributions to a collective product following specific guidelines.
	Collaborative Writing	Use slope to make decisions.	In pairs, students negotiate content and form in writing.

The two tasks in the Preparing Moment have been carefully structured to require students to engage in discussion with their peers to converge in different ways. In the Think-Pair-Share, a select number of students are asked to report to the whole class the experiences of others. In the Sort and Order task, as students place staircases one after another, in each case they are stating an opinion about both a particular staircase related to others already visible, but also about the features of staircases that are most salient to the issue of steepness. The task requires each pair to agree on a common sorting that they then report together to the class.

As students move into the Interacting Moment, however, activities are structured to engage them in close exploration of ideas related to the concept of slope through the reading and discussion of multiple representations. Students jointly clarify ideas, connect multiple representations, and elaborate on the meaning of those representations as they collaborate with a partner in the reading of several texts. The Read and Do task presents an information gap where students must share and co-construct a newer meaning or understanding (Chu & Hamburger, 2019). Here, through the structure of the task, one party has information that others do not have access to, and communication serves to bridge the gap in information and enable all students to complete identical representations.

Through the Interacting Moment and into the Extending Moment, students' interaction with peers supports participation in key mathematical practices. As they "look for and make use of structure" in tables and graphs, they also "attend to precision" and elaborate on vertical and horizontal changes in graphs, ramps, and staircases. They then "make sense of problems and persevere in solving them" across complex and novel situations that model real-life situations, applying their understanding of slope to make decisions. By the end of the lesson, students have negotiated a new genre (the poster) and are positioned as experts as they give advice in writing about how to proceed with new construction projects.

Offer Language Supports to Connect Ideas and Engage in Disciplinary Practices

To engage in doing mathematics, students must use language to develop conceptual and procedural understandings, reason abstractly, construct arguments, justify their solutions, solve problems, and critique the reasoning of others. All these mathematical practices require sophisticated uses of language that go far beyond learning key vocabulary terms. To amplify the curriculum for English Learners and provide them with the supports necessary to carry out these practices, teachers must consider how they will need to use language and what supports must be designed into the lesson to allow them such sophisticated participation.

We offer the following recommendations for teachers to consider as they redesign a lesson to better serve English Learners:

- Structure a variety of opportunities for language use;
- Offer language supports for disciplinary practices;
- Invite students to have greater autonomy in language choices over time; and
- Design for growth in language practices.

Structure a Variety of Opportunities for Language Use. The language opportunities offered in "A Less Slippery Slope" are designed into the materials as well as embedded in the structures and processes of tasks. The rich, complex text "From Stairs to Ramps" that students read has been carefully designed with multiple embedded features to enhance access to the text: subheadings, focus questions, labeled technical diagrams, and illustrative photographs (see Figure 6.4). These features support students as they read the text with a partner, pausing after each section to clarify meaning and attempt to read the

Figure 6.4. Passage from "From Stairs to Ramps" with Engineered, Amplified Text

Rules for Stair Construction

Why are there rules for treads and risers?

Countries often set rules for how long the tread must be and how high the riser can be. These restrictions are to accommodate people with different physical abilities. For example, in the United States, each tread must be at least nine inches long. Each riser can be at most 8.25 inches high.

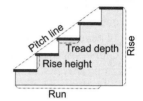

focus question. These features have been designed to model for students how good readers pause to check for understanding, identify areas of ambiguity, and connect to prior experiences.

Offer Language Supports for Disciplinary Practices. The slope lesson further provides models and supports for English Learners as they engage in disciplinary practices and explore diverse purposes for using language, including:

- *Describing* parts or components, quantifying dimensions;
- *Comparing* objects in terms of key attributes or relationships;
- *Identifying* parts related to wholes, instances of types, and salient features; and
- *Characterizing* how *variables co-vary* and relate to one another.

In order to engage in these language practices, the slope lesson models explicit formulaic expressions that students can use as they engage in the tasks and accomplish the conceptual goals for the lesson. These formulaic expressions serve as generative language structures that students can use to enter into and navigate through the tasks. The expressions highlight key conceptual points students must attend to as they develop understanding of the relationship between vertical and horizontal changes. Some formulaic expressions provided for different tasks include:

- *This staircase is steeper because . . . :* Students might say that ". . . is taller but has the same number of blocks on the bottom."
- *Starting from the point . . . to get to the point . . . , there is a horizontal change in the x of . . . , and a vertical change in the y of . . . :* This formulaic expression is much more generative than the usual "up-over" construction, such as "Up 3, over 2." The "up-over" expression emphasizes step-by-step changes, but in so doing obscures the direct variation between the two variables.
- *As one variable increases by . . . , the other variable . . . :* In the example above, one way to summarize and connect would be "As x increases by 2, y increases by 3." Likewise, "As x decreases

by 2, *y* decreases by 3." If students then focus on the unit rate of change, they might say, "As *x* increases by 1, *y* increases by 3/2." This unit rate of change is indeed the slope.

Invite Students to Have Greater Autonomy in Language Over Time. The language architecture of the slope lesson is open and wide in the Preparing and Extending Moments that introduce and conclude the lesson, while narrower and more focused in the Interacting Moment in between. That is, students are relatively freer in the Preparing Moment to use their own language resources to express their experiences and initial understandings. During the Interacting Moment, students are offered carefully selected phrases from which they can choose, as well as an elaborate formulaic expression carefully tailored to the conceptual goal of having students coordinate horizontal and vertical changes. Over time, students are given more choice over how they will use language to achieve their goals. This growing freedom is demonstrated in the Extending Moment tasks in which, while certain components of the Collaborative Poster task are specified, the choices of language are left entirely up to students (see Table 6.3).

Design for Growth in Language Practices. The language that students are invited and supported to use moves across multiple continua over the course of the lesson. Rather than rely on the misleading dichotomy thought to exist between "everyday" and "academic" language, we may consider instead how students over the course of the lesson develop more authority in using more technical language to develop more products that involve writing.

The slope lesson begins with dialogic interactions with classmates who are sharing opinions and information to co-construct understandings or mathematical representations. By the end of the lesson, they are creating written products, such as letters and posters, that require substantial negotiating, editing, rehearsal, and integration of multimodal elements in a poster.

Students also develop more authority about the subject of slope. They begin on an equal footing as they discuss experiences and express initial ideas about the staircase manipulatives. As the lesson culminates in students' becoming experts about slope and wheelchair ramp decisions, they write with greater authority to a more distant, imagined audience.

Language also develops in terms of how students are using more "technical" terms to concisely and precisely refer to ideas. "Academic" terminology is just one species of technical language, because the specialized, technical terminology used to describe football, cricket, or motorcycle maintenance is just as opaque to outsiders as mathematical terms may be initially. In the slope lesson, the language moves from everyday contexts such as climbing hills and ladders, to more specific contexts such as stairs and ramps. The focal text introduces many more technical terms as a means to amplify students' understanding of how language refers to parts of everyday

Table 6.3. Progressions of Language Across Slope Tasks

Task	Language Practices	FORMULAIC EXPRESSIONS		Key Words
		Supplied by Students	Offered as Explicit Models	
Think-Pair-Share	Relating a personal experience with reflection	Relating experiences and telling stories. "One time . . ."		"climb" "easy" "hard"
Sort and Order	Describing and sorting objects; justifying methods		"I think this staircase is *steeper* because . . ." "I think this staircase is *less steep* because . . ."	"steeper" "less steep" "staircase"
Read w/ Clarifying Bookmark	Connecting to prior experiences, clarifying and elaborating on experiences with novel information		Clarifying Bookmark expressions (12) for four different analytic practices for reading	"tread" "riser" "tread depth" "riser height" "ramp" "stairs" "rules" "horizontal" "inclined"
Read and Do	Coordinating representations, describing changes, co-varying variables		"Starting from the point . . . , the point . . . has a horizontal change in x of . . . and a vertical change in y of . . ."	"change in x" "change in y" "table" "graph"
Collaborative Problem & Collaborative Poster	Reporting solutions, posing questions, justifying choices of representation	Original question, justification	Mathematics Clarifying Bookmark expressions (9) for three different analytic practices for understanding a problem	
Collaborative Writing	Explaining rules in context, developing scenarios, and making recommendations	Conventions of business letters (e.g., second-person, salutations, etc.)		

Table 6.4. Questions to Consider and Potential Steps to Take

	Questions to Consider	Potential Steps to Take
Conceptual Focus	• How clearly is the conceptual focus defined? • How does the conceptual approach tap into students' experiences or funds of knowledge? • How rich is the connection potential of the ideas, representations, and procedures in a lesson?	• Anticipate students' prior experiences and provide opportunities to make explicit connections. • Identify the minimal "working definition" students need to get in various lesson activities. • Select metaphors or analogies to frame the conceptual ideas in ways students can recognize.
Quality Interactions	• How are activities structured to ensure maximum participation by all learners? • How are students offered different roles in interacting with each other? • How do these roles support the co-construction of mathematical knowledge? • How do opportunities to participate change across time?	• Employ different structures for participation to ensure all learners are engaged in sustained oral interactions about disciplinary ideas. • Create opportunities for students to offer opinions and information, but also to converge and reach consensus. Aim for co-construction. • Employ a variety of scaffolding tasks to ensure that students have different ways to contribute.
Language Focus	• How are language opportunities structured throughout the lesson? • What language supports will students need to be offered to engage in disciplinary practices? • How do language practices, grow over the course of the lesson? • To what extent do students have greater autonomy in making language choices over time?	• Provide structured opportunities for disciplinary language practice to develop conceptual understanding. • Map language progressions and identify when to introduce key terms in rich, multimodal texts. • Provide formulaic expressions when necessary and attend to degrees of freedom. • Solicit and highlight explicit features of language performances in disciplinary practices, but give students substantial latitude.

experience. Later tasks provide explicit models for the kinds of language needed to describe graphs, tables, and changes within the coordinate plane.

SO WHAT ARE MATHEMATICS EDUCATORS TO DO?

This slope lesson is just one instance of how instruction can be transformed through the three key shifts and redesign actions to better support English Learners as they engage in rigorous mathematics learning. To fully enact this vision, multiple groups of educators will need to contribute in concerted ways because educators not only work in different settings but also stand in different positions with regard to instructional materials and design.

At the lesson level, classroom-based educators can ask themselves critical questions about the lessons they are designing and the instructional materials they are using. Based on these answers, they can potentially take the steps shown in Table 6.4.

For educators who work either in supporting classroom-based teachers or by creating instructional materials and lessons meant to be enacted broadly, a long-term agenda is necessary. This work will need to subsume the work on lessons and include the strategic planning and redesign of units and courses. Educators will need to reframe the design of their curricula to meet the needs of English Learners. Putting the shifts into practice will benefit all learners and will provide equitable opportunities that are particularly critical for English Learners both to gain initial entry and to subsequently participate in increasingly sophisticated ways.

REFERENCES

Chu, H. (2013). Scaffolding tasks for the professional development of mathematics teachers of English language learners. In C. Margolinas (Ed.), *Task Design in Mathematics Education* (pp. 559–567). Oxford, UK: International Commission on Mathematics Instruction.

Chu, H., & Hamburger, L. (2019). Designing mathematical interactions for English Learners. *Mathematics Teaching in the Middle School, 24*(4), 218–225.

Chu, H., & Rubel, L. H. (2013). When the world is not the problem: Real-world contexts in analogies. In M. Berger, K. Brodie, V. Frith, & K. le Roux (Eds.), *Proceedings of the Seventh International Mathematics Education and Society Conference* (pp. 262–271). Cape Town, South Africa: Mathematics Education and Society.

Herbel-Eisenmann, B., & Breyfogle, L. (2005). Questioning our patterns of questioning. *Mathematics Teaching in the Middle School, 10*(9), 484–489.

Heritage, M., Walqui, A., & Linquanti, R. (2015). *English Language Learners and the new standards. Developing language, content knowledge and analytical practices in the classroom.* Cambridge, MA: Harvard Education Press.

Kilpatrick, J., Swafford, J., & Findell, B. (2001). *Adding it up: Helping children learn mathematics.* Washington, DC: National Research Council.

Koeslch, N., Chu, H., & Bañuelos, G. (2014). Language for learning: Supporting English Language Learners in meeting the challenges of new standards. *TESOL Quarterly, 48,* 642–650.

Lampert, M. (2017). Ambitious teaching: A deep dive. In R. Heller, R. E. Wolfe, & A. Steinberg (Eds.), *Rethinking readiness: Deeper learning for college, work, and life* (pp. 147–173). Cambridge, MA: Harvard Education Press.

Lobato, J., & Thanheiser, E. (2002). Developing understanding of ratio-as-measure as a foundation for slope. In B. Litwiller & G. Bright (Eds.), *Making sense of fractions, ratios, and proportions: 2002 yearbook* (pp. 162–175). Reston, VA: National Council of Teachers of Mathematics.

Moschkovich, J. (2002). A situated and sociocultural perspective on bilingual mathematics learners. *Mathematical Thinking and Learning, 4,* 189–212.

Polyá, G. (1957). *How to solve it.* Garden City, NY: Doubleday.

Sleep, L. (2012). The work of steering instruction toward the mathematical point: A decomposition of teaching practice. *American Educational Research Journal, 49,* 935–970.

Stein, M., Engle, R., Smith, M., & Hughes, E. (2008). Orchestrating productive mathematical discussions: Five practices for helping teachers move beyond show and tell. *Mathematical Thinking and Learning, 10,* 313–340.

Stein, M., Smith, M., Henningsen, M., & Silver, E. (2000). *Implementing standards-based mathematics instruction: A casebook for professional development.* New York, NY: Teachers College Press.

Stigler, J., & Hiebert, J. (1999). *The teaching gap.* New York, NY: Free Press.

Stump, S. (1999). Secondary mathematics teachers' knowledge of slope. *Mathematics Education Research Journal, 11,* 124–144.

Walqui, A., & Heritage, M. (2018, Fall). Meaningful classroom talk. Supporting English Learners' oral language development. *The American Educator, 42*(3), 18–23.

Walqui, A., & van Lier, L. (2010). *Scaffolding the academic success of adolescent English language learners: A pedagogy of promise.* San Francisco, CA: WestEd.

Zahner, W. (2015). The rise and run of a computational understanding of slope in a conceptually focused bilingual algebra class. *Journal of Mathematical Behavior, 88*(1), 19–41.

CHAPTER 7

Mapping a Changing World View

Designing Learning Experiences for English Learners in Social Studies

Nicholas Catechis and Pía Castilleja

In a 9th-grade World History class in California serving students who are almost all English Learners, students are vigorously engaged in examining a set of three world maps that represent the world quite differently, even though they were created within a span of fewer than 60 years. As part of a carefully sequenced set of tasks, immediately prior to their investigation of the maps, students had worked together in dyads to articulate their interpretations about what maps do and represent. As we enter the classroom, we observe that they are now identifying variances in the way these maps represent the world. They next determine the order of creation of the maps within a specific time period, based on narrative texts that describe their purposes and the contexts in which they were created. Figure 7.1 shows the three world maps the students are collaboratively analyzing.

Later in the lesson, entitled "Mapping a Changing European World View," students will apply similar conceptual, analytic, and language practices to contemporary maps that require the same kind of reading of multimodal texts, critical questioning, and analysis of maps as primary source documents. Students' learning in the lesson thus focuses on understanding what maps represent and convey; how to read, compare, and interpret them as primary source documents that provide particular historical world views and purposes; and how to engage together in sustained, quality conversations that approximate the thinking, reasoning, and language of social scientists and, in particular, of historians.

These tasks are part of a larger unit, *Contextualizing the Age of Exploration*, that was created by members of the Quality Teaching for English Learners (QTEL) team at WestEd, including the first author of this

Figure 7.1. Age of Exploration Maps

Münster after Ptolemy

Waldseemüller

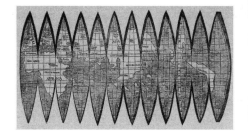

Martellus

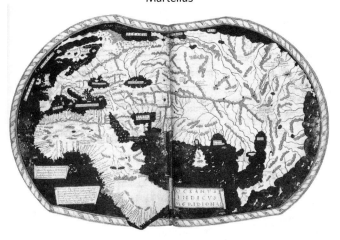

Sources: Waldseemüller, M., Apian, P., & Austro-Hungarian Monarchy. DATE (1507) [Map] Retrieved from the Library of Congress, {see also https://www.loc.gov/item /2009582745/}; Münster, S., Kandel, D., Henricpetri, S., & Münster, S. DATE (1545), {see also https://www.loc.gov/item/2017585793/}; Martellus, Henricus. Martellus' World Maps DATE: (1489–1490) Outline of the 1489 British Library Martellus world map. {see also https://commons.wikimedia.org/wiki/File:Henricus_Martellus'_World_Map.jpg}. All maps courtesy of Library of Congress, Geography and Map Division.

chapter. Both authors are experienced teacher educators on the QTEL team as well as teachers of English Learners at the secondary level. In this chapter, we discuss the "Mapping" lesson as an exemplar for how instruction can be designed to support the apprenticing of English Learners into challenging conceptual, analytic, and language practices in the multidisciplinary sphere of social studies.

SOCIAL STUDIES TEACHERS AS LESSON DESIGNERS: CHALLENGES AND CHOICES

As the examples in this chapter will illustrate, our pedagogical orientation toward the design of ambitious learning experiences for all students, including English Learners, rests on the assumption that teachers must apprentice students into specific disciplinary practices, including supporting the development of the language practices needed to engage in them. Underlying this assumption is our conviction that teachers' work hinges on developing the expertise to make meaningful choices in the selection of purposeful and carefully sequenced learning opportunities. In the case of social studies teachers, that professional choice involves addressing the dual challenges of creating learning experiences that draw from a multidisciplinary subject area and that attend to the disciplinary language practices students need to engage in that work.

In this chapter, we present a lesson that invites students to analyze, compare and contrast, and carefully read primary and secondary sources concerning world maps of a specific period of history while they simultaneously develop the language needed to engage in that work. The lesson thus provides examples of the pedagogical approach detailed in the introductory chapters of this book. Before we dive into the lesson itself, we position lesson design as the process of making choices that maintain the inextricable link between disciplinary language and content knowledge.

Lesson Design as the Process of Making Meaningful Choices

To enable students to apprentice into disciplinary practices, social studies teachers need to make meaningful choices about the purpose, content, and structure of learning opportunities, drawing from a multidisciplinary field—which in the United States has traditionally included anthropology, geography, economics, civics, sociology, and history. As a school subject, social studies involves the development of both academic and life skills, supporting students' abilities not only to analyze and understand history and human society in its multiple dimensions, but also to enhance their skills of participating critically and thoughtfully in the world (Barth & Shermis, 1980; Marker & Mehlinger, 1992; Mintrop, 2004). To invite students to engage intellectually and practically with this multidisciplinary content, social studies teachers need to create a rich and coherent tapestry of interconnected ideas that consistently broaden and encompass deeper and more nuanced understandings (conceptual practices), while apprenticing students to deploy academic tools (analytic practices) to engage in critical thinking and problem solving.

While social studies is a multidisciplinary field characterized by an interdisciplinary approach to knowledge that invites students to inquire about human society through a complex lens, it is the discipline of history that often predominates in social studies and provides the strongest unifying thread among the disciplines covered in K–12 social studies education. History often serves as foundational glue, providing a substantive and procedural framework to the design of instructional experiences (Neumann, 2012). It is also research on history education that provides the richest scholarship regarding pedagogical disciplinary practices.

Engaging English Learners in the Practices of History: Attending to Conceptual and Analytic Practices. To support English Learners, and following from our assumption that disciplinary language and content knowledge are inextricably intertwined (Valdés, Kibler, & Walqui, 2014; see also Chapter 2), teachers need to be able to identify the discipline-based conceptual and analytic practices to which language is linked. Unless the conceptual understandings and analytic work at the center of their lessons are clearly identified, teachers will be unable to create tasks that support the language their students need to use as historians.

A key job of history teachers is to engage students in exploring the meaning and significance of central concepts. In the case of the lesson in this chapter, these include the notions of change over time, how and why world views and perspectives change in relation to historical events, and the nature of historical documents as sources that give us access to perspectives on events of the past. These generative notions, central to the curriculum, are also the basis of an inquisitive stance toward the world that resonates with the experiences and intuitions of English Learners.

At a time when a critical stance toward texts and events has proven to be not only an academic but also a civic necessity, disciplinary practices related to developing a critical stance with respect to sources should be central to our work. During the last few decades, scholars of history education have advanced our understanding of how historians approach texts (Neumann, 2012; Seixas & Peck, 2004; van Drie & van Boxtel, 2008; Wineburg, 2001). They have, for example, identified key source-related analytic practices such as contextualization, sourcing, and corroboration (Wineburg, 2001, 2013). van Drie and van Boxtel (2007, p. 5) describe these practices as follows:

> **Contextualization:** situating a document in a concrete temporal and spatial context;
> **Sourcing:** looking first at the source of the document before reading the body of the text; and
> **Corroboration:** comparing documents with each other.

Engaging in disciplinary practices such as these entails participating in a variety of embedded analytic practices (Neumann, 2012; Wineburg, 2013), such as identifying evidence, questioning sources, and interrogating provenance, some of which will be addressed in the mapping lesson described in this chapter. Once teachers have identified a generative subset of analytic and conceptual practices related to the focus of the unit, these choices can now guide their lesson design.

Creating Opportunities for Quality Interactions and Engagement in Language Practices. In addition to disciplinary ideas and operations, the design of lessons needs to include opportunities for the practice of language appropriate to the discipline. As noted in Chapter 2, language does not grow independently of the development of conceptual understandings and is, therefore, inseparable from the concepts and analytic practices central to lessons. Thus, effective lesson design includes careful orchestration of students' participation in tasks. Through structured opportunities to engage in dialogue that is not scripted, teachers invite students to apprentice into both content and language that are inextricably linked. Engagement in structured interactions provides students affordances to co-construct ideas, deepening their conceptual and analytic understandings, and supporting their increased ownership and control over disciplinary uses of language (van Lier, 2004).

When structuring interactions, a central aim is to create opportunities for students to dialogue. This implies not only the purposeful selection of the right task to provide the scaffolding required at a particular moment in the lesson, but also the careful crafting of prompts centered around the key ideas of the lesson. By posing purposeful open-ended questions or statements for students' consideration, teachers support their engagement in critical thinking and disciplinary inquiry, thus mobilizing the analytic practices motivating the lesson.

In the lesson presented here, "Mapping a Changing European World View," this design consideration is illustrated by the task that opens the lesson, the Anticipatory Guide (see Table 7.3 on p. 153). In this task, students are invited to consider and respond to statements that focus on concepts and analytic practices central to the lesson, while simultaneously engaging in the language practices that make the interaction with the content possible (i.e., explaining their rationales for their responses to the statements in the Anticipatory Guide). Through this process, students are apprenticed into the use of disciplinary language and the practice of discourse in that discipline (Coffin, 2006; Schleppegrell, 2005).

Carefully planned—"designed-in"—scaffolding (Hammond & Gibbons, 2005) allows us to predict our students' participation, based on prior experiences teaching similar lessons. At the same time, the plan invites the novel and unpredictable reaction on the part of students through original expressions that render their learning tangible (Walqui & van Lier, 2010). Peer discussion and writing tasks promote learning in the context of historical inquiry activities. In the lesson, as students are invited to interact with three historical maps, a compare-and-contrast activity provides English Learners the opportunity to analyze sources using language to present their evidence and make their thinking explicit. They first discuss and construct their understanding, and through interaction, increasingly control their language as they commit their thinking and meaning-making in writing (Christie & Derewianka, 2008; van Drie & van de Ven, 2017).

The learning opportunity provided by the task occasions engagement, not in short responses and teacher-directed interactions, but in creative meaning-making and authentic academic peer conversations that involve comparing and contrasting a variety of sources and posing clarification questions. By providing these opportunities, the task itself contributes to the socialization of students into processes of thinking, talking, reading, and writing in the discipline.

DESIGNING LEARNING OPPORTUNITIES FOR ENGLISH LEARNERS IN SOCIAL STUDIES

Teachers need to provide their students with opportunities to develop ways of thinking, inquiring, and critically approaching ideas (analytic practices) as historians do; to engage with interconnected and generative ideas and themes (conceptual practices) central to history; and to approximate the ways of using language (language practices) that are common among historians. As we illustrate in the lesson, carefully crafted instructional experiences involve language practices that are inseparable from the conceptual and analytic ones. In the remainder of this chapter, we guide teachers through the design of the lesson, elaborating on choices made about the content and structures of the lesson.

As noted earlier, this lesson and the unit of which it is a part were developed to be used for professional development of teachers at the secondary level. Our aim was to provide teachers the opportunity to experience a lesson presenting: (1) the Three-Moment Architecture of the lesson described in Chapter 3 and (2) the weaving together of discipline-based conceptual, analytic, and language practices. The purpose was to make visible the decisions teachers need to make as they design powerful, generative lessons for their English Learners and other students. As we often do during professional development, we also supported and collaborated with teachers as they enacted the lesson in their classrooms.

Contextualizing the Age of Exploration: Mapping a Changing European World View

Drawing on the pedagogical tenets and designs presented in Chapters 2 and 3, the lesson described in this chapter is the first in a series of three conceptually linked lessons that make up the Unit, *Contextualizing the Age of Exploration*. Throughout the Unit, students develop understandings of the nature, purpose, and structure of a variety of sources that they will continue to encounter in the history curriculum and that they will be able to respond to appropriately in increasingly complex ways. The three lessons provide students with multiple opportunities to develop, test, deepen, and refine their conceptualization of key themes and analytic practices.

The spiraling nature of the Unit is illustrated in Figure 7.2.

Lesson Design

As explained earlier in this chapter, we began the design of this lesson by committing ourselves to a set of key disciplinary practices that would continue to be deepened throughout the Unit. Additionally, we deliberately selected powerful texts to represent different perspectives on the world to support the development of students' historical thinking and analytic skills.

Figure 7.2. Three-Lesson Spiraling Unit

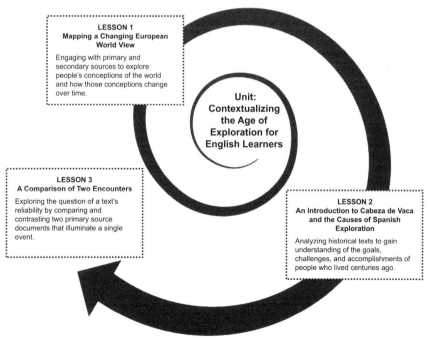

LESSON 1
Mapping a Changing European World View

Engaging with primary and secondary sources to explore people's conceptions of the world and how those conceptions change over time.

Unit: Contextualizing the Age of Exploration for English Learners

LESSON 3
A Comparison of Two Encounters

Exploring the question of a text's reliability by comparing and contrasting two primary source documents that illuminate a single event.

LESSON 2
An Introduction to Cabeza de Vaca and the Causes of Spanish Exploration

Analyzing historical texts to gain understanding of the goals, challenges, and accomplishments of people who lived centuries ago.

Attending to Disciplinary Practices. While a lesson may address many themes and a variety of learning standards at once, we posit that in order to support students' understanding and deep engagement with practices and notions, a deliberate and explicit focus on a well-chosen cluster of practices is in itself a crucial scaffold to their learning. The practices introduced in this lesson will continue to be revisited—spiraled—in subsequent lessons as students deepen and expand their understandings.

Figure 7.3 shows the conceptual, analytic, and language practices that will be intertwined and provide the focus to this lesson and to subsequent lessons in the Unit. These practices are aligned with the K–12 College, Career, and Civic Life (C3) Framework for Social Studies (National Council for the Social Studies, 2013) and draw on the analytic practices outlined by educational historians described earlier.

Selecting Texts for Our Objectives. Having determined the objectives of our lesson, the crucial step of text selection followed. In choosing texts, we

Figure 7.3. Disciplinary Practices Addressed in *Contextualizing the Age of Exploration*

Conceptual Practices

- Understand that historical events and development were shaped by unique circumstances of time and place as well as broader historical contexts.
- Understand how historical contexts shaped and continue to shape people's perspectives.

Analytic Practices

- Use questions generated about multiple historical sources to pursue further inquiry and investigate additional sources.
- Analyze evidence from multiple primary and secondary sources, taking into account the circumstances and period of their creation.
- Analyze evidence from multiple primary and secondary sources by interrogating their provenance.
- Analyze evidence from multiple primary and secondary sources by comparing and cross-referencing multimodal evidence.

Language Practices

- Explain orally and write about comparisons and contrasts among a variety of primary and secondary sources.
- Ask clarification questions and pose hypotheses when engaging in sense-making with oral, written, and visual texts.
- Explain ideas and information gathered from sources for different purposes and audiences.

attended to the analytic opportunities different texts could provide students as well as the language environment that they would allow us to create.

The central idea we wanted students to understand through this lesson was how maps graphically portray people's conceptions of the known world within a certain time period, and how, as people's conceptions change, so do their maps (Rumsey & Williams, 2002). We also reasoned that by selecting historical maps—multimodal primary sources—in conjunction with other texts (e.g., secondary sources such as history textbooks), we could create an environment that provides a "rich semiotic budget of resources" that stimulates students' meaning-making activities in interaction with others (van Lier, 2004, p. 81). Furthermore, the selection of multimodal texts supports students' ability to identify and discern information from multiple sources. This capacity, a crucial 21st-century skill, becomes an invitation to make sense of or inquire about the relation between images and written text when properly articulated in the lesson (Prangsma, van Boxtel, Kanselaar, & Kirschner, 2008; Walqui & van Lier, 2010).

The maps selected for this lesson illustrate an important consideration of text selection specific to the social sciences, namely the generativity afforded by the inclusion of conflicting or contradictory sources. The dissonance created by different views of the world not only sparks interest but also helps students interrogate notions of objectivity in history. That interrogation, in turn, provides the opportunity to develop skills to analyze and evaluate sources of information, including its authors, purposes, and significance.

While there were numerous options available, we selected three maps to inquire into the European exploration of the Americas during the 15th and 16th centuries (Figure 7.1). We believed that these maps offered diversity of origin, time period, and geographical expertise that would allow students the deepest possible analytic engagement.

Lesson Design Decisions. Now that we had the main texts selected, we asked ourselves how the lesson should begin and end. We made the decision to start with students making initial judgments about general statements on maps, using a task called the Anticipatory Guide. The statements in our guide were designed to be broad enough to enable students to identify their assumptions, generate understandings, and enable them to articulate opinions at the onset of the lesson. The statements were also carefully crafted and connected to the texts so that at the end of the lesson, students could return to them with evidence to support or refute their initial opinions. To close the lesson, we invited students to collaboratively write a couple of paragraphs based on what they had learned throughout the lesson, applying their skills and practices to a different set of maps.

Because we are concerned with building and extending students' ability to engage in academic practices and make meaning, the lesson asks students to use language to achieve communicative disciplinary purposes and provides numerous and coherent scaffolded opportunities to support students in engaging in those language practices.

SOCIAL STUDIES LESSON IN THREE MOMENTS: MAPPING A CHANGING EUROPEAN WORLD VIEW

Table 7.1 provides an outline of the lesson depicted in the Three Moment lesson architecture introduced in Chapter 3.

Preparing Learners

The lesson begins by activating prior knowledge on the topic and themes to be analyzed in the selected visual texts.

Anticipatory Guide. We selected an Anticipatory Guide, a task designed to initiate students' thinking about some of the key ideas that will be explored in the forthcoming content on maps, to make connections between the content and their own experiences, and to learn new vocabulary in context. The Anticipatory Guide is also a means for teaching students the importance of being aware as a reader of one's own preconceived notions in relation to a text. In one way, the task is analogous to the comprehension questions that commonly follow reading assignments, but with important variations. Instead of providing questions for students to answer, the Anticipatory Guide presents several statements to students for their agreement or disagreement. Rather than responding after examining the texts, students consider the statements beforehand, sharing their opinions and reasons first with a partner and then with the whole class. Anticipatory Guides can also serve as a diagnostic tool, helping teachers identify what students already know or think about the topic being studied.

When constructing a Guide, the aims are to develop statements that grab students' attention and to provide assertions that generate both agreement and disagreement. For example, we designed an Anticipatory Guide (Table 7.2) in which students respond to several teacher-created statements about maps and their creators. The statements are general and subject to interpretation, yet each one will be important in students' understanding and enactment of key historical practices, such as sourcing and contextualizing.

To support the interactive nature of the task and foster discipline-specific language development, the task calls for students to work in dyads, taking turns. One student reads a statement and considers whether they agree or disagree with it, inviting the partner to express their opinion. Then it is the partner's turn to go through the same process. Formulaic expressions

Table 7.1. Mapping a Changing European World View

Lesson Objective: Students learn that maps graphically portray people's current conceptions of the world and that, as people's conceptions have changed over time, so have their maps.

PREPARING LEARNERS		
Activate prior knowledge on topics/themes to be analyzed in visual and written texts.		
Task	**Objective**	**Description**
Anticipatory Guide	Activate students' background knowledge about maps while also introducing key concepts and language.	Students make initial judgments about statements on maps.
Semantic Map	Tap into prior knowledge and organize existing knowledge on the topic of maps.	In groups of four, students create a Semantic Map displaying their existing knowledge of maps.
Gallery Walk	Take note of patterns and trends within the classroom to support the building of conceptual interconnections and to invite students to envision how they might accomplish tasks in the future.	Groups review Semantic Maps using Post-it™ to leave comments.
INTERACTING WITH TEXT		
Support and promote structures and processes that assist students to reason, read, write, and participate in historical conversations.		
Map Comparison	Delve deeply into the selected primary sources (historical maps) by comparing and contrasting different maps.	In dyads, students analyze maps with a specific purpose in mind.
Round Robin	Build understanding of the texts based on different student responses.	Group members take turns stating their comparisons.
Map Description Card Match	Reach a consensus on the available evidence and previous analysis.	Groups of four match description cards with the maps previously examined.
Collaborative Chart	Weave the decontextualized knowledge from the maps and texts matched into a chronologically structured narrative.	Groups of four create a chronologically structured narrative from the maps and texts matched.

(continued)

Table 7.1. Mapping a Changing European World View (*continued*)

Task	Objective	Description
Presentation of Evidence	Take ownership, articulate findings, and build awareness of what constitutes quality work.	Groups of four present their narratives.
Collaborative Writing	Answer open-ended questions in response to an exam-like prompt.	Partners write in response to their newly acquired knowledge.
EXTENDING UNDERSTANDING		
Provide an account that consolidates and makes clear how students can apply the relationships among the key ideas and details explored in novel contexts.		
Map Analysis Carousel	Identify and analyze key features of novel texts.	Groups of four compare and contrast four contemporary maps illustrating different projections of the world.
Blue Marble Extension	Identify aspects of a text that reveals author's point of view and purpose.	In a whole classroom scenario, students discuss the famous Blue Marble photograph of Earth, comparing the way it was distributed to the public with a north-up orientation rather than the south-up orientation the original photo showed.

Table 7.2. Anticipatory Guide

	Agree	Disagree	Brief Explanation
1. Maps help us understand how people, goods, and ideas move from place to place.			
2. Technology available to people is evident in the maps they create.			
3. Flat maps of the world are just as accurate as globes.			
4. Maps are accurate representations of what exists.			

Figure 7.4. Formulaic Expressions

FORMULAIC EXPRESSIONS FOR WORKING ON AN ANTICIPATORY GUIDE I

Student 1	I will read statement _____. It says _____.
	I agree/disagree with it because _____.
	So, I am going to mark it agree/disagree. What do you think?
Student 2	I agree/disagree with you because _____.
	So, for statement one, I will mark agree/disagree.
	Now let me read statement _____. It says _____.
	I agree/disagree .....

(Figure 7.4) assist students in apprenticing language for academic conversations. Partners may disagree in their answers, which will be revisited at the end of the lesson, when students will be asked to explain if they agree with their original responses, stating the reason why this was—or was not the case.

Semantic Map and Gallery Walk. At this point in Preparing the Learner, we introduce another task, the Semantic Map. Our purpose in doing so is to provide opportunities for students to organize their existing ideas about maps. Often, Semantic Maps are used at the end of a lesson by including an idea in the middle of the map and having students brainstorm single words connected to it. However, we take a different approach and utilize the Semantic Map to organize ideas by developing guiding questions for students' responses, such as, "*What purposes do maps have? What are some elements in a map? What do maps say about their creators?*" At the onset of the activity, we may show students a sample Semantic Map as a model. Then, during enactment, we invite students in groups of four to brainstorm and discuss their responses, while encouraging the groups to generate products with subthemes and categories that organize ideas into phrases and sentences rather than one-word bullets.

Groups make sure that their Semantic Maps are clear to anyone who may see them. They should ask themselves whether a visitor would be able to understand everything in their Semantic Map without any other explanation. When finished, groups post their signed products around the classroom. Sample phrases might include: "*Maps can be physical, political, or economic. Elements of maps are: scale, legend, and compass rose.*" Groups would then have the opportunity to rotate and view the products, leaving comments and/or questions on Post-it. Figure 7.5 provides an example.

Figure 7.5. Semantic Map on Maps

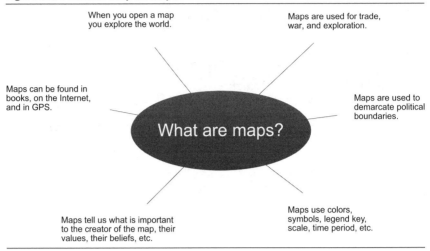

At this stage of the lesson, with the Anticipatory Guide and the Semantic Map, we have offered opportunities for students to use their prior knowledge and to experience vocabulary in context. We have also foreshadowed new concepts that students will encounter as they delve deeper into the Age of Exploration.

Interacting with Text

Having prepared learners, we now move into the Interacting with Text Moment of the lesson. Through careful scaffolding, we strive to present students explicit structures and processes that provide them opportunities to reason, read, write, and participate in historical conversations that are focused on central and generative ideas in social studies. Our main goal is to invite students to examine multiple sources of information presented in diverse formats, graphic as well as in words.

Map Comparison. The Compare-and-Contrast Matrix is a graphic organizer that helps students analyze key features of two or more ideas, objects, and so on. These charts are valuable for English Learners because they help to highlight and compare central notions in a text, whether in written or visual format. Students can also use the matrices to organize their understanding of a text they are examining. Their notes can then be very helpful in subsequent tasks.

For this lesson, we designed a Compare-and-Contrast Matrix (Table 7.3) to invite students to analyze selected land masses in the historical maps from

Table 7.3. Compare-and-Contrast Matrix

A COMPARISON OF THREE MAPS

Directions: With a partner, examine the three maps from the Age of Exploration and the modern world map. Compare the Age of Exploration maps using the criteria in the first column below. Fill in the matrix with what you notice about each map. Point out the differences and similarities in the maps.

Where is the landmass located in each map? How does each location compare to the modern world map?	MAP A	MAP B	MAP C
MADAGASCAR			
AFRICA			
INDIA			
NORTH and SOUTH AMERICA			

the Age of European Exploration. It is important to note that students had knowledge of this period of history from earlier lessons. For each dyad, we prepared a modern world map and the three Age of Exploration Maps. Students work with a partner on the graphic organizer. In this case, we use dyads rather than groups of four because the interactions among pairs can lead to more rigorous and sustained interactions. Additionally, they ensure that each student has more opportunities to engage in talk.

Specifically, the task involves each dyad locating four land masses (Madagascar, Africa, India, and North and South America) on the modern map and then finding them on the earlier maps. By focusing on these four land masses, students are able to notice their similarities and differences in size, geographic location, and shape when compared to a modern world map. They record these findings in the appropriate cell for each Age of Exploration Map. As enactments of this lesson have shown, students' initial assessments of the maps tend toward assertions such as "This map is wrong!" This is exactly the kind of assumption we want to surface as we apprentice students into a disciplinary stance toward primary sources.

This task provides students the opportunity to build arguments when comparing and contrasting the maps and finally to reach a consensus. As the lesson proceeds, teachers circulate around the room to contingently support and promote analytic conversations.

Round Robin. Once partners reach a consensus on their responses, they write down their findings and agree on which parts of the answers each one will report on. The sharing takes place in a Round Robin. During this task, each student takes a turn to speak without being interrupted by others, who jot down in their matrices any novel information they did not have. Each person contributes their agreed-upon part of the answers for one of the four land masses without being interrupted.

Map Description. For the next task, we selected a Sort and Label activity where students work in small groups of four to sort materials prepared by the teacher. With each placement, students must be able to explain the reasoning behind their decision. The materials we prepared are three written descriptions—each one printed on a card—of the three previously examined maps that provide information about the cartographer who created each of the historical maps (Figure 7.6). Each description was written so as to provide just enough information to make the match but also includes some ambiguity so as not to make the task too simple. For example, Card 1 begins, "This map was based on the Greek cartographer Ptolemy . . .", but later states, "When this map was republished, the editor, Sebastian Münster, . . ." The students are thus required to read carefully before deciding to which map the card corresponds. The three cards are distributed to each group. Students read the cards aloud in their groups with the purpose of matching each card to a corresponding map based on evidence from the text and the graphic.

When students engage in this task, we remind them to read all the cards carefully before making their decisions since they are to base their pairings on evidence from the cards and maps. The purpose is to have students negotiate meanings and solve problems when matching the maps

Figure 7.6. Map Description Cards

MAP CARDS 1-3

1

This map was actually based on the work of the Greek cartographer Claudius Ptolemy, who historians believe lived from 90–168 AD. His maps were so advanced for their time that the map that you see here was republished some fourteen hundred years after Ptolemy first created it.

When this map was republished, the editor of this map, Sebastian Münster, included information about the world that was not known at the time of Ptolemy, such as the existence of both North and South America. The map does not give a lot of information about each land — there are very few names of countries, mountains, or rivers on the map. However, this map does give a much more accurate depiction of the shapes of all the continents and the distances between them than previous maps had shown.

2

This map was created by Henricus Martellus, a German cartographer. Working as a cartographer in Italy, Martellus produced a map that may have helped change the course of history. Some historians believe that a copy of his map reached the hands of Christopher Columbus. At the time, Columbus was looking for more proof that a sea voyage to Cathay (the name for China at the time) and the riches of the Indies lay only 5,000 miles to the west of Europe. Martellus's map, which incorrectly shortened the distance of a westward voyage between Europe and Asia, may have helped convince the King and Queen of Spain to use their money to finance Columbus's voyage to the Indies. What neither Columbus nor Martellus knew at the time was that the entire continents of the Americas would stand in Columbus's way!

3

This map, created by the German cartographer Martin Waldseemüller, was not printed on a piece of paper in a book for people to look at. Nor was it meant to be hung on a wall. Instead, this map was to be cut out and placed on a globe, a round sphere that would simulate the shape of the earth. From the second century on, mapmakers knew that a globe was the most accurate way to represent the earth.

On this map, Waldseemüller chose to honor an Italian explorer and cartographer who had written about his recent travels to the "new world." Most historians believe that this Italian explorer was the first person to recognize that this land was a new continent, and not part of East Asia, as Columbus had thought. His name was Amerigo Vespucci, and his name is represented for the first time on any map. Can you see where?

---

with the card descriptions, as they are invited to pay attention to the information provided as clues that will help them put together pieces of this historical puzzle.

Collaborative Chart. Building on the previous task, we offer students the opportunity to engage in further analysis of the maps and texts by weaving the sources and their thinking into a chronologically structured chart (Table 7.4). Students take control of their own learning and focus their attention on disciplinary practices, as they debate with each other the correct

Table 7.4. Collaborative Chart

Map Creation Date	Map Letter	Card Number	What evidence did you use?
1489			
1507			
1545			

chronological ordering of the sources, marshaling appropriate evidence to support their sequencing. It is through these meaningful opportunities to support their ideas with evidence from the texts that students apply their newly gained knowledge and skills to the solution of the puzzle.

Presentation of Evidence. Once they have found and articulated the evidence that supports their matches and chronological orderings, groups decide what to write to display their evidence in the collaborative charts. When groups finish, we ask them to post their charts and invite one group to present their findings to the class. If there are disagreements, another group presents their alternate conclusions to the class. Additional evidence from groups is elicited until a class consensus is reached.

Collaborative Writing. As we close this Moment of the lesson, we want to give students the opportunity to individually list two or three possible responses to the following question:

After examining these three maps from the Age of Exploration, what do we know about European exploration from 1485–1545?

To provide students with further practice in sustained interactional sequences, we then have partners share their responses, deciding on the top two replies. Dyads then write collaboratively, expanding on their responses. During enactment, once they are finished with their draft, each dyad exchanges their writings with another and everyone provides feedback on an idea that they think should be further developed.

The goal of this task is for students to construct new understandings, as evidenced by the metacognitive discussion they engage in when formulating their collaborative writing. Examples of the kinds of points that may surface from students' discussions include:

- Significant developments in the art and science of cartography are evidenced by the inclusion of lines of longitude and latitude in the more recent maps examined.
- Before 1488, Europeans had not even explored Africa as far as Cape Horn (or *C. de Bona Speranza* as seen in the 1489 map).

Depending on the ideas the students raise, the teacher might also use this moment to remind them of the European exploration of the Americas starting with Columbus in 1492, call students' attention to the name used for North America (Terra Florida) in the updated Ptolemy map of 1545, and foreshadow that they will learn more about this area, named La Florida when the Spaniard Álvar Núñez Cabeza de Vaca and his men were commissioned to explore it in 1528.

Extending Understanding

In the final moment of the lesson, Extending Understanding, students are invited to apply their thinking beyond the historical context of the Unit to new contexts.

Map Analysis Carousel. To help students make connections to more current times, we invite them to use the practices developed during the lesson to investigate and make inferences about assumptions informing contemporary map projections of the world (Figure 7.7).

Through this task, students apply their inquiry about the Age of Exploration maps to contemporary cartography by analyzing four world maps created by 20th-century map-makers. In particular, they focus on specific land masses such as Australia, Africa, South America, and Europe. Ultimately, students come up with their own hypotheses regarding map-makers' purposes, biases, and world views.

In this task, each student takes one map and responds individually to the following questions in the Map Analysis Carousel Matrix (see Table 7.5).

1. What does the map represent?
2. What are two important findings from this map?
3. What questions does this map raise for you?

Students have only a few minutes to analyze their individual map, and then maps are rotated. The rotation continues until they have each written down responses to the three questions for all four maps.

Figure 7.7. Contemporary World Maps

Mercator Projection

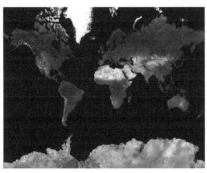

Source:
https://commons.wikimedia.org/wiki
/File:Mercator-projection.jpg

Peters Projection

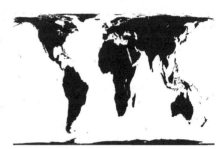

Source:
https://commons.wikimedia.org/wiki
/File:Peters_projection,_black.png

South-Up

Source:
https://commons.wikimedia.org/wiki
/File:Blank-map-world-south-up.png

Pacific-Centered

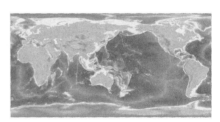

Source:
https://commons.wikimedia.org/wiki
/File:WorldMap-B_with_Frame.png

Table 7.5. Map Analysis Carousel Matrix

	South-Up	Pacific-Centered	Mercator Projection	Peters Projection
What does the map represent?				
What are two important findings from this map?				
What questions does the map raise for you?				

Lastly, students share their analyses one map at a time in a Round Robin by explaining their responses to the questions above. The teacher can provide students the following formulaic expressions to use as they share their responses:

Expressing Findings:

- One thing I noticed was that . . .
- An important finding from my map is . . .
- One fact that stood out for me was . . .

Asking Questions:

- One question this map raises for me is . . .
- I wonder why . . .
- I still don't understand why . . .

Blue Marble Extension. Finally, as a follow-up activity, the teacher provides students an image of Earth taken on December 7, 1972, by the crew of the Apollo 17 spacecraft (Figure 7.8, left). The astronauts took the photograph as they were traveling to the Moon at a distance of about 18,000 miles from the surface. The image was named the Blue Marble, because to the astronauts the Earth had the appearance and size of a glass marble. The teacher invites students to study the photograph and identify land masses depicted such as the Arabian Peninsula, Madagascar, and almost the entire

Figure 7.8. The Published and Original Orientation of The Blue Marble

Source: commons.wikimedia.org/wiki/File:The_Earth_seen_from_Apollo_17.jpg; https://commons.wikimedia.org/wiki/File:Apollo17WorldReversed.jpg

coastline of Africa. Then, the teacher shows students the image of Earth as the astronauts had actually seen it on December 7, 1972 (Figure 7.8, right). The teacher explains that this iconic image of the world was widely disseminated the other way around. The teacher then asks students to discuss, first in their groups of four and then opening to whole-class discussions, reasons as to why the image was flipped from its original orientation. Possible responses will likely include widespread assumptions of a north-up orientation of the world. Teachers will invite them to make connections to what they have learned throughout the lesson about contexts informing the representations of our world.

By the end of this lesson, students have co-constructed understandings about the rapid changes occurring during the Age of European Exploration. More importantly, they have developed an awareness of maps as human constructions that reflect contemporary understandings of the world. This is evident from student interactions, for example when they discuss the various representations of the world. These instances and the artifacts they create indicate that the students are apprenticing into historical thinking skills, such as locating events and sources in space and time, using a chronology to make sense of the past, and comparing sources to learn about how maps are constructions of their time. As students apprentice into these ways of thinking, they become more familiar with how sourcing and contextualization support analysis of primary and secondary sources.

Apprenticing English Learners into Discipline-Based Practices and Developing Their Autonomy

Let us now reflect back on how the lesson scaffolds students' engagement with conceptual, analytic, and language practices, and supports their autonomy. The first two Preparing Learners tasks—the Anticipatory Guide and the Semantic Map—activate prior knowledge and introduce key vocabulary and themes to support students' performance in the subsequent Interacting with Text tasks. During the Anticipatory Guide, students use formulaic expressions as needed to assist them in apprenticing key structures for academic conversations. As the lesson progresses, the carefully sequenced tasks, such as the Compare-and-Contrast Matrix and Map Description, offer students more complex opportunities to engage with two key analytic practices using language with increased control: close reading and corroboration of sources. Students engage in close reading when the Compare-and-Contrast Matrix invites them to focus on specific land masses and cite concrete evidence from the sources. This task supports the growth of their ability to read maps closely and carefully, as well as to be aware and move away from presentism, as they are initially likely to judge the five-centuries-old texts through the lens of the present. Later on, and using insights gained through close reading, students engage in corroborating sources, that is, matching the actual text with its source by identifying the card that describes each historical map.

While emergent, these practices will continue to be spiraled throughout the instructional opportunities provided by the lesson as students are invited to think, talk, read, and write like historians. Through the coherent intellectual journey planned for them in this lesson, students deepen their understandings and, in the final activities, as evidence that they are capable of addressing novel problems, students deploy the ways of thinking cultivated throughout this lesson.

Developing autonomy is further evidenced when students are invited to participate and interact in a variety of tasks with partners or in small groups. In the Anticipatory Guide, students listen to their partner's ideas and the reasons for agreeing or disagreeing with each statement, while also expressing their own views. Although the use of formulaic expressions may be scripted, what gets expressed is particular to each student. In the Map Description Card Match, students take control of their own learning by assessing their decisionmaking. For example, students reflect on evidence provided by the maps and the map description cards to match the visual with the written texts, in an effort to contextualize and deepen understanding about each map. In these interactions, students are required to engage in sustained and focused dialogue that builds on each other's contributions with evolving purposes. They first deepen their understandings as they negotiate meanings to reach consensus about which card matches each source, and later in the co-construction of their Collaborative Chart. Further evidence of students' growing ownership of their own learning is apparent in the discussion of their interpretations of the Map Analysis Carousel.

As we suggested earlier, text selection is essential to lesson design. The three historic maps explored in this lesson—multimodal primary sources— are generative complex texts that invite students to inquire into a different world view. The three historic maps hold information that requires the integration of images and written text such as toponyms, frontiers, and landscapes that have been altered by modern exploration and events. These historical maps capture the attitudes of their creators and represent world views shared during a dynamic period in European history. With the inclusion of these texts, students who might otherwise be challenged by written sources can productively locate the visual discrepancies among the sources in the lesson and generate hypotheses for why the maps might disagree.

CONCLUSION

To support the fulfillment of English Learners' immense potential, it is imperative that teachers design learning opportunities that move their students "beyond their current state of development and make their knowledge generative, so that [they] can use it to support new learning" (Kibler, Walqui, & Bunch, 2014, p. 14). The lesson described in this chapter is characterized by its emphasis on scaffolding students' development of autonomy through a process of apprenticeship that takes place in social contexts as they engage in analytic, conceptual, and language practices simultaneously by interacting with carefully selected primary sources.

The Three Moment Architecture of the lesson introduced in Chapter 3 provides a framework to assist teachers in reasoning through the experiences that will be necessary for English Learners to develop the discipline-based practices related to the lesson. This architecture supports the triggering and connecting of ideas that students already have, priming their knowledge for new and deeper understandings. Each task has been designed to deepen students' engagement in the stated discipline-specific conceptual, analytic, and language practices. Most importantly, tasks have been sequenced in ways that challenge, balance, and support students' current abilities so that they can participate in the more complex disciplinary setting of today's history and social studies classrooms.

Earlier in this chapter, we claimed that our job is to support teacher expertise by engaging in robust design practices that support generative learning experiences for English Learners. Specifically, by representing language development as a social process of apprenticeship and not as an isolated effort of individuals, and by inviting teachers to make meaningful choices—including the selection and crafting of amplified, rich, and complex texts rather than simplified, superficial ones—we hope that this lesson exemplar will enhance teachers' own understandings, agency, and autonomy.

REFERENCES

Barth, J. L., & Shermis, S. S. (1980). Social studies goals: The historical perspective. *Journal of Research and Development in Education, 12*(2), 1–11.

Christie, F., & Derewianka, B. (2008). *School discourse*. London, UK: Continuum.

Coffin, C. (2006). *Historical discourse: The language of time, cause and evaluation*. London, UK: Continuum.

Hammond, J., & Gibbons, P. (2005). Putting scaffolding to work: The contribution of scaffolding in articulating ELS education. *Prospect, 20*(1), 6–30.

Kibler, A. K., Walqui, A., & Bunch, G. (2014). Transformational opportunities: Language and literacy instruction for English language learners in the common core era in the United States. *TESOL Journal, 6*(1), 9–35.

Marker, G., & Mehlinger, H. (1992). Social studies. In P. W. Jackson (Ed.), *Handbook of research on curriculum* (pp. 830–851). New York, NY: Macmillan.

Mintrop, H. (2004). Fostering constructivist communities of learners in the amalgamated multi-discipline of social studies. *Journal of Curriculum Studies, 36*(2), 141–158.

National Council for the Social Studies (NCSS). (2013). *The College, Career, and Civic Life (C3) Framework for Social Studies State Standards: Guidance for enhancing the rigor of K–12 civics, economics, geography, and history.* Silver Spring, MD: Author.

Neumann, D. (2012). Training teachers to think historically: Applying recent research to professional development. *The History Teacher, 45*(3), 383–403.

Prangsma, M. E., van Boxtel, C. A. M., Kanselaar, G., & Kirschner, P. A. (2008). *History learning with textual or visual tasks: Student dialogue.* Proceedings of the 8th International Conference for the Learning Sciences, ICLS '08, Utrecht, The Netherlands. Retrieved from www.researchgate.net/publication/220934229

Rumsey, D., & Williams, M. (2002). Historical maps in GIS. In A. K. Knowles (Ed.), *Past time, past place: GIS for history* (pp. 1–18). Redlands, CA: ESRI Press. Retrieved from https://www.davidrumsey.com/gis/ch01.pdf

Schleppegrell, M. J. (2005). *Helping content teachers work with academic language: Promoting English language learners' literacy in history.* Final report to the UC Linguistic Minority Research Institute (Individual Research Grant Award #03-03CY-061G-D).

Seixas, P., & Peck, C. (2004). Teaching historical thinking. In A. Sears & I. Wright (Eds.), *Challenges and prospects for Canadian social studies* (pp. 109–117). Vancouver, Canada: Pacific Educational Press.

Valdés, G., Kibler, A., & Walqui, A. (2014, March). *Changes in the expertise of ESL professionals: Knowledge and action in an era of new standards.* Alexandria, VA: TESOL International Association.

van Drie, J., & van Boxtel, C. (2008). Historical reasoning: Toward a framework for analyzing students' reasoning about the past. *Education Psychological Review, 20*(2), 87–110.

van Drie, J., & van de Ven, P. H. (2017). Moving ideas: An exploration of students' use of dialogue for writing in history. *Language and Education, 31*(6), 526–542.

van Lier, L. (2004). *The ecology and semiotics of language learning: A sociocultural perspective.* Boston, MA: Kluwer Academic Publishers.

Walqui, A., & van Lier, L. (2010). *Scaffolding the academic success of adolescent English language learners.* San Francisco, CA: WestEd.

Wineburg, S. (2001). *Historical thinking and other unnatural acts.* Philadelphia, PA: Temple University Press.

Wineburg, S. (2013). *Reading like a historian.* New York, NY: Teachers College Press.

CHAPTER 8

What Makes Me Who I Am?

Engaging Beginning-Level English Learners in Quality Learning

Lee Hartman and Elsa Billings

Teachers of beginning-level English as a Second Language (ESL) courses, also called English Language Development (ELD), English as a New Language (ENL), or English for Speakers of Other Languages (ESOL), experience a unique set of instructional challenges. They are faced with the task of supporting the rapid English language development, enhancement of analytic thinking, and high-challenge subject matter learning of diverse groups of students who enter their classrooms with a range of English language exposure and educational histories. As noted in Chapter 1, all English Learners, including those who are just beginning the process of learning English, bring with them often unrecognized language abilities, life experiences, problem-solving skills, and knowledge of the world. Therefore, providing quality learning experiences to beginning English Learners that build on their strengths to realize their extraordinary potential, while being significantly challenging for teachers, can also be profoundly rewarding.

Unlike the previous set of chapters in this book, this chapter focuses not on a single discipline, but rather on a specific group of learners: beginning-level English Learners who are also often newcomers to the United States and to U.S. schools. The literary text at the center of the lesson we describe, Sandra Cisneros' *House on Mango Street*, and the theme of the unit in which the lesson is embedded, identity, were selected by teachers at the International Newcomer Academy (INA) in Fort Worth, Texas, a school where beginning-level English Learners who are also newcomers spend a year before they go to high schools in their neighborhood. The teachers who designed this unit, including the first author of this chapter, participated in professional development with the Quality Teaching for English Learners (QTEL) initiative to improve their ability to design effective learning opportunities for students who arrive at their school not speaking any English.

DEFINING BEGINNING ENGLISH LEARNERS

In the United States, a small but important subset of English Learners at the high school level is comprised of immigrants who are enrolled for the first time in U.S. schools and who have attended classes taught in English for fewer than 2 years (Francis, Rivera, Lesaux, Kieffer, & Rivera, 2006). Throughout this chapter, we use the term "beginning English Learners" to refer to this group of newcomer students; when we refer to newcomer students, we are referencing those who are also beginning English Learners. As Chapter 1 describes, multiple terms are used for the complex array of students designated by their schools as English Learners. Different terms highlight not only students' language proficiency but also their experience in education and in U.S. schools. The U.S. Department of Education (2016) uses the term "newcomers" to describe "any foreign-born students and their families who have recently arrived in the United States." More recently, the term "Recently Arrived Immigrant English Learners" (RAIELs) was coined to represent students who have been in U.S. schools for up to three academic years and who, upon entry into U.S. schools, were classified as English Learners (Umansky et al., 2018). Other terms refer to ways these students' experiences differ, including the nature of their prior schooling. For example, many schools identify "Students with Interrupted Formal Education" (SIFE). While it is important to understand specific experiences and backgrounds of students that these terms attempt to capture, it is also critical to build on the significant potential English Learners bring with them in order to provide them with the optimal opportunities to achieve academically, participate civically, and engage in productive careers.

EMERGING SHIFTS IN BEGINNING-LEVEL ESL CURRICULUM AND INSTRUCTION

Offering quality learning opportunities for beginning-level English Learners in high school, especially when those students are newcomers, is essential. As discussed in Chapter 1, 21st-century careers, life, and civic participation require that all students have access to and succeed in deep disciplinary learning. Beginning-level English Learners' challenges are compounded by the fact that they are in the initial process of developing English, the language in which they are expected to learn concepts and engage in analysis across multiple subject areas (Valdés, Kibler, & Walqui, 2014). This chapter addresses one of the main premises of this book: that teaching English Learners, including beginning-level English Learners, must help students *simultaneously* learn English and develop the complex competencies required of 21st-century learners.

Shifts in Programming for Beginning English Learners

The most common programming for beginning English Learners at the high school level in the United States involves grouping them and having them take ESL classes focused exclusively on learning English. These classes are often paired with "sheltered" content instruction in English (Short & Boyson, 2012; Umansky et al., 2018) and are intended to be temporary until students are "ready" to transition to more rigorous mainstream academic courses. Such programming presents numerous challenges for English Learners. Often students are not deemed knowledgeable enough in English to transition into advanced academic coursework for multiple years, resulting in their not acquiring the necessary credits to graduate on time (Lang, 2017). While some sheltered content courses do offer credit, there is wide variation in the extent to which they represent opportunities for the robust development of the conceptual, analytic, and language practices of the disciplines. The extended isolation of English Learners from mainstream academic coursework minimizes their opportunities to participate in and learn from challenging academic discourse with their peers, both English-speaking and non-English-speaking (Valdés, 1998, 2001). On the other hand, placing beginning-level English Learners into mainstream classes without the necessary supports for accessing complex text and ideas is also untenable (Umansky et al., 2018).

In response to this dilemma, some districts in recent years have re-envisioned ways to provide comprehensive support and accelerated learning for beginning-level English Learners while endeavoring to provide safe and supportive spaces for learning. They do so by providing students with an orientation to navigating U.S. school systems, finding opportunities for language and literacy development in English while building on their home language resources, and accessing rigorous academic content (Lang, 2019; Short & Boyson, 2012; Warren, Thompson, & Hartman, 2015).

This book describes one such model of conceptualizing instruction, designed to allow teachers simultaneously to address English Learners' development of discipline-specific practices, including language, in an interactive social learning context. The development of what some call "hybrid" models for simultaneous learning of language and disciplinary literacy (Lang, 2019), exemplified in the unique instructional design described throughout the book, is applied in this chapter to beginning-level English Learners. We describe how teachers can design instruction that aims deliberately to *amplify* students' access to challenging ideas, texts, and learning activities, in stark contrast to the low-level tasks or drills that students at the beginning levels of English language proficiency are often asked to complete. The lesson we describe in this chapter demonstrates how the key tenets and lesson architecture described in Chapters 2 and 3 can apply to instruction focused on beginning-level English Learners in a way that includes the unique accommodations that may be needed for such students. Specifically, we describe how teachers of recently arrived English Learners can design language development opportunities that integrate English Language Arts concepts and analytic practices from the moment students begin school in the United States.

Shifts in the Work of ESL Teachers

Although teachers may in many cases have not participated in the determination of program policies and structures for English Learners, it is teachers who must carry out the day-to-day work of apprenticing students rapidly into a new language and engaging them in rigorous academic curriculum. Most teachers of beginning-level ESL courses find themselves in situations where shifts that support the kind of integrated development of language and content described above have not yet occurred. The responsibility of "teaching language" to students is often seen as resting solely on the shoulders of the ESL teacher. However, all teachers need to share responsibility for apprenticing students into the uses of English necessary to accomplish the disciplinary goals of their class. The bottom line is that students do not have the luxury of waiting a semester or year before they engage in real academic work. If content-area classrooms need to become sites of language development, so too does the ESL classroom need to become a place where authentic, disciplinary learning occurs. Without both of these shifts, students are condemned to an educational trajectory of constantly trying to catch up and possibly never transcending the English Learner label.

Consequently, in the same way that teachers in mainstream courses ideally would see themselves as responsible for providing opportunities for language development appropriate to their discipline, ESL teachers need to recognize their roles in building students' basic practices in the core disciplines. These two challenges for ESL professionals coincide with both 21st-century societal demands and those of new state content standards and redefine the work of teaching beginning-level English Learners (Valdés, Kibler, & Walqui, 2014).

A LESSON IN THREE MOMENTS

In this chapter, we describe a lesson designed for the first weeks newcomers spend in school, demonstrating how beginning-level ESL classrooms can function as spaces where English Learners develop conceptual and analytic practices related to English Language Arts while simultaneously acquiring language. As discussed above, the lesson challenges current practices found in many beginning-level ESL classes and provides an alternative conceptualization of what is possible and what students are capable of doing and learning, even at the early stages of English language development.

Lesson Planning and Design

This lesson is part of a larger unit based on the theme of identity that was created by a team of three teachers (Mary Chow, Evan Mirolla, and Lee Hartman) at the International Newcomer Academy in Fort Worth, Texas (INA). Although students' ages and number of years of prior schooling completed varied considerably, they were all officially designated as 9th-graders, since they arrived in the United States with no credits. As in other ESL classrooms, the students brought with them diverse backgrounds in language proficiency and content knowledge. Some had nearly finished high school in their home countries, while others had experienced severe interruptions in their education and were unable to read or write in their first languages.

All the students were in the same classroom and were receiving state credit for English Language Arts I. The curriculum objectives thus matched the standards required of their native English-speaking peers. There was no time to waste on countless vocabulary drills and fill-in-the-blank grammar worksheets to prepare them for a "sheltered" class in the following year. Rather, this was a high-challenge Beginning ESL/ELA course with the goal of apprenticing students into becoming accomplished readers and writers who by the end of the year could do well in mainstream classes. The unit and this specific lesson support the development of discipline-based content understanding (in English Language Arts), analytic skills, and language practices that students can apply in their current and future studies.

Teachers introduced this unit during the first 6-week grading cycle of the first semester of students' first year of school in the United States, after students had been in classes for 3 weeks. Those first 3 weeks had oriented students to the classroom, the school, schedules, and the discourse protocols and patterns needed for successful participation in U.S. schools. During this introductory period, students had engaged in a series of structured tasks that invited them to begin to use English in sustained interactions with one another from day one. These structures and lessons facilitated the construction of new knowledge, quality interactions, and language acquisition while serving to introduce students to the workings of the educational system. These interactive activities and routine structures would prove invaluable as students then progressed into deep disciplinary practices in English Language Arts.

Once students had begun to grasp how school operates in the United States, teachers moved to compelling concepts and the analytic practices and related language needed to engage with such content. Since the teachers at INA wanted students, even at this budding level of language learning, to be challenged and to authentically engage with rigorous texts, the same unit theme (Identity) and text from the mainstream English Language Arts curriculum were used, rejecting the simplified text that had been designated as the district's adopted textbook for ESL classes. Lessons were constructed around that text, concentrating on linking the text's themes to students' own identities: who they are, including who they are in the context of their respective families and communities.

Rather than creating activities in which students simply talk superficially and in disconnected ways about themselves, their families, and their communities, students were invited to use vignettes from Sandra Cisneros' *House on Mango Street* as a base for reflecting on their own identities and how these were shaping their own lives. The aims of the discourse went beyond students' producing statements such as "My name is . . ." and "I like to . . . ." The goal in this first unit was to express complex ideas and apprentice into becoming accomplished readers and authors in English, acquiring and using new language along the way. Identity was used as a meaningful connector to the exploration of their identities and how they were being transformed in a new setting.

While the focus of this chapter is on one lesson, the unit as a whole consists of three lessons, each presenting selections from the main text and revisiting varied aspects of identity. Figure 8.1 shows how the three lessons spiral around the central theme. The lessons generate from text selections and build upon one another, starting with the concrete and most personal theme of students' views of themselves and moving toward more

Figure 8.1. Three Lessons in a Spiraling Unit

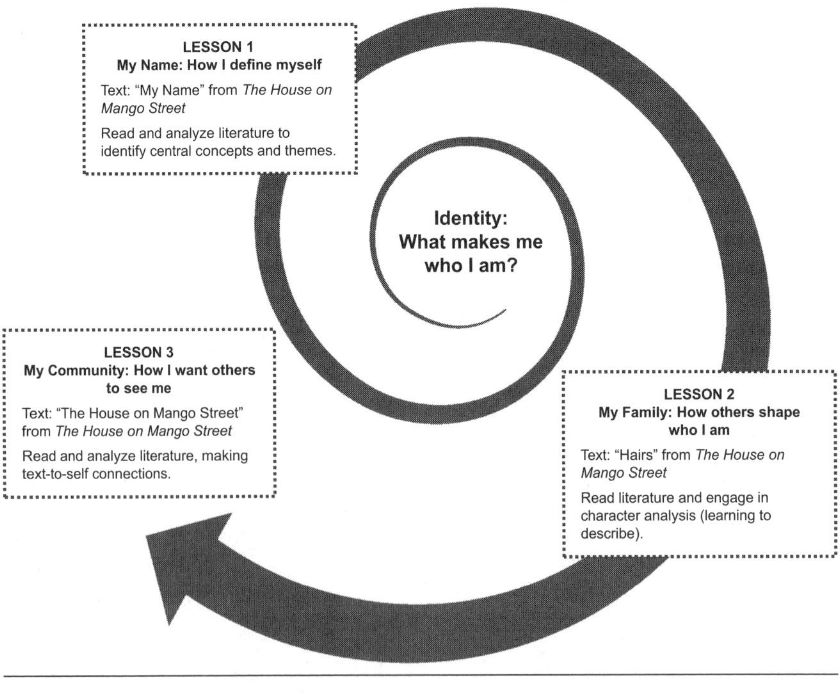

LESSON 1
My Name: How I define myself

Text: "My Name" from *The House on Mango Street*

Read and analyze literature to identify central concepts and themes.

Identity:
What makes me
who I am?

LESSON 3
My Community: How I want others to see me

Text: "The House on Mango Street" from *The House on Mango Street*

Read and analyze literature, making text-to-self connections.

LESSON 2
My Family: How others shape who I am

Text: "Hairs" from *The House on Mango Street*

Read literature and engage in character analysis (learning to describe).

abstract themes of how students identify as part of a family and of a wider community.

The English Language Arts practices are introduced and engaged in spirally to enable students to appropriate them over time. For example, in each lesson students first engaged in tasks that tapped their prior knowledge and experience and built new fields of understanding and language about the main themes and literary devices, which are always interconnected. Furthermore, students read and discussed the text as needed in order to invite them to interpret its meaning, and to extend their understanding by applying those ideas and literary structures in their own writing. By the end of the unit, students produced and edited three pieces of original writing in English for assembly in a small book that became part of their classroom library.

Lesson Objectives. The lesson described in this chapter is Lesson 2, "My Family: How Others Shape Who I Am." The main learning objectives center on determining central ideas of a text and analyzing characters—in this lesson, the learning objectives focus on descriptions of family members. Tasks include not only reading, but also speaking, listening, and writing in the same genre (autobiographical narrative). Objectives in these lessons are mindful of and reflect those required in new standards such as the Common Core to "read and comprehend literature, including stories, dramas, and poems, at the high end of the [grade-level] text complexity band independently and proficiently" (CCSS, 2010, p. 38).

The teachers developing this unit did not, however, place a grade-level text in front of newcomers who were beginning English Learners and expect that they would be able to read and understand every word completely. In order to engage beginning English Learners in language, conceptual, and analytic practices in deep and accelerated ways, they knew it was necessary to construct high-challenge lessons coupled with high support, building the scaffolding students needed to access the language and meaning of the text. Table 8.1 shows the main Common Core Standards addressed in the lesson.

Table 8.2 shows the disciplinary practices in literature that correspond to the ELA standards in Table 8.1. As students work toward achieving the lesson objectives, they appropriate these practices and over time become part of the larger community of expert readers and writers.

Text Choice. To reach our objectives and invite students to engage with this deep and thought-provoking theme, we needed a robust text. The ESL textbook was not much help, so the INA team decided to go outside the classroom textbook and use parts of the text being taught in mainstream English I classes. For this lesson, the vignette "Hairs" by Sandra Cisneros from the book *The House on Mango Street* was chosen.

We included this text in the lesson not only because it made it possible to reach the objectives set as a destination for the lesson (understanding

Table 8.1. English Language Arts Standards for 9th–10th Grades Addressed in Identity Lesson

- Cite strong and thorough textual evidence to support analysis of what the text says explicitly as well as inferences drawn from the text.
- Analyze how complex characters develop over the course of a text, interact with other characters, and advance the plot or develop the theme.
- Determine the meaning of words and phrases as they are used in the text, including figurative and connotative meanings; analyze the cumulative impact of specific word choices on meaning and tone.

Source: CCSS, 2010, p. 38

Table 8.2. Conceptual, Analytic, and Language Practices Addressed in Identity Lesson

Conceptual Practices	Analytic Practices	Language Practices
• Understand the concept of identity • Understand that identity is shaped by interactions and relationships	• Identify the key ideas of a text and supporting details • Identify how the author uses figurative language to describe characters	• Formulate questions to gain insight on how others understand a text • Use figurative language to construct deep descriptions of people

key ideas and character descriptions), but also because it constituted an example of the kinds of complex texts with which beginning English Learners can interact when supported with careful and strategic lesson design. Furthermore, this text was chosen because it was required reading for mainstream English classes in the district. Trusting the immense potential of these learners, we offered them the original version as opposed to a simplified or "ESL-friendly" text. We amplified the text by elaborating on it (e.g., chunking the text and adding guiding headlines), thereby giving beginning-level English Learners access to literature that might otherwise be beyond their reach—because of its style and use of figurative language.

At the same time, we structured tasks in a way that invited students to co-construct new knowledge through peer interactions, thus equipping them with strategies to access other comparable texts in the future. While the lesson may appear different from what beginning-level English Learners' peers in mainstream English Language Arts classes might encounter, the learning goals for students were the same.

Often the tendency is to find a text that is "at the right level" for students to complete these objectives (Bunch, Walqui, & Pearson, 2014). It is not unheard of for beginning-level adolescent English Learners to be offered books designed for students in the primary grades. Because the unit designers wanted students to be successful in attaining learning objectives, offering them simplified texts would not have conveyed belief in their intellectual ability, nor would it have inspired in them the motivation to grapple with more difficult texts. Our proposal turns the notion of simplification on its head and offers students *amplified texts*—those that keep the author's authentic expressions, ideas, and themes intact while providing enhancements helpful for English Learners. Designers divided the text into meaningful segments and added subheadings to each part to focus students' attention on the purposes accomplished by the text segment. An example of this kind of "text engineering" appears in Table 8.2. The amplified text may *look* different from what students in other classes may encounter. The structure and wording of this portion of the text is the original, but the presentation has been engineered with subtitles to support students' accessing the meaning.

The focus of amplified learning opportunities is on the big ideas, and we do not require that students understand every word in the text. Since we are apprenticing them into the practices that skilled readers use when they encounter complex texts, we want them to be comfortable with not understanding each word and to trust that they will acquire the language as they move from what may be ambiguous now to what is increasingly clear over time.

LESSON ARCHITECTURE: THREE MOMENTS IN A LESSON

The team designed the lesson using the Three Moment Architecture described in Chapter 3, choosing a culminating task and planning backward to ensure that each task built upon the one before in a way that students were prepared to successfully complete the Extending Understanding task. We also paid attention to ensuring that students developed the language practices and the understandings needed to encounter a similar text in their new language. In this lesson (as in all lessons), the beginning focuses first on what students *can* accomplish, with sufficient support, and steadily builds upon that foundation. Of course, as beginning English Learners, the students need extra linguistic support, such as the vocabulary needed to describe people, language models for discourse, and use of their home language(s) to negotiate difficulties. However, acquiring new words is not the objective of the lesson, but rather a means to an end. As we move through the lesson, each task and the flow of the lesson as a whole support students as they move toward reaching the ultimate goal of apprenticing into the conceptual, analytic, and language practices of English Language Arts.

To accomplish this, the lesson works toward engaging students in writing, using figurative language to describe people in their families as preparation for reading the text. For beginning English Learners, using figurative language is no easy feat. Therefore, they are invited to engage in a series of scaffolded tasks in order to be able to work at the edge of their competence.

Throughout the lesson, students work collaboratively, interacting with each other and their teacher through robust, generative tasks. These tasks do not elicit one-word or one-phrase responses written on worksheets by students working independently in silence. Rather, they are designed to invite students to generate knowledge and ideas as they analyze and explore the central concepts the lesson addresses.

Preparing Learners

Some readers may question the number of tasks in this first Moment of the lesson (Table 8.3), especially in light of the advice offered in Chapter 3 to not overextend this Moment. Typically, scaffolding tasks are more common in the second Moment when students interact with complex text. For beginning English Learners, however, the Preparing Learners Moment is critical to ensuring that they are prepared to access a text that is challenging because it is in a language, and perhaps a genre, with which they are unfamiliar. The tasks prepare students to think about the central ideas, what they already know or may not know, and the language associated with those ideas. As they increase their background knowledge and language proficiency, students move toward greater autonomy and need less support.

Self-Sketch. The lesson begins with tasks in which students draw on what is familiar in their everyday lives, themselves, and the people around them. In the first task, the teacher invites students to draw the outline of a person while the teacher projects an outline of her own. Modeling the task, the teacher describes what she is doing, using a Think Aloud to articulate what she is thinking as she does her own self-sketch. The teacher might say, "I have long, dark brown hair with highlights, so I'm going to draw and color it like this. My eyes are big and brown too, so I'll represent them like this." As she describes herself, she labels the various body parts and colors that she is using to model the language the students will need for the task. The students individually complete their own sketch of themselves with similar labeling.

Dyad Pair-Share. When the sketches are complete, the teacher strategically groups students into heterogeneous dyads based on language proficiency and has them explain their drawings to their peers. By moving from imitating the teacher to interacting with one another, students practice and learn language and concepts from one another's descriptions. They also learn the important functions of communicating information and co-constructing knowledge in this community of practice.

Self-Portrait. Moving from the concrete, the next task focuses on more in-depth portraits. As the teacher explains the criteria for what the portrait

Table 8.3. Tasks for Preparing Learners

Lesson Title: My Family: How Others Shape Who I Am (Analyzing Important Characters in a Text and in My Life)

MOMENT ONE: PREPARING LEARNERS		
Task	Description	Purpose
Self-Sketch	Students sketch themselves, labeling body parts, facial features, and associated colors.	Introducing key concepts; contextualizing key vocabulary
Dyad Pair-Share	Dyads share their sketches of themselves.	Co-constructing key concepts and vocabulary
Self-Portrait	Students focus on thoughts and personality traits as they include more information in a self-portrait.	Activating prior knowledge
Interview a Peer	Students interview one another to find out how each one has described himself/herself.	Building schema
Sketch a Peer	Using the information they gain from their interviews, students sketch their classmates.	Making connections
Peer Portraits	Students describe their peers' thinking and personality.	Using vocabulary in context
Family Tree Questions	Students begin to gain new vocabulary by analyzing Pedro's family tree.	Contextualizing vocabulary; introducing key concepts
Quick-Write	Students write a quick description of a special family member.	Contextualizing key concepts and vocabulary; bridging prior knowledge
Dyad Pair-Share	Students share and listen to their peers' ideas.	Structuring interaction

will contain, she models using examples of the language she wishes for students to imitate. Her portrait includes a sentence that represents who she is, a picture that shows what she is like as a person, and a symbol that represents some aspect of who she is "on the inside." As she adds each of these to her own self-portrait, she continues to articulate what she is thinking so students begin to use those same metacognitive processes as they complete their own self-portraits.

Although the teacher has modeled the language of the tasks, students may still need support with English expressions needed to describe themselves. The teacher provides some of the words students may find useful in completing the task, especially in describing what their character is like. The students may also benefit from the use of their home language at this stage and may depend on peers to scaffold the learning of these new terms that they are encountering or access to L1 resources such as dictionaries and translators. The goal at this stage is not perfect language use. Rather, students are being apprenticed into the use and structure of certain tasks, conceptual understandings, analytic practices, and English practices, all of which will benefit them throughout the lesson and entire course of study.

Interview a Peer, Sketch a Peer, Peer Portrait. Once students have completed their self-portraits and used language describing themselves in greater depth, they are invited into more collaborative tasks. Using a list of questions such as those in Figure 8.2 prepared by the teacher, students first interview one another. Next, they sketch their peers as they did themselves. Finally, they complete a Peer Portrait by filling in the sketch with information from the interview.

Family Tree Question and Answer. Once students have collaborated in acquiring and using language to describe themselves and their peers, they are prepared to extend their practices by learning to describe their own families.

Using a handout that depicts a family tree showing three or four generations with names of individuals (which is accompanied by a chart of titles showing relationships, e.g., father, aunt, grandmother, father-in-law, stepmother, sister, cousin, etc., in both English and in the L1 of students), students engage in one-on-one dialogues in which they ask and answer questions of each other about the family depicted on the family tree handout (e.g., "What is Alicia's aunt's name?" "Who is Pedro's grandson?"). Without using precious class time to memorize long lists of vocabulary words, students are invited to use the words in a meaningful context. As they work together to formulate questions and answers, students begin to appropriate the new terms. These handouts are not lists of vocabulary to be memorized, but tools necessary to perform a task.

Figure 8.2. Peer Interview Questions

What is your name? Where are you from?

What do you like to do?

How would you describe yourself?

My Family Tree. Once students have become more familiar with the language of family relationships in English, they construct their own family tree, labeling names and relationships of their family members to themselves, with the teacher modeling aloud her metacognitive processes. The students can fill in words that they may not know in English in their primary language and then go back and find the names of the terms in English. In this way, students build the lexicon they will need to access the text.

Quick-Write and Pair-Share. Now students are ready to be introduced to the theme of the specific text they will encounter in the Interacting with Text moment of the lesson. Using their own family trees and the descriptions they made of themselves and their classmates, students choose one family member who is especially significant for them and do a quick-write to describe that person in a short paragraph.

Using the prompt, "Describe someone in your family who is special for you," students work independently to get their thoughts on paper. The teacher provides formulaic expressions with models of the language that can be used to complete the task. Students are also free to include ideas and thoughts in their primary language that can lead to the creation of more substantive descriptions. The task ends with students' sharing what they have written with a peer in dyads, writing down descriptors they hear to be ready to share with the entire class.

In all of these tasks, generative routines are established. This use of highly ritualized and structured activity is especially important with students at emerging levels of language proficiency. When the structure of the task becomes familiar, students begin to focus less on the procedures and more on the ideas and analyses. When the tasks remain constant, students' responses become more novel.

The lesson thus far has been preparing students for interacting with the central text. The teacher has provided the linguistic support and arranged the tasks in a way that allows students to build a field of knowledge that will prove useful in the next Moment of the lesson. If the lesson had begun with the Quick-Write task, students might not have been able to complete it. Therefore, we begin with what they know and give them the support they need to be able to successfully complete a task that then moves them to the next, and the next, and so on.

Interacting with Text

Once students have engaged in quality interactions with their peers around the central themes of the upcoming text, using the language they will need to make sense of the text and anticipating the central theme by drawing on their own experience, the teacher introduces them to the text through

Table 8.4. Interacting with Text Tasks

MOMENT TWO: INTERACTING WITH THE TEXT		
Task	Description	Purpose
Read Aloud with a Focus	The teacher models how to read and find the gist of a text.	Modeling metacognitive reading purposes
Reading in 4 Voices	Students are assigned parts or chunks of the text to read out loud.	Alerting students to the structure of a text and the literary devices the author uses
Character Description Matrix	Using the text as a model, students describe one of the characters.	Building schema

a number of tasks summarized in Table 8.4. English Learners can become frustrated when they encounter a text that has language with which they are not familiar. If many of the words are new to them, the task can seem overwhelming. It is important in this moment of the lesson to reassure students that they do not have to understand every word of a text to understand the themes and concepts it presents.

Reading Aloud with a Focus. To begin, the teacher apprentices students into comprehending the gist of what they read. By using a Read Aloud with a Focus task, the teacher once again models for students the metacognitive processes that accomplished readers use and demonstrates how tolerating ambiguity, or being comfortable with not understanding every detail in a text, is vital to learning a new language. Furthermore, since every chunk signaled by a different font corresponds to a unit of meaning, students become aware of how breath pauses function in the oral rendering of a text. She begins by reading the first paragraph, describing to students what she is thinking as she reads. For example, she might say, "I recognize the word 'family' and know that KiKi and Nene are names, so I think the author is describing her family. I see five names so I know that there are five people in the family. Three of the names are not Mama or Papa, so they are probably brothers and sisters." As she moves through this Think Aloud, the students watch as the teacher fills in her Reading with a Focus Chart (Table 8.5). They listen and record the information as well. When she is finished with the first paragraph, she returns to the text to read and analyze additional paragraphs in the same way as needed.

It is important to note that, although they are not reading aloud, students are indeed interacting with the text. They are following the example of the teacher and know that one day they will do what she is doing. She is apprenticing them into a practice that is vital for good readers. As apprentices,

Table 8.5. Reading with a Focus Chart

	Selections from the text	Using my own words, this is what I understand from the passage.
1		
2		

their participation is far from autonomous. This does not mean, however, that they are not engaging in deep conceptual and analytic practices. They are engaged in what Lave and Wenger (1991) describe as "legitimate peripheral participation" (p. 29). Their teacher believes in their potential to one day be expert readers and treats them as such. Accordingly, her students are engaged in rigorous work that is central to the discipline and building the foundation for skills that will benefit them for a lifetime.

Reading in Four Voices. Because they have already begun to identify the gist of the text, students are now able to look more closely at its details and analyze its structure. In order to give students practice with the language and the way in which the author constructs the text in an almost poem-like fashion, the teacher purposefully divides the text into chunks of meaning. She does this by changing the physical type of the text into **bold**, *italics*, underlined, or regular type (see Figure 8.3). In groups of four, each student reads a different text type. As they read the text together aloud, students can hear how each character is described and the kind of figurative language the author uses to make comparisons.

Character Description Matrix. Once the students have worked through these tasks on perceiving the big picture of what the text is about, they are able to engage in a more detailed analysis of the descriptions of the author's family. If this is the first time students have been exposed to figurative language in English, the teacher guides them by explaining the way metaphors and similes are structured and how some descriptions are personifications of objects (e.g., lazy hair). Depending on the needs of students, she may need to explain by referring to the author's description of Papa how similes draw comparisons between two things using the words "like" and "as." The narrator is comparing Papa's hair to a broom because they look similar. Using visuals of a broom, she leads the class in a discussion of how someone's hair

Figure 8.3. Reading Aloud in Four Voices

Hairs

Sandra Cisneros

Section 1: Esperanza describes the people in her family.

Everybody in our family has different hair. <u>My Papa's hair is like a broom, all up in the air.</u> And me, my hair is lazy. It never obeys barrettes or bands. Carlos' hair is thick and straight. He doesn't need to comb it. **Nenny's hair is slippery—slides out of your hand.** <u>And Kiki, who is the youngest, has hair like fur.</u>

Section 2: Esperanza describes a special family member—her mother

But my mother's hair, my mother's hair, **like little rosettes,** <u>like little candy circles</u> all curly and pretty because she pinned it in pincurls all day, sweet to put your nose into when she is holding you, **holding you and you feel safe,** <u>is the warm smell of bread before you bake it,</u> is the smell when she makes room for you on her side of the bed still warm with her skin, **and you sleep near her,** <u>the rain outside falling and Papa snoring.</u> The snoring, the rain, and Mama's hair that smells like bread.

---

can look like a broom and then draws a picture of how she imagines Papa based on this comparison.

Students then work together again in dyads to complete the Character Description Matrix (Table 8.6) for the other three family members in paragraph 1. Using pictures to understand vital new words like "slippery," "fur," "thick," and "straight," they work together to identify the part of the text that describes each character and then represent what they see in their minds when they read the description. Using formulaic expressions such as, "I'm going to draw _____ because the text says _____," students build on each other's ideas before drawing their pictures. Without this added structured interaction, students' descriptions might be less imaginative. Notice that students are given a choice for the formulaic expressions they can use.

Students then complete their Character Description Matrix with the support of a peer to give a deeper analysis of the description of Mama. Since the author uses richer and more vivid descriptions for Mama, students read the text again and identify what words the author uses to paint a picture of what Mama is like and what she looks like in a conversation such as the following:

> *S1:* I think Mama's hair is _____. I know this because the text says _____.
> *S2:* I agree with you, and I can add _____.
>   I disagree with you because _____.
> OR

Table 8.6. Character Description Matrix

Family Member's Hair	Comparison/Description	Picture
Papa's hair		
Esperanza's (me) hair		
Carlos' hair		
Nenny's hair		
Kiki's hair		
Mother's hair		

> *S1:* What the author is saying is that Mama's hair is _____.
> I know this because she describes it as _____.
> *S2:* I agree with you. Furthermore, I can add that _____.
> I do not think that is the case, and my evidence is that the author
> says _____.

The students work together to generate new ideas and come to a richer and deeper analysis than they might do independently. Through this kind of sustained quality interaction, students are acquiring not only the language needed to interact with one another but also the skills necessary to participate in the activities of the discipline, in this case, character analysis and descriptive writing.

This second Moment can prove challenging for beginning English Learners. When they encounter a new genre or type of text for the first time in English, supports to access the full meaning and to understand unique literary devices can be critical.

For this reason, the Interacting with Text tasks started with modeling how to read to understand the overall gist of the text. This engagement was followed by tasks focused on more detailed reading and analysis of the author's descriptions of the characters. Beginning with the ending in mind is thus crucial in designing the flow of tasks.

Extending Understanding

Once students have read the text multiple times, each with a different purpose, considered the central ideas, and begun to analyze character descriptions, they move to the Extending Understanding Moment. In this Moment, as shown in Table 8.7, students use the knowledge they have gained to create portraits of their own families, focus on one member, and write a two-paragraph description of that family member following the structure of the text.

Character Portrait. The students now combine what they learned in the self-portrait task in the first Moment with the analysis of character descriptions in the second Moment to develop a deeper exploration into and description of the character of the author's mother. In a character portrait of Mama (like their self-portraits), students now include an original phrase from the text that synthesizes the character, a picture representing a vital part of the text, a symbol that represents the character, and a quote that encapsulates how the speaker feels about her.

Family Member Description Matrix. With the ultimate goal of moving students from apprenticeship to the appropriation of the concepts, skills, and

Table 8.7. Extending Understanding Task

MOMENT THREE: EXTENDING UNDERSTANDING		
Task	Description	Purpose
Character Portrait	Students make a character portrait of their own that is similar to the character from the text.	Learn to describe people to others who do not know them. Synthesize key concepts and language and apply them to a novel situation.
Family Member Description Matrix	Students use a similar matrix to that used in the interacting moment to describe their own family members.	Practice describing people to others who do not know them. Apply disciplinary practices outside of the text.
Writing	Students use their portraits and matrices to construct a two-paragraph description of their own families, similar to the text they have just read.	Practice describing people to others who do not know them. Apply newly acquired conceptual, analytic, and language practices.

language practices, the lesson ends with more independent work in which students create written descriptions of their own.

Using an almost identical Character Description Matrix to the one used to analyze the characters in the text, the students work individually to describe members of their own families in a Family Member Description Matrix, comparing what they look like and who they are as individuals. They then focus on one member of the family who is particularly special to them and compose a more in-depth description following the example in the text. This is the goal of this final Moment in the lesson: that students synthesize all the understandings they appropriated by interacting with each other and the text.

Writing. Once they have organized their thoughts in the Family Description Matrix, students complete the lesson by writing a description of their families using a similar structure to the one in the text they have just analyzed. The teacher can provide structure and language if needed (see Figure 8.4), but students formulate their own ideas and write them as a text to be read by others. During the activity students need to be aware that the purpose of their writing is to create compelling descriptions, painting with words pictures that others can see. As students begin the practice of appropriating the skills and engaging in the activity of legitimate authors, they are now authors themselves.

Figure 8.4 provides a model of the type of formulaic expressions students may use in their writing. The model is to be used only if needed, knowing that students will quickly appropriate the writing structures and that these can be eliminated as soon as learners are ready to increase their autonomy. This future-oriented view of what our students will be able to accomplish without the support of the teacher drives our choices, even at the beginning stage of language learning.

The Extending Understanding Moment in the lesson is crucial because it is here that students apply what they have learned and appropriate the skills they have been apprenticing. This culminating writing activity provides an opportunity for the teacher and students to assess their development of the conceptual, analytic, and language practices related to this literary discipline.

CONCLUSION

This lesson is driven by the high expectations needed in ESL classrooms today to prepare beginning-level English Learners for the demands of the 21st century. It is not simply a series of exercises to build a lexicon of "survival" English vocabulary that will be added to other words until students are "ready" for a "real" English class. The lesson illustrates how teachers can invite newcomers to participate in carefully scaffolded tasks that engage

Figure 8.4. Writing Structure Model

1. **Introduce the purpose of your writing**
   I am going to describe my family so that you get an idea of who they are.
   OR
   I am going to write to you about my family.
   OR
   Let me introduce my family to you.

2. **Say how many people there are in your family**
   There are_____ people in my family.
   OR
   I have a small family. We are only _____.
   OR
   I have a large family. There are ____ people in my family.

3. **Begin introducing your family as a whole**
   We are from a (small OR medium OR large) town in _____.
   We come from the capital of _____.
   We have been in the United States for _____.

4. **Choose a member of your family who is special to you and say something about this person so that others begin to imagine them.**
   One person in my family who is very special to me is _____, because _____.

them in real academic work, weaving in deeper and deeper practices as they progress through the unfolding lesson. It also shows how teachers can treat English Learners as young scholars capable of grappling with deep concepts and rigorous ideas. The lesson—with its rigorous conceptual and language goals—allows teachers themselves to enact roles beyond simply providing language exercises, fun games, and new words until students are ready for "real work." Like their colleagues in the other disciplines, teachers of ESL can apprentice students into becoming accomplished readers, writers, and thinkers.

Using the Three Moment Architecture, students move toward development of the critical skills they need. This does not mean that every student in the class understands perfectly every part of the text or its analysis. At this point in their educational careers, beginning English Learners are just beginning to be apprenticed into these new practices. As the year progresses, the teacher will offer them numerous additional opportunities to engage with one another, complex texts, and rigorous concepts in much the same way. Through the constant weaving of these processes throughout the year, students simultaneously appropriate the conceptual, analytic, and language practices they need. The teacher not only sees what her students are capable of during this lesson, but also anticipates what they are capable of by the end of the year and far into the future. We trust in students' potential, confident that they can and will be successful.

REFERENCES

Bunch, G. C., Walqui, A., & Pearson, D. P. (2014). Complex text and new common standards in the United States: Pedagogical implications for English learners. *TESOL Quarterly, 48*(3), 533–559. doi:10.1002/tesq.175

Common Core State Standards Initiative. (2010). *Common Core State Standards for English language arts and literacy in history, social studies, science, and technical subjects.* Washington, DC: National Governors Association and Council of Chief State School Officers. Retrieved from http://www.corestandards.org/wpcontent/uploads/ELA_Standards1.pdf

Francis, D., Rivera, M., Lesaux, N., Kieffer, M., & Rivera, H. (2006). *Practical guidelines for the education of English language learners: Research-based recommendations for serving adolescent newcomers.* Houston, TX: Center on Instruction, University of Houston.

Lang, N. W. (2017, March). Adolescent newcomers doing school in the US: Program design and language practices. Paper presented at the annual conference of the American Association of Applied Linguistics, Portland, OR.

Lang, N. W. (2019, February 20). Teachers' translanguaging practices and "safe spaces" for adolescent newcomers: Toward alternative visions. *Bilingual Research Journal.* doi:10.1080/15235882.2018.1561550

Lave, J., & Wenger, E. (1991). *Situated learning: Legitimate peripheral participation.* Cambridge, UK: Cambridge University Press.

Short, D. J., & Boyson, B. A. (2012). *Helping newcomer students succeed in secondary schools and beyond.* Washington, DC: Center for Applied Linguistics.

Umansky, I., Hopkins, M., Dabach, D. B., Porter, L., Thompson, K., & Pompa, D. (2018). *Understanding and supporting the educational needs of recently arrived immigrant English learner students: Lessons for state and local education agencies.* Washington, DC: Council of Chief State School Officers.

U.S. Department of Education, Office of English Language Acquisition. (2016). *Newcomer Tool Kit.* Washington, DC: Author.

Valdés, G. (1998). The world outside and inside schools: Language and immigrant children. *Educational Researcher, 27*(6), 4–18.

Valdés, G. (2001). *Learning and not learning English: Latino students in American schools.* New York, NY: Teachers College Press.

Valdés, G., Kibler, A., & Walqui, A. (2014). *Changes in the expertise of ESL professionals: Knowledge and action in an era of new standards.* Alexandria, VA: TESOL International Association.

Warren, T., Thompson, R., & Hartman, L. (2015, April). Building teacher metacognitive abilities: A narrative of practice. Paper presented at the annual meeting of the American Educational Research Association, Chicago, IL.

CHAPTER 9

Where the Rubber Meets the Road

What Teachers and Students Report When Implementing High-Quality Learning Designs for English Learners

George C. Bunch, Heather Schlaman, and Sara Rutherford-Quach

Is pursuing the kind of amplified instruction outlined in the previous chapters possible, especially after years of reductive approaches to language and literacy for English Learners? What can English Learners achieve when engaged in classrooms that follow the tenets and design features discussed earlier in this book? What challenges do they and their teachers face in implementing curriculum designed to provide enhanced opportunities for engagement in rigorous, well-supported disciplinary practices that simultaneously provide opportunities for language development?

In this chapter, we discuss what students and teachers in three U.S. cities had to say about the challenges and opportunities they experienced when implementing a pilot unit designed to exemplify amplified curriculum for English Learners in their classrooms.[1] Grounded in approaches consistent with the tenets discussed in Chapter 2 and developed using the architecture outlined in Chapter 3, the unit was created to illustrate how such a curriculum could be designed to provide rich learning opportunities for English Learners and their "mainstream" peers. Although this particular unit was developed for English Learners at or beyond the intermediate level of language proficiency, the underlying principles and design features are applicable to students at more beginning stages of English language proficiency as well (see Chapter 8).

The 7th-grade English Language Arts unit, *Persuasion Across Time and Space: Analyzing and Producing Persuasive Texts*, was designed for the Understanding Language initiative by Aída Walqui, Nanette Koelsch, and Mary Schmida (2012) at the Quality Teaching for English Learners (QTEL) initiative at WestEd (see also Bunch, Walqui, & Kibler, 2015; Kibler, Walqui, & Bunch, 2015).[2] The unit is available in its entirety on the Understanding Language website (ell.stanford.edu), and classroom vignettes of its implementation can

be accessed on the Teaching Channel website (https://www.teachingchannel
.org/blog/2013/10/25/video-playlist-ell-instruction).

The unit was developed just after the Common Core Standards had
been adopted by most states and as they were starting to be implemented.
Because the new standards called for a radical departure from prevailing
assumptions about learning for all students, language development, and instruction for English Learners, the unit was designed to illuminate a number
of theoretical and pedagogical shifts in the design and enactment of learning
opportunities for English Learners (Bunch et al., 2015; Kibler et al., 2015;
Walqui et al., 2012).

Among the shifts exemplified in the unit are those that embody the notion
of *amplification* discussed in this book, for example shifting from instruction
centered around isolated ideas or texts to considering ideas and texts as interconnected, and moving from the use of simplified to more complex texts.
A number of shifts also relate to specific tenets discussed in Chapter 2, as
shown in Table 9.1.

Table 9.1. Shifts and Tenets Enacted in Design of Persuasion Unit

Tenets Discussed in Chapter 2	Related Shifts Illustrated in *Persuasion Across Time and Space*
Development emerges in social interaction. It is a consequence of, not a prerequisite for, learning.	From considering language acquisition as an individual process to understanding it as apprenticeship in social contexts.
Quality learning is deliberately and contingently scaffolded.	From activities that pre-teach content or simply "help students get through texts" to those that scaffold students' development and autonomy.
Quality school learning focuses on substantive and generative disciplinary practices.	From separate "content" and "language" objectives to objectives that highlight the role of language in engaging with disciplinary practices.
During learning, English Learners simultaneously develop conceptual, analytic, and language practices.	From identification of discrete structural features of language to exploration of how language is purposely patterned to do rhetorical work.
When it comes to the development of language practices, quality learning opportunities for English Learners focus on form in contextual, contingent, and supportive ways.	From viewing language acquisition as a linear process aimed at accuracy, fluency, and complexity to understanding it as a nonlinear and complex developmental process aimed at comprehension and communication.

THE UNIT AND THE PILOT

The unit is comprised of five lessons of approximately one week each as shown in Figure 9.1. Each lesson contains a number of pedagogical tasks that support English Learners as they engage in making meaning of historical speeches, such as President Lincoln's *Gettysburg Address*, Dr. Martin Luther King Jr.'s *I Have a Dream*, and Robert Kennedy's *On the Assassination of Martin Luther King*.

In the introductory lesson, students engage with a variety of media to examine the use of emotional appeal in advertisements to interest readers and persuade them to take action. The second lesson takes students deeper into analysis of persuasive techniques through close reading of and interaction with the *Gettysburg Address*. In the third lesson, students learn Aristotle's Three Appeals (ethos, pathos, and logos) and use this knowledge to critically analyze three Civil Rights-era speeches. In the fourth lesson, students collaboratively analyze the structural, organizational, grammatical, and lexical choices made in Barbara Jordan's *All Together Now* (1994) in order to examine how authors construct persuasive texts at both macro and micro levels. Finally, in the fifth lesson, students demonstrate their learning by analyzing a more recent address delivered to the United Nations by a 12-year-old and by writing their own persuasive texts.

Consistent with the notion of *spiraling* discussed in Chapter 2, the arrangement of the lessons and activities is designed to provide iterative opportunities for students to discuss, read, and write about common themes throughout the unit in order to recursively develop deeper understandings.

The unit provides various levels of scaffolding (Walqui & van Lier, 2010). At the *macro* level, the spiraled lessons allow students to move from analyzing persuasive discourse in forms with which they are more likely to be familiar, such as advertising, to genres that are less familiar to them, such as historical and political speeches. At the *meso* level, each lesson's tripartite structure allows students to (1) prepare to engage with upcoming texts by activating and building background knowledge, (2) interact with those texts in various ways, and (3) connect what they are reading and discussing to texts from other lessons, units, and courses, as well as to their lives and the larger world (see Figure 3.3 in Chapter 3). Finally, various interactive activities at the *micro* level provide opportunities for students to engage with each other and the teacher in collaborative tasks that they might not initially have been able to do by themselves. Suggestions for differentiation are provided, based on the level of scaffolding (light, moderate, heavy) needed for students to make meaning from a text.

After feedback on a draft of the unit was collected from teachers at several school districts across the United States, and after parts of the unit were "pre-piloted" by a group of summer school teachers in Oakland and New York City, three urban school districts were chosen to pilot the full unit.[3]

Figure 9.1. The Persuasion Unit's Spiraled Design

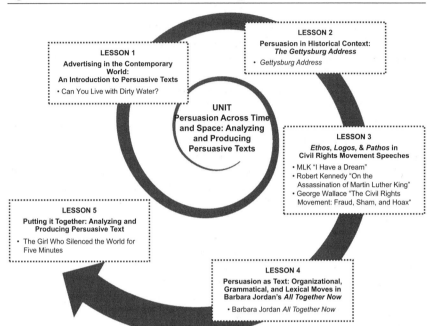

Source: Walqui, Koelsch, & Schmida, 2012.

The districts were chosen based on the large numbers of English Learners they served, as well as the geographic and demographic diversity that the districts represented. One district was in a large Midwestern city with a long history of immigration and where English Learners represented 20% of the district's student population. Another was in a Southwestern city with almost 40% English Learners. The third district was in a city in the South with a lower, but dramatically increasing, English Learner population.

Sixteen teachers in nine schools piloted the unit. Two days of professional development designed by the creators of the unit allowed teachers to learn about its theoretical underpinnings, experience several lessons as students, and discuss potential challenges that might arise in their classrooms. All classrooms participating in the pilot had at least 25% English Learners.

Two or three times during implementation of the unit, project staff visited pilot classrooms, videorecording lessons and meeting with teachers to plan and debrief as well as discuss challenges and opportunities as they arose. Midway through the unit's implementation, web conferences were held for participating teachers to share questions, concerns, and successes across the three piloting districts. Teachers were not, therefore, implementing the unit without guidance and support. At the same time, this was not a "laboratory" setting or one that featured unusual levels of outside intervention, and teachers faced challenges common in many schools attempting to implement new initiatives.

The pilot was designed as an initial exploration to gauge the feasibility of the unit's approach to instruction and to address several questions: How would teachers and students experience the unit? How would students manage the increased demands? How effective would teachers perceive the supports to be? How would teachers embody the conceptual and pedagogical shifts? What implementation challenges would present themselves, and could these be overcome?[4]

Overall, teachers reacted positively to the unit. In their post-unit responses, almost all teachers expressed higher levels of comfort addressing the Common Core Standards with English Learners than they had had before teaching the unit. Teachers stated that the unit contained helpful models for providing scaffolding, differentiating instruction, and supporting English Learners' access to complex, rigorous texts. Participating teachers also highlighted ways that their teaching would change in the future as a result of the unit.

Students talked about the unit in positive terms as well, highlighting their engagement in the activities and noting the benefits of working collaboratively with their peers. Both teachers and students also described implementation challenges, some related to the shifts called for by the unit and others associated with institutional barriers to changing practice. Notably, many teachers expressed surprise at what their students, especially English Learners, were able to do, given the difficult texts at the heart of the unit.

In the remainder of this chapter, we first share teachers' and students' comments about specific practices that students were able to engage in and develop during the unit and then turn to their perspectives on features of the curriculum itself.

WHAT STUDENTS WERE ABLE TO DO

During and after implementation of the unit, teachers and students consistently reported their satisfaction with both the substance and processes of students' engagement and learning. As articulated in this section, participants highlighted the quality of the ideas English Learners and their classmates addressed together, their use of language to co-develop understandings of complex text, and their persistence and sense of agency as they tackled the challenging curriculum.

Students Engaged with Complex Texts and Themes

Consistent with the goals of the unit, teachers expressed satisfaction with the ways that students, including English Learners, were able to engage with complex texts. Several acknowledged that they were initially concerned about the complexity of the texts and skeptical that students would be able to read them without more explicit instruction. Typical was the response of one teacher who said that, initially, "We thought . . . we're never going to be able to do the *Gettysburg Address.*" But this teacher's expectations were exceeded once students began engaging with the unit activities: "Some of the things they're saying about it are amazing."

Teachers expressed surprise at their students' ability to understand the central concepts of the unit, including the persuasive appeals of ethos, logos, and pathos, and to recognize and apply those understandings across texts. One teacher said, "You never thought you could bring Aristotle into the 7th-grade classroom and they'd be just rolling it off the tongue." A number of teachers also noted the connections students made among texts, among subject areas, and between the unit concepts and their own lives.

Many teachers were impressed with what previously "struggling" students were able to accomplish during the unit. One teacher said,

> I really do think that each student walked away with something, whether or not they got the big picture of everything. I still think that even my students who struggle the most will walk away from that unit remembering something about persuasive speeches, and . . . that was kind of surprising to me.

Several teachers specifically pointed out that the unit was accessible to and effective for students of varying English language proficiency levels. As one teacher noted, the unit helped *everyone* to "elevate" their thinking and language.

Students Collaborated with Each Other

A prominent theme in the reflections of both teachers and students concerned the value of student collaboration, despite inherent challenges. Students reported feeling positively challenged by the expectation that they present to peers and work collaboratively to decipher and use the language and ideas of the mentor texts (*The Gettysburg Address*, Martin Luther King's *I Have a Dream*, etc.), which they identified as linguistically demanding. One student commented, "I think it's different because . . . we used to work independently. . . . We were working alone and now we work in groups . . . and now [our teacher] trusts us more." Although the expectations for collaboration stretched their capacities, students recognized the experiences as educative and believed their presentation skills had improved. As one student commented, "Group is good because the first one, he knows something, and another person, he knows another thing. We, you know, combined we formed the speech."

Teachers reported that they observed students in groups collaborating purposefully, not just "socializing." Several teachers commented that it was challenging for students to contribute verbally and be accountable for listening to and learning from their peers. Yet many teachers reported being surprised at how confidently and productively students communicated their learning with each other. These teachers observed students relying on one another, providing mutual scaffolding as they deciphered the language of the text.

Students Produced Oral and Written Language in New and Elaborated Ways

Both teachers and students discussed how students took up opportunities for language use and development provided by the unit's activities. Teachers talked about students' enhanced language use in terms of increased quality and quantity of conversations, arguments, presentations, writing, and engagement with texts.

One teacher pointed out that students moved beyond the procedural language she had often heard in group work previously (e.g., "How do I fold this paper?" and "Where do I draw this line?") to now include "purposeful" language, such as what kinds of symbols students should use to represent George Wallace's ideas on a collaborative poster about Civil Rights-era speeches. According to the teacher, along with these kinds of discussions came opportunities for attention to language: "They're pushing each other's language. I mean, if you can hear them, 'No, . . . it's said like this' or 'Maybe there's another word for it.'" The teacher further explained with an example:

> Like today, I was just watching one of my students and he was struggling, but he was having a tremendous discussion at a very high level about something that was quite meaningful to him. I believe . . . it's the structure of the collaboration, and . . . it's just really wonderful hearing my kids talk again in class, . . . [to] have it so purposeful, and to push that language.

A number of teachers were impressed with students' conversational engagement during group activities and the depth of their textual discussions. Referring to an activity during which students analyzed advertisements for different persuasive techniques, one noted, "They were arguing with each other: 'No, this is the hard sell 'cause it has this.' 'No, this is the soft sell.' So they were really actively engaged . . . in helping each other learn through the process." The animation in students' discussions pleased teachers because they felt it reflected and led to new understandings.

Teachers reported that throughout the unit students became more confident not only in their ability to deconstruct complex texts, but also in their capacity to understand and use the language and ideas of the assigned texts. One teacher described her surprise at not having to unpack textual language herself as much as she had anticipated:

> I thought for sure I was going to have to go back and help out with the language in terms of what was a hard, medium, and soft sell. But because that was laid out for them and we had done so much work prior to that, they took to it immediately.

During the unit, students were asked to write short, paragraph-length responses and analyses throughout each lesson, a page-long reflection at the end of each lesson, and a longer persuasive piece at the end of the unit. According to teachers, most students' writing reflected their understanding of the unit's texts and elements of persuasion. One teacher described a particularly impressive piece of student writing: "It was something we had read and she just pulled out right away: 'This is pathos and this is why.' And I hadn't even instructed her to do that." Teachers also noted that students, in their own writing, utilized specific persuasive strategies that they had seen in the unit's texts, including strategic repetition, logical and emotional appeals, and counterargument.

Additionally, teachers reported that students were frequently using core conceptual terminology. Several teachers admitted being "surprised" or "amazed" by students' academic vocabulary use, and that students were appropriately "using words that they didn't know a few weeks before." Students themselves also highlighted how the unit texts and structure promoted vocabulary growth. As one student explained, "I'm learning more English because of the speeches and everything; they're using more big, fancy words." Another student said, "Big words get smaller for me now."

Students Demonstrated Persistence, Confidence, Maturity, and Leadership

Finally, teachers expressed a belief that students demonstrated significant personal growth in several other areas over the course of the unit, including maturity, independence, persistence in the face of difficulty, and confidence, particularly with respect to reading and speaking. One teacher noted that students' skills and confidence related to producing language grew after completing the unit:

> I feel like the confidence level of my ESL students has grown just by being required in a way, to talk about things out loud. So now, for example, 4 weeks after we finished, they're volunteering to read passages when they would have never

volunteered to speak out before. . . . Their confidence is growing. That means that their language ability and their confidence in reading and speaking is growing.

Teachers and students indicated that students demonstrated more ownership over the curriculum during this unit than they had previously, noting that students regularly challenged each other's claims, language, and actions. Students appeared to be learning from each other and engaging in more authentic, academic, free-flowing conversations—what one teacher called the "freedom to talk."

THE AMPLIFIED CURRICULUM: SUCCESSES, CHALLENGES, AND TEACHERS' ADAPTATIONS

Teachers and students attributed students' success to the unit's overall design and the structure of specific activities. Not surprisingly, both teachers and students also experienced challenges related to the rigor of the unit and to implementing a new instructional approach. In many cases, as will become clear throughout this section, the challenges were what led to the successes. Some teachers also expressed limitations of the unit, such as lack of guidance for evaluating the progress of individual students. In response to their concerns, teachers described adaptations they had made during the unit or offered suggestions for future iterations. In this section, we discuss the specific features of an amplified curriculum that teachers and students highlighted as contributing to their experiences enacting the unit, as well as modifications that teachers made in relation to their own contexts and concerns.

Engaging Themes and Texts

Students said that the overall theme of the resonated with them, pointing out that learning how to persuade someone else about something was a useful skill, both in school and in life. They also said they were interested in the unit's texts, including speeches about race and the environment, videos exploring contemporary notions of body image, and historical speeches like the *Gettysburg Address*. Students indicated that the materials connected with their lives in powerful ways, particularly around issues of race, civil rights, and equality. One student commented,

> I think that in these speeches . . . it [doesn't only] teach you about . . . racism and everything, you actually get into it. You wonder what would happen if [struggles against] racism wouldn't have happened. We would probably be separated. We wouldn't have had friends to hang out with. . . . That's the great thing about this. It actually makes you interested in what you are learning.

Several teachers noted a correlation between the use of texts related to students' lives and their increased language use. As one teacher explained,

> They're very interested in the rights of minorities. Because [the] focus of all the readings . . . [was] around that, I heard a lot of discussion from their own personal lives, that they have experienced a time that they felt they weren't being treated equal[ly] or a time that their parents [or grandparents] shared with them.

Teachers also argued that many students who had been disengaged or even excluded from prior conversations about texts were revived by these materials. Collectively, the students' and teachers' comments indicate the importance of the selection of interesting, compelling, meaningful, and relevant themes and topics around which to design learning activities, lessons, and units—for English Learners and all students. Many teachers noted that suspending the notion that every student had to master every element of lessons freed them to recognize what each student was able to gain from engaging in the texts, topics, and themes at the heart of the unit.

Unit Structure and Spiraling

As teachers reflected on the unit before, during, and after implementation, they highlighted positive aspects of its sequencing and structure. Several commented on the value of inviting students, in the first lesson, to analyze persuasive elements of visual and print advertisements, including public service announcements, before moving on to the *Gettysburg Address* in the second lesson: "It started out very visually and, on the same theme throughout the unit. . . . I really liked . . . starting with the hook of the video, and the visual, and something that's very relatable to the students." Another pointed out that "getting the kids interested visually first, rather than through [written] text . . . kind of sold them" on the type of analytical work they would be doing with the more difficult historical speeches.

Teachers also discussed how the unit was structured to provide students just enough supportive background information in advance of reading texts. The activities, according to teachers, facilitated comprehension without removing the challenge of grappling with the meaning of the texts once students began reading them. In the words of one teacher, "That was a good model for me, to see . . . the balance there of giving them background information, but letting them struggle to pull out some of the bigger ideas and vocabulary throughout the text."

One teacher highlighted the importance of the activities that allowed students to activate and build background information, pointing out how critical it was to get students' "prior knowledge enacted." Another said that it was "eye opening" to watch students struggle with text and "really think about things," and that providing some background information provided the opportunity to apply and synthesize what students had learned to the text itself:

> Watching them struggle with texts that were hard and the answers weren't right there in front of them, like, 7th-grade texts, like in a textbook, [where it] might be a lot easier to find answers. . . . for them to have to struggle and . . . really think about things, read the background information and apply that information, and do all that synthesis was really impressive for me—to see that they were capable of doing it and thrived on it.

Finally, one teacher pointed out that the process of engaging students with difficult text served not only to help "level the playing field" for students with different amounts of background knowledge, but also to introduce students to a process for approaching difficult texts in general:

> I think the biggest thing was the ability to analyze the mentor texts. And then, for them to see, I think in sort of a meta way, the steps that it takes for them to prepare for such a thing. So that it's not just about putting a document like the *Gettysburg Address* in front of you, but it is about the process that you take, with which to make it have . . . meaning. And the documents that they read leading up to it, how that helps to build their schema, I think is really important for all the students, because then it sort of gave them a level playing field with which to engage the text.

When discussing the unit's implementation, teachers across multiple school sites discussed the spiraling embedded throughout the unit as one of the more important and helpful elements. Some teachers highlighted as helpful the opportunities students had for "listening/viewing multiple times with a different purpose each time," pointing out that asking different questions each time they watched a single video led students to new understandings each round and prevented boredom. Many teachers also discussed the importance of spiraling for increasing students' ability to read, comprehend, and analyze difficult texts. They pointed out the benefits for English Learners when students were invited to engage with a single text multiple times in different ways, as well as to spiral back on themes with texts in different genres, time periods, and social contexts. One teacher put it this way:

> Having . . . a central theme made [the lessons] consistent and purposeful as opposed to: "We're going to learn about persuasion and here's eight different speeches and this has this and this has this." [Instead, the texts] were linked together and . . . it was clearer that there were connections between them. And that helped them build their confidence and [ability] to analyze from text to text: "Oh I got this in the *Gettysburg Address*" and "Oh I see the same thing."

So I feel like . . . the purposeful nature of it was helpful for them to make those deeper connections to the text.

Teachers also highlighted the importance of spiraling for students' writing. One teacher explained,

It was good being able to say to the kids you know when it comes to your own writing . . . let's think back from day one . . . and they were able to. Let's go back to the advertising, let's go back to—I mean I could say to them, "What did . . . all of the writers do that was the same?" And they would know. . . . [T]he spiraling of everything really worked for them.

Although a few teachers worried that multiple activities around a single text challenged some students' stamina and may have been repetitive for more advanced readers, several mentioned that the spiraling approach featured in the unit was something that they would apply to their future teaching and would share with other teachers. One teacher reported, "I can't picture going through another year without [using] the spiraling technique that's going on here." This teachers also mentioned that others implementing the unit at this school had talked about "how much this could affect [the] rest of our staff when we start sharing this."

Promoting and Supporting Student Collaboration

Teachers found that the collaborative nature of the unit, especially the structures calling for students to work with each other in groups of various sizes, placed more responsibility for learning on the students and less on teachers in their traditional roles at the front of the classroom. One teacher described this new role for teachers as "more of a facilitator" than the "leader." Some teachers found it challenging to relinquish control, knowing that not all groups would arrive at the same interpretations of the texts, or even gain complete comprehension. One teacher described the challenge of not "giving [the students] everything they need" but instead "trusting" the collaborative process. At the same time, most teachers recognized the value of turning the reading and analysis of texts over to students in this collaborative setting. One teacher described the benefit of allowing students to "struggle" rather than stepping in as the teacher to "remedy" the problems a group was encountering. Teachers agreed that, in the words of one of them, "letting go of [the feeling that] I have to be up there" resulted in deeper learning and more genuine engagement for students than would have been the case with solely teacher-directed reading and discussion.

Although most of the teachers had prior experience asking students to engage in collaborative work, several of this unit's activities engaged students in ways teachers had not seen before. One teacher suggested that the intentional structure of the tasks led students to work together rather than allowing one or two students to complete all the work for the group. A different teacher noted that, when students had information they were responsible for sharing with the rest of the group, they "took that very, very seriously." In fact, teachers at several schools commented positively on these "Jigsawed" activities (see Chapters 2 and 4), highlighting how this structure helped build students' background information, promoted collaboration, and led to student agency. This teacher pointed out that having students focus on different texts allowed them to become experts in a particular area, giving students "a sense of agency or purpose within that unit."

From students' perspectives, working collaboratively was challenging but allowed them to get feedback from others, support each other in the readings, and share ideas to arrive at understanding together. One student commented, "We can't just depend on the teacher to give us the answers to everything. We have to work together to actually do the work."

To be clear, fostering the desired levels of collaboration was clearly not easy or automatic. Some teachers said that the student collaboration presented behavioral challenges, and many noted that it would have been helpful for students to have engaged in the kinds of collaboration called for by the unit earlier in the year. One teacher specifically noted frequent interpersonal conflicts among students that made forming groups challenging. Another teacher mentioned the tendency for "middle school drama" to interfere with students' ability to focus on the academic tasks. Teachers also noted in some cases that students found ways around genuine collaboration, for example by copying each other's graphic organizers rather than sharing information verbally and discussing it. One teacher commented that some students tended to work ahead, completing the work on their own rather than staying on pace with the group, and had to be reminded to collaborate. This teacher acknowledged that collaboration can feel less "efficient" than individual work. But she also acknowledged that "It's a good lesson to learn that even though you can do it more efficiently that's not really the point."

The sheer amount of collaboration was also identified as a challenge in one of the teacher focus groups. Teachers commented that they felt the group work needed to be interspersed with independent work and, in the words of one teacher, "periods of quiet reflection too" to help students remain focused. One teacher commented on the challenge of keeping students focused when there was no "output" in the form of an individual product to be turned in.

But in contrast to some teachers' comments about collaborative work increasing the number of behavioral problems, many students indicated that each individual's unique responsibility for the group tasks actually made it *easier* for them to stay on task. One student mentioned that, prior to the unit, "Some people in our class were usually, you know, with their head down and stuff. But now with the activities that they made us do . . . in groups, [those students] were able to participate a bit more . . . and understand the content a bit more." Another student commented, "In a normal English class, they can get away without doing anything."

One student noted increased participation among English Learners specifically: "Before the unit, when we used to work . . . the people that couldn't speak English would want to play around. But now [in this unit] they learned a lot and they participate in group work and everything." Another student put it this way: "I think it was better than just any other language arts class. We got to work with our . . . friends, so we got more work done, and we understood more."

Scaffolding and Differentiation

Teachers highlighted challenges related to the diversity among their students in English language proficiency, academic backgrounds, and learning needs. They also discussed ways in which the unit attended to some of those challenges—not by assigning different tasks to students at different levels of competence, such as is often done based on traditional notions of differentiation, but rather by offering different levels of scaffolding within each task to support students' engagement and learning in the central endeavors of the unit (Walqui et al., 2012). As one teacher put it,

> I thought it was interesting just being more aware of minimal scaffolding versus maximum scaffolding. And I feel like, no one's ever kind of separated those two for me. It's always been like, "scaffold or differentiate!"

Several teachers in at least two different schools discussed how teaching the unit helped them understand that, in classes with mixed levels of language and academic proficiency, it was possible to present challenging material in ways that benefited all students, albeit perhaps in different ways for different students. One teacher said that, before teaching this unit, she was afraid to "push the rigor" for "ESL kids":

> Through some of these lessons where there are some difficult questions . . . I know that all levels of students in my class aren't necessarily going to get each little part of it, they're gonna get a part . . . I think the way that this [unit] is developed [helps]—everybody's getting something out of it.

A teacher at a different school said that the biggest lesson from the unit was that "Not everyone has to know everything. . . . You can be an expert in one area. And allowing that person to become the expert gives them a sense of agency or purpose within that unit. So that seemed to help quite a bit." This teacher remarked that in this unit, "I wasn't, you know, beating the heck out of it by trying to get everybody to comprehend every single speech, every single reading piece."

One teacher linked the capacity of the unit to reach multiple students to the elements of scaffolding embedded in specific tasks. For example, rather than tackling the entire thing, students were only responsible for filling out an assigned part of a graphic organizer. But they still benefited from hearing from others who filled out other sections.

Challenges and Adaptations

Before concluding, we discuss the ways in which teachers themselves adapted the unit's tasks and materials to respond to several common challenges they were encountering along the way.

Responding to Group Work Challenges. Teachers responded to the variety of challenges that collaborative work presented by grouping students strategically—both to avoid interpersonal conflict and behavior problems and to ensure that students who needed the most support were grouped with students who could provide it. Some teachers and students also commented on the fact that the collaborative nature of the unit presented challenges in terms of students' different speeds in completing activities. One teacher mentioned that the unit did not provide guidance for what some groups should do while waiting for others to complete the activities. To address the challenges of keeping students on task and ensuring effective collaboration, teachers suggested adaptations such as setting firm time limits to keep students focused, using a prop that students could pass around to establish who held the floor, and assigning roles for each student to ensure equal participation. One teacher added independent reading time at the beginning of each class period to help students gain focus before moving into the group activities.

Assessing Individual Students. Another concern that arose from teachers about the collaborative nature of the unit was that it was often difficult to determine how well individual students were learning the concepts and when some might have been struggling. These teachers' comments on assessment point to the size of shifts they were being asked to make, the challenges inherent in formatively assessing students' group conversations for evidence of student progress, and the need for more explicit tools and guidance for teachers in these areas.

Collaborative activities call for a focus on learning processes instead of products and suggest that the social context of learning and assessment should be inseparable from one another. Thus, they disrupt traditional conceptions of assessment, which evaluate individual student oral or written output, and instead ask teachers to look at student growth in the context of interaction with peers. But without explicit evaluation tools, some of the teachers found it challenging to examine and determine the language and disciplinary practice development that was taking place when students were engaged in shared endeavors with peers and how this engagement supported overall growth.

In response, some teachers created their own assessment strategies for evaluating what students were learning during the interactive activities. Some used formative assessment strategies such as exit slips or mini-essays to evaluate what individual students were learning each day as well as to guide their modifications of the lessons, grouping strategies, and their teaching to address individual student needs. One teacher described her formative assessment process:

> The biggest thing for me was whether or not the students actually were understanding what they [were] writing. Because so much of it was collaborative groups, I did a lot of exit slips and entrance slips (just quick, you know, put your poster up, a quick check board), so that I knew that they remembered what was going on early in the week. And then at the end, [if there was] someone in a group that wasn't paying attention . . . I could pull them, and give them a little bit of extra guidance the next day.

Another teacher described using mini-essays to formatively assess students for strategic grouping purposes. As she explained,

> I had them write these mini essays. . . . It gave me something to fall back on. Like, to go back and say "Okay, where does this person get it and maybe I should group these two together?" It helped with the grouping. To see where, where they would go next or . . . taking into consideration the next lesson, "How am I gonna group you?"

Given the teachers' comments, it is clear that more support for their assessment practices is warranted, both in the unit itself and in larger efforts at professional development. In the spirit of the tenets discussed in Chapter 2, particularly helpful would be guidance and tools that prompted teachers to use diagnostic formative assessment practices to evaluate content knowledge, disciplinary literacy practices, and language competence. Such assessments would need to be framed in a way that view the three as developing interdependently as students collaborate in communities of practice but that also provide important information about individual students' progress along the way.

Promoting Accessibility for Students at Lower English Proficiency and Reading Levels. Despite their overall appreciation of the unit's approach to scaffolding, some teachers and students pointed out that challenges remained, even with different levels of scaffolding. One explained:

> Some of the reading levels [of the texts] were just [challenging to] . . . some of my students, about five of my students. . . . So that's where I had to use guided

reading, to fold that in and make sure that we [were] able to do some reading, where they . . . could break it down into smaller chunks.

Although the unit was not designed for beginning-level English Learners, in some cases such students were in the ESL, sheltered, or even mainstream English language arts classes piloting the unit. Several teachers pointed out the challenges facing these students and detailed the types of adjustments to the curriculum they made, such as individually working with students to decipher texts, grouping students who speak the same home language but have various English proficiencies together, and encouraging students to translate for each other. One teacher was adamant that while she did have to make some changes to the curriculum, this unit met the needs of her linguistically heterogeneous class much better than any other she has taught, noting:

> I have not seen any unit in over 20 years that . . . addresses English Language Learners and their need for discourse, their need for real juicy material to talk about, [with] the rigor that this provides. . . . Constantly, we had to make some adjustments, but nowhere near the adjustments I've had to make in past units.

CONCLUSION

Returning to the questions that guided the pilot, it appears that both teachers and students experienced the unit positively. Although there was concern from a few teachers about the unit being too difficult for beginning-level English Learners and for some students with special needs, a majority of teachers overwhelmingly expressed their surprise at how students who had "struggled" in the past, especially English Learners, were able to engage productively with the complex and challenging texts and the key ideas at the heart of the unit. Teachers and students attributed the success of the unit to the themes addressed and to the collaboration, spiraling, and scaffolds embedded in the structure of the unit.

In a few cases, teachers' adaptations appeared to run counter to the conceptual and pedagogical shifts the unit was intended to promote, such as one teacher's conclusion that some students needed "baby steps" to get through the content of the unit and another's desire for a standardized instrument to measure students' language development. Overall, however, teachers' comments demonstrated their understanding of and movement toward the larger spirit of "amplify, don't simplify" (Walqui & van Lier, 2010), the specific shifts called for by the unit (Walqui et al., 2012), and the tenets presented in Chapter 2. Many challenges remained, but teachers made various adjustments to address them. In the end, a number of teachers remarked how piloting the unit had made an impact on how they would teach in the future, including one teacher who said that it would be impossible to "go back" to the way this teacher had taught before.

We should, of course, acknowledge that it is possible that teachers and students were emphasizing their positive experiences with the unit because they knew they were speaking with people who were involved with its design. And we are certainly not claiming that these contexts explored here constitute a representative sample that can be generalized to all settings. But the explicitness of students' and teachers' remarks, and the clear patterns that emerged across comments from participants at different schools, districts, and states, give us confidence that what was shared represents credible indications of how teachers and students experienced the unit—and that their experiences could be helpful for teachers attempting to amplify the curriculum in other contexts.

Since one of the intentions of this book is to guide teachers in designing curriculum for English Learners, it is important to clarify that, in this case, the teachers themselves were not the designers of the lessons they were piloting. However, the unit was designed precisely as an exemplar of what curriculum might look like so that teachers and others (e.g., school districts, open source developers) could eventually develop themselves, given time and structures for collaboration. Consistent with the book's call for teachers to engage in the design of learning opportunities, the teachers discussed in this chapter, even using the materials others had created for them, made a number of adaptations, representing various levels of consistency with the shifts the unit was designed to illustrate.

To conclude, it is important to reiterate that the instruction that students and teachers describe in this chapter did not happen without preparation and support. Teachers had 2 days of professional development specifically designed to help prepare them to understand and implement the unit, schools and districts had volunteered to participate in this pilot, and some support was provided from those involved in the broader efforts to design and pilot the unit. Where might teachers who have not had access to such an orientation begin? What would it take to prepare new teachers for this work? And how can we support teachers throughout their careers to develop and enact curriculum across various subject matter areas that realizes opportunities for the kind of ambitious and supportive instruction at the heart of this unit and discussed throughout this book? It is to these questions that we turn in Chapter 10.

NOTES

1. We have been engaged in this work in different ways. George Bunch chaired the working group that initially invited Aída Walqui and WestEd to produce the unit, and he reviewed several drafts of the unit during its conception. All three authors contributed to the analysis of the data and the writing of this chapter. We

also wish to acknowledge Rebecca Greene, Eduardo R. Muñoz-Muñoz, and Renae Skarin for their contributions to the data analysis.

2. Pia Castilleja, Rob Lucas, Lydia Stack, Aída Walqui, and Steven Weiss were instrumental in the implementation of the pilot. The Understanding Language initiative, cochaired by Kenji Hakuta and Maria Santos, was funded by the Carnegie Corporation and the Bill and Melinda Gates Foundation. Understanding Language's ELA Work Group, which included George Bunch, Martha Castellón, Susan Pimentel, Lydia Stack, and Aída Walqui, provided guidance and input throughout the development of the unit.

3. The Council of Great City Schools helped select the districts that piloted the unit.

4. During the pilot, we videotaped selected lessons, collected student work, interviewed and surveyed teachers, collected pre- and post-implementation questionnaires, and facilitated student and teacher focus groups. We systematically coded the data using both *a priori* and emerging codes. We met throughout the process to calibrate our coding practices and articulate emerging themes. Given the short time frame and minimal financial resources available, the piloting was not intended to produce the kind of student outcome data that could be analyzed to "prove" whether the approach was effective in meeting individual standards or in increasing test scores. However, we were able to learn much about the promises of such instruction and the associated challenges, from the standpoint of teachers and students, across multiple sites of implementation.

REFERENCES

Bunch, G. C., Walqui, A., & Kibler, A. K. (2015). Attending to language, engaging in practice: Scaffolding English language learners' apprenticeship into the Common Core English Language Arts standards. In L. C. De Oliveria, M. Klassen, & M. Maune (Eds.), *The Common Core State Standards in English Language Arts for English Language Learners: Grades 6–12*. Charlotte, NC: TESOL Press.

Kibler, A. K., Walqui, A., & Bunch, G. C. (2015). Transformational opportunities: Language and literacy instruction for English language learners in the Common Core era in the United States. *TESOL Journal, 6*(1), 9–35.

Walqui, A., Koelsch, N., & Schmida, M. (2012). Persuasion across time and space: Analyzing and producing complex texts. Retrieved from https://ell.stanford.edu /teaching_resources/ela

Walqui, A., & van Lier, L. (2010). *Scaffolding the academic success of adolescent English language learners: A pedagogy of promise*. San Francisco, CA: WestEd.

CHAPTER 10

Developing Teacher Expertise to Design Amplified Learning Opportunities for English Learners

Aída Walqui and George C. Bunch

This book has provided a framework for teachers to design powerful, exciting, and challenging learning opportunities to engage and support English Learners (and all students) in the concepts, analysis, and language at the heart of disciplinary inquiry. We have argued that moving away from *simplification* toward *amplification* as a guiding principle is necessary for recognizing and building on the resources English Learners bring with them, for maximizing their immense potential, and for envisioning them as both contributors to and beneficiaries of a more equitable, just, and sustainable 21st-century world. We have also shown how amplification enhances, rather than restricts, opportunities for the development of language and literacy alongside other disciplinary practices and content. We have provided elaborated examples of such designs in various disciplines, walked the reader through the kinds of decisions teachers face when developing lessons and units that follow the proposed tenets, and shared teachers' and students' reflections in classrooms where such designs are being used.

However, as is well known by both teachers and those who work to prepare and support them, designing and implementing high-quality instruction—for any students, but especially for English Learners—requires more than access to a rationale, framework, and examples, no matter how compelling they may be. Accomplished teaching is a remarkably complex achievement—one that teachers need to envision and apprentice into deliberately and over extended periods of time. The ability to construct coherent and engaging lessons or units is a necessary component of this teaching expertise, but it is not sufficient for negotiating successful *implementation* of high-quality instruction in complex classroom environments.

The key to teachers' long-term success, for both developing amplified learning designs and implementing them, is the gradual building of deep pedagogical expertise as a lifelong activity. In fact, studies demonstrate that when teachers do not have a deep and sophisticated pedagogical understanding, they may unwittingly transform innovative lessons into traditional instruction, maintaining core elements of their instruction that the design was attempting to transform (Wilson & Berne, 1999). That is, teachers may selectively take up innovative ideas and implement them in shallow or incoherent ways (Coburn & Stein, 2016), or they may adopt only surface level features of the design and ignore those that are most important to the approach (Spillane & Zeuli, 1999).

We devote this final chapter, therefore, to exploring the complex nature of the expertise that teachers need to develop over their careers to most effectively design and implement the kind of amplified learning for English Learners, and all students, discussed throughout this book. To be clear, however, our message is *not* that only the most accomplished teachers who have undergone years of development have a chance at successfully designing and implementing amplified curriculum. So, we begin by offering concrete suggestions for what practicing teachers, regardless of their backgrounds, can do *right now*, with their colleagues, to leverage and build their collective expertise as they engage in the kind of design we advocate for in this book. We then discuss the nature of the relevant expertise that teachers develop over the course of their careers. We conclude with how those who offer professional development can facilitate the development of this expertise, and what preservice teacher educators can do to help lay the foundation for the development of expertise that will come throughout teachers' careers.

WHAT TEACHERS CAN DO RIGHT NOW

What can teachers themselves do to develop their capacity to design and implement the kinds of learning opportunities introduced in this book? In this section, we provide some immediate guidance for the question most frequently asked by teachers: Where do we start, especially if we do not have access to professional development initiatives to help support us? In fact, even teachers who do participate in such initiatives face the moment when the workshop is over and they begin to tackle the hard work of developing and implementing their own learning designs. We paraphrase here high school teachers' responses to a recent professional development session that Aída conducted as part of her Quality Teaching for English Learners (QTEL) program. We suppose that these sentiments might be shared by other teachers reading this book:

> We love the architecture of lessons and spiraled units presented. As we worked through the designs, we ourselves were motivated and engaged. As we reflect on the lesson and its deliberate architecture, we recognize that our own organization of curriculum is typically framed around individual (one-period) lessons, formulaic standards and objectives, scripted lesson plans, and/or periodic

district testing goals. Given these contextual constraints and tensions, *where and how do we begin* to refocus planning and implementation of units and lessons to shift design and instruction to this architecture?

Indeed, this is the predicament in which many teachers find themselves. How do teachers break out of it? Part of the answer is "ambitiously" and "holistically"—not in piecemeal ways. The other part is "work with a colleague who teaches the same assignment as you do." Working collegially is not only more productive, it also builds community and support. What follows are specific suggestions for how this collaboration may proceed, based on the conceptual tenets and design principles discussed throughout the book and linked to the model of teacher expertise to be described later in this chapter:

- Start with the end in mind: What conceptual, analytic, and language disciplinary practices do you want your students to begin to develop? Remember that you are not after mastery, but gradual development.
- Choose robust and enticing texts, problems, or phenomena that are appropriate vehicles for the development of proposed practices. Read them carefully and discuss together which concepts, analytic practices, and disciplinary language you want your students to practice throughout.
- Begin planning the itinerary. Following the Three Moment Architecture presented in Chapter 3 and used throughout the book, start by considering how you might *prepare students* so that they are ready to get the most out of the text and goals. Then decide what tasks will help your students *interact with and make sense of the ideas and* text central to the lesson. Then, of course, decide how you will invite students to *extend their understanding* and apply what they learned in novel situations. Throughout, think of engaging students in substantive interactions. This planning is going to take you several hours, and it will offer you a week's work.
- Share with your partner designer your reflections on the implementation of the lesson, including what seemed to work well in the design and why, what seemed to create difficulties, and what students' participation and work indicate. If you have a supportive principal, ask your principal to substitute for the two of you for a couple of periods so you can visit each others' classes.
- Refine the lesson based on your reflections. Do so immediately after implementation, since a semester or a year later, many of your good ideas for improvement may not be as salient as in the moment.
- Continue working on your old lesson plans, superimposing on them the three-part lesson architecture and beginning to create spiraled units. You may discover that the texts you use do not

support a high challenge/high support design, in which case, it is time to replace texts for rich, complex, alluring ones. Using potent, compelling texts is not only important for students. It is important for you, because if you cannot be excited about what you are teaching, your students will not be enthusiastic about learning.

- A month later, work with your colleague on another lesson, or on the original lesson as part of a larger, spiraled unit that invites your students to deepen and expand practices from other perspectives on the same theme. Follow the same process outlined above. Over a few years, you will have developed your own powerful curriculum. At the same time, you will have strengthened your own expertise to amplify future learning opportunities for English Learners and other students—part of the long-term development of teacher expertise to which we turn to next.

THE NATURE OF EXPERTISE IN TEACHING: COMPLEX, INTERSECTING, AND CONTINUOUSLY DEVELOPING DOMAINS OF UNDERSTANDING

As we discussed earlier, teacher expertise entails both the knowledge needed to teach plus the ability to translate it into fruitful action. More specifically, efforts to advise, prepare, and support teachers to fulfill the vision of designing amplified curriculum presented in this book must be based on a clear and coherent understanding of the knowledge and actions that underlie effective teaching, in its situated nature in particular disciplines with particular students.

In order to help both teachers and teacher educators understand the different interrelated components of expertise, we present a model of teacher expertise that has been helpful to us as we engage in our own work with teachers at various stages of their careers. We then share an example of this expertise "in action," describing how two teachers took one of the lessons described in this book and adapted it for their own students in their own classrooms.

Working on a project that considered what it meant to support practicing teachers in communities of learners as they developed their situated expertise, that is, the knowledge and action needed to be successful with the specific students with whom teachers work in a class, Lee Shulman (1995) developed what was at the time the most comprehensive model of teacher understanding available. Because the original model was not specifically developed taking English Learners into account, Walqui (1997, 2007a) adapted it to consider this important population of students. Before proceeding further in describing the adapted model, we want to underscore two foundational notions from Shulman's original proposal: the consideration of teachers as professional lifelong learners, and the belief that this knowledge develops not in isolation, but in community, with the goal that teachers' autonomy, through collaboration and apprenticeship, emerges over time. Readers of this book will recognize important parallels between this conception of teacher development and the tenets regarding student learning described throughout these chapters. Teachers develop agency as professionals in ways that mirror the development of students' autonomy and agency as learners.

Walqui's adaptation of Shulman's model, as shown in Figure 10.1, presents six interrelated and mutually impacting domains of understanding: vision, motivation, knowledge, reflection, context, and practice, all of which develop, to various degrees, synergistically as a result of preparing to become teachers, and all of which either continue to grow or begin to stagnate during the years of professional practice. As will become apparent, the model is not set up in such a way that simple causal relations can be adduced, such as "first teachers develop motivation and then they craft a vision." Instead, the relationship is envisaged as a complex, dynamic one in which all parts play a crucial role in mutually strengthening or debilitating ways, and development is organic rather than linear or modular.

Figure 10.1. A Model of Teacher Understanding

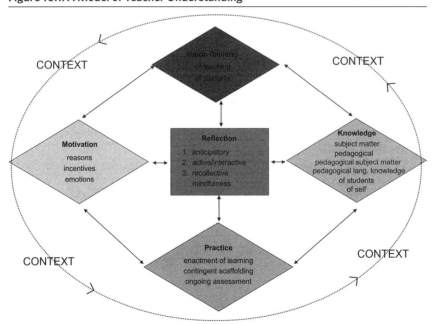

Source: Walqui, 1997, adapted from Schulman, 1995.

Vision

The domain of vision, essential for teachers to be able to develop learning opportunities that are truly *amplified* for English Learners, has two main components: (1) teachers' conceptualization of how capable their students are and who these students can become in the short term (as the result of the course the teacher is teaching), mid-term (as a result of their whole schooling), and long term (in their lives as adults in society); and (2) teachers' understandings of the types of opportunities students will need to develop that capability, the learning activities they need to be invited into to keep growing. This vision includes a recognition that building what has not grown in students yet is the result of teachers' increasingly professional and intentional work.

In Chapter 9, we saw how teachers reacted as they observed their students respond actively and productively to invitations to engage in using the three Aristotelian appeals in a lesson on persuasive texts. Teachers were surprised and excited as they saw their students working together beyond their capability, supported by both the structure and process of scaffolding. Through experiences such as this one, teachers develop—or strengthen—a vision of their students as immensely capable, with potential that can be unlocked by robust, amplified participation in well-crafted lessons. Such a vision contradicts the more common "*pobrecito* syndrome"—a conception of learners as "poor things" who need simplification and mini-steps in order to succeed (Walqui, 2007b).

Motivation

Of course, to do the work we are proposing teachers do with English Learners, motivation is essential as well. This domain is composed of the reasons teachers go into teaching and remain in the field, and the incentives they derive as they carry out their work. As with the others, motivation is not a fixed domain, one that teachers have or do not have. Motivation is enhanced or diminished as a result of professional trajectories. At the beginning of their educational studies, most teacher candidates are motivated to become teachers moved by one or more reasons: their passion for a particular content area; positive experiences working with children and youth as tutors, coaches, or babysitters; a desire to make a difference in the lives of young people; and commitment to contributing to a more equitable and just world. Their reasons can be the result of having themselves had one or several good teachers who had a big impact in their lives or, on the other hand, being frustrated by the lack of such teachers.

As they begin their teaching, experiences at work strengthen or debilitate their motivation. For example, when teachers have the opportunity to work alongside colleagues in the design of lessons they will teach, to share experiences and student artifacts resulting from their enacted plans, and to focus on what worked or didn't work to strengthen it in future lessons, as we suggested before, they find that these interactions strengthen their desire to teach, enhance their joy of working with colleagues productively, and develop their professionalism. If, instead, teachers work in an environment where they are left on their own, behind closed doors, afraid to share experiences or worried that if they ask for help that may signal a personal weakness, then initial motivation will be eroded. Multiple other factors affect motivation: for example, what teachers see as excessive emphasis given to testing that uses valuable time on preparing students for tests instead of engaging them in interesting subject-specific activity. Mandated pacing, with strict adherence to superficial lesson plans, is equally demotivating.

Knowledge

Shulman (1986) distinguished three areas of teacher knowledge: subject matter knowledge, general pedagogical knowledge, and pedagogical subject matter knowledge (which he also referred to as pedagogical content knowledge), all central to the design and implementation of successful learning opportunities. From the perspective of working with English Learners, Walqui added three other crucial components: knowledge of English Learners, pedagogical language knowledge (teachers' understanding of the role of language in teaching and learning), and knowledge of self. We discuss each of these components briefly.

Subject Matter Knowledge. Teachers need deep understanding of the subject matter they teach when designing and implementing curriculum for English Learners, because they need to know what it is about a particular concept, theme, or text that is essential and consequently needs to be focused on, and what, although interesting and valuable, is not indispensable for English Learners to grasp during a first learning encounter. When they guide students in simultaneously developing conceptual understandings, analytic, and language practices, teachers need to know how to streamline these in order to focus on the most generative, productive ones first. Teachers also need to understand which key conceptual relationships students will be initially invited to work with as they develop their knowledge of the discipline, and which others will be built later on as the curriculum spirals to revisit, deepen, and expand concepts. Once again, knowledge of the discipline—while essential—is not a fixed state, nor something that is acquired exclusively before or during preservice education. In addition to teachers' own ongoing personal explorations and development of their content knowledge, opportunities to design lessons or units, whether introduced in preservice teacher education programs or further developed once teachers have their own classrooms, serve as opportunities to deepen subject matter knowledge.

Pedagogical Knowledge. This kind of knowledge refers to general ideas about how to invite students into learning opportunities: the architecture of lessons; the role of tasks; how to structure units of study; the importance of providing students with substantive opportunities to talk, ask each other questions, and respond to interlocutors' ideas; the value of teacher wait time; the notion of scaffolding; and the types of scaffolding that exist for different purposes. All these ideas are important for teachers, but, as we will discuss next, they need to be implemented in specific classes with concrete and unique groups of students.

Knowledge of Students (including English Learners). Growing knowledge of the students who are going to be the agents of learning in the classroom is equally important when designing opportunities to learn. In the same way in which a master tailor does not cut and sew a suit destined for a person without knowing and measuring the future owner in order to determine what may both suit and fit them, lessons are designed to suit and fit the learning needs of specific students. Knowledge of who the specific students in a class are, how they learn, what topics attract them, what they find enticing, how much English they know at the moment, where they seem to be progressing well, where growth needs to be scaffolded, and what barriers they may have to overcome (e.g., being painfully shy) are critical to creating learning environments and lessons that are equitable and that invite and support every student to grow. This knowledge, which begins to develop in preservice programs (e.g., through reflection and discussion on readings as well as candidates' own case studies of students that can be tied to teachers' visions and motivation), is ultimately derived from teachers' keen observation in the classroom as students are engaged in activity. It certainly goes beyond students' test scores, since these scores may actually obscure what students are capable of accomplishing. In fact, during the lessons we have proposed in this book, where students are actively learning with each other, it is possible for teachers to observe students (rotating their focus as needed) to take notes that will later on be useful during their lesson design. After all, as we established in Chapters 2 and 3, a lesson needs to be placed beyond students' ability to work on their own in order to spur their growth.

Knowledge of students includes developing answers for questions such as the following: Why do particular students react the way they do? How should teachers deal with oppositional responses from students? What should teachers do when they are tempted to give up their high expectations and design simpler lessons for their students?

Pedagogical Language Knowledge. Galguera (2011) proposed this important component of teacher expertise, which was later elaborated by Bunch (2013) to refer to teachers' knowledge of the role of language in teaching and learning in the various subject areas. Such knowledge includes, for example, how to structure learning activities that invite students to experience and unpack how explanations work in history or in science, what their purposes are in the different disciplines, and what general organization different kinds of disciplinary texts tend to follow.

The notion of *pedagogical* language knowledge challenges the idea that content-area teachers need to "teach English" in didactic and atomistic ways, whether for English Learners or any other students. For example, we disagree with current proposals that lessons for English Learners should start with the presentation of lists of vocabulary items (the "frontloading" of vocabulary) contained in the lesson. While explicit focus on vocabulary can be helpful at various points in teaching content-area lessons (including sometimes early on), it must always be approached in ways that support rather than curtail English Learners from developing larger and more important understandings of language. Language is a way of acting in the world, and as such, *what is accomplished by using it* needs to be the entry point for explorations of language.

Pedagogical Subject Matter Knowledge. This area is the knowledge of how to build disciplinary understandings for all students in a class, emphasizing, especially for English Learners, how key ideas are advanced in specific types of text in English, while ensuring throughout that all learners are being challenged and supported. Chapters 4 through 8 in this book illustrate this process in diverse subject matter areas. It stands to reason that while subject matter and general pedagogical knowledge begin to develop in preservice education, pedagogical subject matter knowledge unfolds as a result of practice and deep self-knowledge.

Self-Knowledge. An often-neglected aspect of teacher knowledge, one not usually associated with curriculum development, is *knowledge of self*. But in order to envision and enact successful learning designs, teachers need to understand and consider themselves as simultaneously knowledgeable and in the process of learning. It is not possible for any teacher to know everything they need to know at any moment of teaching, but it is important for them to prepare with their best current knowledge for most every teaching event, and to keep their eyes open so they can learn from observing their students. Teachers also need to have a sense of humor about their own limitations and model for students the practices to repair whatever did not work optimally in a lesson. We often hear from English Learners that they appreciate teachers saying "I really do not know the answer to that question, but I will find out and report on it later on," and then coming back at a later point with a response. For students, it constitutes an example both of intellectual integrity and curiosity on behalf of their teachers.

Reflection

The domain of reflection for teachers is most typically considered an area of expertise that involves reviewing their teaching to identify what succeeded and what didn't—as a way of improving and refining lessons for individuals or for groups of students. This looking into the past to learn for the future has been part of educational theory since Dewey (1925) and, following van Manen (1991), we call it recollective reflection. Van Manen proposed three other types of reflection that are especially useful to us and that Walqui added to Shulman's model. *Anticipatory reflection*, directly related to design, refers to the deliberation among alternatives that teachers engage in as they select future pedagogical courses of action. Van Manen adds two other types of reflection to teachers' deliberations. One, related to enactment, is the deliberations that teachers engage in contingently as the lesson is proceeding. As teachers observe how invitations to engage in action are being interpreted by students, "on their feet" they contemplate appropriate additions or deletions to their original plan. This essential component of any good teaching is *interactive reflection*. It makes teaching contingent, responsive to the moment and evolving student needs. In current educational formulations, this reflection is called Formative Assessment (Heritage, Walqui, & Linquanti, 2015).

Finally, van Manen introduces the concept of *Mindfulness*, which refers to the ability to exploit the pedagogical moment, to act thoughtfully, to have "pedagogical tact" in less intentional ways than in interactive reflection. We could say that the cumulative goal of reflective activity in the classroom is to arrive at teachers developing pedagogical tact, where their vast knowledge, built on constant reflection of practice, has led them to develop a presence of mind that leads them to do the right thing at the right moment in a class. In our model, reflection is at the center of all other domains because it is the engine that drives teacher expertise.

Context

That context matters for teachers is almost self-evident, especially now, when as discussed in Chapter 1, standards, accountability, and testing are an ever-present reality. Knowledge of the context is essential. This knowledge entails the requirements of society, of school authorities, new educational mandates, conflicts in the surrounding environment—and how to navigate them for the ultimate benefit of all students, with English Learners at the center of our focus.

The contexts within which teachers operate are especially important to consider in the growth or erosion of their expertise. Beginning with the school, and moving beyond to the district, state, and national policy mandates, all these arenas of decisionmaking impact teacher expertise. For example, Walqui (2000) studied high school contexts that supported the growth of English Learners. In one of the schools highlighted, The International High School at La Guardia Community College in New York City, the care invested in the building of productive contexts was exemplary. Teachers worked in cohorts that taught the same two groups of students for 2 years; time was created during the school day for teams of teachers to collaborate with each other; teams of teachers hired new colleagues, and supported and assessed them; and the universal definition of the principal by teachers was "he is a buffer for us"—meaning that he fought the necessary fights, such as creating time, to support teachers' work in the service of their students. Such a context promotes the development of teacher expertise, and educators need to see how to re-create it in their own venues.

Practice

We address teacher practice as the last domain in teacher expertise because knowledge alone does not a good teacher make. Expertise resides in the artful enactment of knowledge in classrooms that becomes the mark of a good teacher. Practice is the one domain that cannot be developed in isolation. Coaching, or what Latin Americans call "accompanying teachers," is indispensable. Coaching represents opportunities for teachers to enact a lesson that has been either designed jointly by teacher and coach, or at least reviewed by the coach, and discussed by coach and teacher. Coaches and teachers need to share a common understanding of lesson goals, lesson design, and the appropriacy of tasks. Only then can coaches serve as mirrors for teachers, helping them see what is working according to plan and what needs to be refined. Over time, teachers appropriate the stances of coaches, and, as accomplished ballerinas, can practice and use imaginary, internalized mirrors to enhance their implementation.

Often a good lesson design can go wrong during its implementation because certain aspects of the lesson have not been completely understood, and a teacher may not observe the confusion and frustration building up in some students and be able to respond contingently. As a result, good designs are derailed or misinterpreted (Anderson, 2017; Coburn, 2003). Vision, motivation, knowledge, and reflection are all required to offer real students in a specific class powerful learning opportunities that build on what they know to push and support their development. The never-ending process of planning, enacting, reflecting, redesigning, and the evolving expertise of teachers enriches the lives of students as well as their own professional lives.

TEACHER EXPERTISE IN ACTION: AN EXAMPLE

To illustrate the relevance of the teacher expertise elaborated upon above as it relates to the design process explored in this book, we share the experiences

of two teachers who worked with Aída as part of a professional development initiative that was intended to build the expertise of a few educators
to apprentice as professional developers. The vignette illustrates how these
teachers use multiple domains of expertise to make important adaptations
to lessons as they are preparing to videorecord their own teaching to help
colleagues reflect on lesson design and implementation.

Amanda Bradley and Brooke Battles, the two accomplished teachers
of English Learners, undertook a rigorous process of apprenticeship and
have now taken leadership positions in their school, South Hills Middle
School in Fort Worth, Texas. Amanda is the Assistant Principal in charge of
instruction, and Brooke is the pedagogical coach at the school. Weeks prior
to the filming, they visited the classes they would be borrowing to familiarize themselves with the students and the class culture. At the same time,
they started adapting the lesson (from the Power, Protest, and Change unit
discussed in Chapter 3) using materials and notes shared by Aída. Having
developed knowledge of the specific students in the classes they would be
borrowing, they decided that these students needed a bit more scaffolding
as they engaged in the reading of the text *The Third Man: The Forgotten
Black Power Hero* (Montague, 2012), also discussed in Chapter 3. Students
had not been accustomed to engaging in metacognitive interactive activities
during reading. After considering several suggestions, they decided to add
a structure that had not been part of the initial lesson design: Raphael's
Question/Answer Relationship (1986). As adapted by the QTEL team, the
task requires that having thought of a question, the student whose turn it
is first announces the type of question, according to Raphael's taxonomy,
they are going to ask. Then the student proceeds to ask their question and
listen to the partner's response. After the response, students may have a brief
discussion. Then it is the turn of the student who answered to now follow
the same procedure. Raphael's taxonomy proposes four different types of
questions:

1. **Right There Questions**: look for information that is explicitly stated
   in the paragraph.
2. **Think and Search Questions**: the answer to these questions is
   implicit in the text, so you need to infer, conclude, and so on.
3. **On My Own**: the question asks for information that is not present
   in the text, but is related to the theme of the text.
4. **The Author and Me**: these are questions that readers would ask the
   author if they had the opportunity to meet (Raphael, 1986).

The purposes of this task are twofold: to have students explore a difficult passage of a text so that together they aid each other in gaining clearer
understandings, and to provide students practice in recognizing and naming

the types of questions they ask each other as part of their metacognitive development. Amanda and Brooke decided that students first needed to recognize the types of questions and get some practice classifying examples.

The teachers selected a section of the text and prepared a list of questions that invited students, again working in dyads, to classify and justify their rationales after reading two sections of the text. Figure 10.2 provides an excerpt of the questions they offered.

In sum, while the original lesson (described in Chapter 3) was designed by Yael Glick and Aída to meet the needs of Yael's students at Voyages Academy in New York City, Ms. Bradley and Ms. Battles decided that their students at South Hills Middle School in Texas needed a bit more support. In both instances, teachers were aware of their students' age, their background knowledge, the analytic practices they possessed, and their command of English. They were determined to trace different pedagogical paths for their students but with similarly ambitious goals. Returning to the model of teacher expertise we presented earlier, both implementations were successful because of the teachers' knowledge of their students, knowledge of the practices presented, and subject matter knowledge. The success could also be attributed to how the teachers, building on their anticipatory and recollective reflection and their vision of their students' potential and future, crafted invitations that rendered good results.

This vignette demonstrates how when educators have deep expertise, they can take a good lesson and adapt it to make it successful in contexts different than the one for which it was originally intended. When teachers, however, have superficial understanding, as discussed earlier on, they adapt what is novel to fit their prior understandings, thus undermining the possible impact of the innovation (Cohen, 1990). There are no lessons that are equally impactful across a wide variety of circumstances; they all need to be situated in the specific context of a class to respond to the specific needs of students.

Figure 10.2. Questions to Be Sorted into Raphael's Four Categories

Read *An Obscure Pick* and *Unexpected Threat* silently and after that, working with a partner, classify the following questions into the four types offered by Raphael, justifying your choice:

1. Did Peter Norman grow up rich or poor?
2. Mr. Montague, why do you say Norman found the high altitude of Mexico City helpful? Isn't altitude typically bad for runners?
3. What did White Australia's policy reveal about their beliefs?
4. Why was Peter Norman an obscure pick to go to the Olympics?
5. What was going on in the United States during the Olympics?

SUGGESTIONS FOR PROFESSIONAL DEVELOPMENT
AND TEACHER PREPARATION

How might teachers at various stages—not only along their journeys as teachers but also in terms of their experience with the concepts discussed in this book—be supported in developing the knowledge, dispositions, and teaching practices described in this chapter? We first discuss what those who engage with teachers in professional development initiatives can do to support the development of teachers' expertise. We then address what can be done in preservice teacher education programs to lay the groundwork for the development of teachers who will be able to amplify instruction for English Learners in the ways we have discussed.

Guidance for Professional Development

Practicing teachers take real-life issues and questions of immediate importance to professional development venues. Often, they want to know how they can improve their practice—and their lessons for tomorrow. While honoring and responding to these needs, those designing professional development initiatives also must attend to the fact that the future is most productively built thoughtfully and gradually as well as tooled with the best understanding. With that goal in mind, we offer a few guidelines for professional developers as they guide teacher learning sessions on lesson design based on the QTEL team's extensive experience working with teachers.

- Before tackling lesson design, teachers need to experience and analyze lessons that model the structures and processes proposed in this book. This process is the same way in which children taking ballet lessons need to have an idea of what accomplished ballet dancing is before they engage in the exercises that will eventually lead them to apprentice into ballet dancing. Good educative materials that both model and discuss purposeful lesson architecture and decision points made along the way are essential in this task of creating visions of good lessons and their components.
- It is helpful if the professional developer works with subject-specific groups of teachers. In this way the work, including analyzing the conceptual, analytic, and language practices at the heart of each discipline, can be carried out with the whole group and with teams of two or four. These teams work on the same lesson, albeit bringing their own choices and creativity to the lesson within the same pedagogical parameters. An advantage of this approach is that the professional developer can have groups compare their proposed

lessons, drawing generalizations that would be appropriate for the whole group.

- Once teachers select objectives for the lesson, choose standards, and have a clear idea of where the lesson is headed, what follows is the decision of which text or texts (written, electronic, pictorial, etc.) will be used. Not every team needs to use the same texts; in fact, it is quite productive to get to the same pedagogical destination via alternative lesson routes.

- Next comes the analysis of the text, a central endeavor for good lesson design. Aída likes to call this part of lesson-planning during teacher professional learning "x-raying the text." The point is to read the short story, essay, novel, and so on, and decide what core ideas (the backbone) and relationships (the system and interrelationships, how key bones connect and articulate to give movement to the body) the text presents in order to then select which ones the lesson will seek to invite students to understand. As discussed throughout this book, not all information presented in a text merits being the focus of a first encounter with the text, but if that first encounter makes the work rewarding for students, chances are that when they have an opportunity in the future, they will revisit the text. In our experience, teachers enjoy the opportunity to discuss with peers which ideas they find essential in selected texts and the rationale for their choice. It is advisable that teachers read texts prior to the session and come ready to review their notes and begin the collaborative work.

- Then it is time to revisit—and perhaps readjust—the objectives of the lesson, refining initial work and agreeing on what conceptual (ideas), analytic (the operations ideas will be put through), and language practices constitute the chosen lesson objectives.

- Finally, teams begin their lesson design. Knowing the destination, it is time to design how students will be invited to prepare, interact with text(s), and extend their understanding. It is important at this point to identify the culminating task that will demonstrate students have developed initial (or other degrees of) understanding of the practices set as the goals of the lesson.

- Design teams of teachers present their lessons, discussing the rationale for their choices. As they listen to each other, teams take notes about specific task choices they like and can replace tasks in their lessons.

Laying the Foundation in Teacher Preparation Programs

What can preservice teacher educators do to begin to lay the groundwork for developing the knowledge, dispositions, and practices needed to create amplified learning opportunities for English Learners and other students? One answer, of course, is to provide novice teachers with authentic, supported contexts to do the kind of lesson planning and enactment—with real students in real classrooms—advocated for in this book. This is possible when multiple aspects of the teacher education program are aligned. Ideally, teacher candidates have access to student-teaching placements where the regular classroom teachers themselves have developed such understandings and practices—or at least are open to the student teachers' designing and implementing amplified lessons—and where other important elements of the teacher preparation program (coursework, field supervision, teacher evaluation mechanisms) are aligned enough so as not to send mixed messages to candidates. Unfortunately, given the challenges facing teacher preparation programs, including the multitude of "moving parts" influenced by a wide range of conceptual, pedagogical, financial, and political factors, true alignment throughout a candidate's teacher preparation program is difficult to achieve.

These limitations do not mean, however, that individual teacher educators cannot introduce teacher candidates to important ideas relevant to amplifying instruction for English Learners—and to have these candidates engage in activities that will make those ideas "come alive" in ways directly related to their development of the elements of professional practice described above. After some initial introduction to the rationale, conceptual grounding, and design architecture for amplified instruction, courses in teacher preparation programs can incorporate many of the approaches described in the professional development section above: asking candidates to analyze and discuss model lessons such as those presented in this book; meeting in disciplinary teams to discuss target disciplinary practices embodied in those lessons or others they observe in their fieldwork (or, less ideally, the "counter-examples" that they observe); and beginning to design, with the support of classmates and the instructor, their own lesson (hypothetical or real, depending on the context). Given the limited real-world experience most teacher candidates initially have in designing or implementing *any* lessons, what teachers produce and how they reflect upon it will obviously differ from more experienced teachers.

One advantage teacher preparation programs have in terms of the model of teacher expertise presented earlier in this chapter is the time and space they have to engage teachers in the *reflection* that is at the center of the model and connected to the other domains. Teacher preparation coursework and mentoring in student teaching classrooms can provide spaces for novice teachers to reflect on the *knowledge* they are developing and the *practice* they are observing and beginning to engage in themselves. Teacher educators can also provide opportunities for those entering the profession to reflect on their *motivation* and *vision*, including teachers' own upbringing and education, the reasons they decided to become teachers, differences between the ways that they were taught and the teaching practices to which they are being introduced, and the implications of teaching students who may be different from themselves in multiple and significant ways. Increasingly, teacher preparation programs, either on their own or because of state requirements, include courses on English Learners that can develop teachers' knowledge of the range of backgrounds, characteristics, strengths, and needs of English Learners; help teachers understand the need for support for English Learners while simultaneously challenging them to amplify rather than simplify learning opportunities; and consider implications for working with English Learners relative to the components of teacher expertise discussed in this chapter.

Courses focused on English Learners can also introduce practices that are central to amplifying the curriculum. For example, George has developed an assignment in one such course to introduce teachers to the notion of scaffolding—a key component of designing the kinds of lessons described in this book. The course is designed for secondary teacher candidates in various content areas who are in early stages of their one-year combined masters and teacher credential program at the University of California, Santa Cruz. The course comes early in the program year, when candidates have just begun to spend time in their student teaching placements, observing their cooperating classroom teachers, and beginning to participate marginally in instruction (working with individual or small groups of students or perhaps teaching part of one of the cooperating teacher's lessons).

After reading an introduction to scaffolding (Walqui & van Lier, 2010) that is consistent with our discussion of the concept in Chapters 2 and 3 and the examples throughout this book, students are asked to discuss how the reading challenged their previous notions of "scaffolding." Invariably, candidates discuss having heard the term used ubiquitously during their previous coursework but primarily as a synonym for the general concept of "help." Examples they provide of what they have heard called "scaffolding" thus include using visual cues to help English Learners' comprehension (e.g., writing things on the board or using pictures or graphic representations), "frontloading" or "pre-teaching" key vocabulary terms, providing students with sentence frames for writing products, or providing clear instructions and examples before asking students to complete assignments by themselves. In class, we discuss the fact that each of these may provide some basic support for English Learners. However, by themselves, none of them represent *scaffolding* in the service of amplification as described by Walqui and van Lier (2010) and as elaborated upon in this book.

After discussion of the reading, and viewing videos of some compelling examples from practice similar to those featured in this book, candidates are asked to work together in small groups over several weeks to design an activity for English Learners to engage in disciplinary practices valued in the target content area—and to either teach and record it in one of their "real" student teaching placements (not an option in all cases), or to lead our class in a simulation of the activity. After students show their video or conduct their simulation, we discuss as a class the structures and processes observed, the planned and unpredictable aspects of the activity, and what might be done in future iterations to improve the activity. Candidates complete the assignment by writing an individual reflection on the goals of their activity, the elements of scaffolding it entailed, and learnings that they might take with them for future planning.

We also discuss the fact that the assignment itself is designed to model key aspects of the vision of scaffolding that we are trying to help candidates develop and enact. For example, the assignment provides a clear structure (the requirement to work in small groups to design and teach a learning activity, clear evaluation criteria, etc.). It is designed to lead to unpredictable outcomes (the activities that each group ultimately designs and presents). It also provides opportunities for various kinds of contingent supports along the way: as candidates of relatively equal strength work through their ideas together, groups check in and receive suggestions from the instructor as they develop their plans, and students receive feedback from their classmates and the instructor after they implement their activity. We also discuss that the assignment models the kind of "handover" from the teacher and "takeover" by the students that ultimately moves toward student autonomy.

As might be expected with novice teachers who have not yet even begun to do any independent student-teaching, the quality of the designs produced is varied, as is the extent to which they represent the intended understanding of scaffolding. But part of the learning is in reflecting on what didn't quite work and engaging in discussions on how the activity could be redesigned to better match the key elements of scaffolding we are emphasizing.

Another option, to be implemented either in conjunction with or instead of the example provided here, would be to ask teacher candidates to carefully observe, over time, the classes they are working with, recording examples of various kinds of student support and identifying the presence or absence of the elements of scaffolding proposed by Walqui and van Lier (2010). Such an activity could also be scaffolded for teacher candidates, so that they see models of how the instructor would conduct such an observation, do the observations in pairs or small groups so as to benefit from working with peers of various strengths, and move toward independent, autonomous observations by the end of the quarter. Whichever version is implemented, these examples show how the notion of "scaffolding" can itself be scaffolded; that is, how one of the key conceptual foundations necessary for the kind of lesson and unit development portrayed in this book can begin to be laid, albeit in modest ways, even in the earliest stages of teachers' journeys.

CONCLUSION

As we conclude this chapter and the book as a whole, we acknowledge that there is still much more to be said regarding how to best prepare and support *all* teachers to transform their practice from *simplification* toward *amplification* as the guiding principle, for the education of English Learners and other students. For example, as we have noted but not had the space to fully address, schools, teacher preparation programs, and in-service professional development initiatives can all be better structured to create optimal conditions for teachers—throughout their careers—to develop the expertise necessary to do the difficult work discussed throughout this book. And further research is necessary to better understand the promise, possibilities, and challenges in preparing teachers to design instruction with amplification as its goal. Nevertheless, we hope we have offered enough guidance for teachers to begin the ambitious work of designing learning opportunities of the highest quality for English Learners. We also hope we have offered productive suggestions for those involved in teacher preparation and professional development to support teachers in this work throughout their careers. Amplifying the curriculum is not easy, but the enormous potential that English Learners offer to addressing our society's current and pressing challenges make these efforts both absolutely essential and eternally rewarding.

REFERENCES

Anderson, E. R. (2017). Accommodating change. Relating fidelity of implementation to program fit in educational reform. *American Educational Research Journal, 54*(6), 1288–1315.

Bunch, G. C. (2013). Pedagogical language knowledge: Preparing mainstream teachers for English learners in the new standards era. *Review of Research in Education, 37*, 298–341.

Coburn, C. (2003). Rethinking scale. Moving beyond numbers to deep and lasting change. *Educational Researcher, 32*(6), 3–12.

Coburn, C., & Stein, M. K. (2016). Key lessons about the relationship between research and practice. In C. Coburn & M. K. Stein (Eds.), *Research and practice in education: Building alliances, bridging the divide.* Lanham, MD: Rowman & Littlefield.

Cohen, D. (1990). A revolution in one classroom. The case of Mrs. Oublier. *Educational Evaluation and Policy Analysis, 12*(3), 311–319.

Dewey, J. (1925). Experience and nature. In J. A. Boydston (Ed.), *John Dewey: The later works, 1925–1953 (Vol. 1).* Carbondale, IL: Southern University Press.

Galguera, T. (2011). Participant structures as professional learning tasks and the development of pedagogical language knowledge among preservice teachers. *Teacher Education Quarterly, 38*(1), 85–106.

Heritage, M., Walqui, A., & Linquanti, R. (2015). *English Language Learners and the new standards. Developing language, content knowledge, and analytical practices in the classroom.* Cambridge, MA: Harvard Education Press.

Montague, J. (2012, April 25). The third man: The forgotten Black Power hero. *CNN.* Retrieved from https://www.cnn.com/2012/04/24/sport/olympics-norman -black-power/index.html

Raphael, T. (1986). Teaching question answer relationships, revisited. *Reading Teacher, 39*(6), 516–522.

Shulman, L. S. (1986). Those who understand: Knowledge growth in teaching. *Educational Researcher, 15*(2), 4–14.

Shulman, L. S., & Associates. (1995). Fostering a community of teachers and learners. Unpublished progress report to the Mellon Foundation.

Spillane, J. P., & Zeuli, J. S. (1999). Reform and teaching: Exploring patterns of practice in the context of national and state Mathematics reform. *Educational Evaluation and Policy Analysis, 21*(1), 1–27.

van Manen, M. (1991). Reflectivity and the pedagogical moment: The normativity of pedagogical thinking and acting. *Journal of Curriculum Studies, 23*(6), 507–536.

Walqui, A. (1997). The development of teacher understanding. Inservice professional growth for teachers of English language learners. Unpublished dissertation, Stanford University School of Education, Stanford, CA.

Walqui, A. (2000). *Access and engagement: Program design and instructional approaches for immigrant students in secondary school.* Washington, DC: Center for Applied Linguistics and Delta Systems.

Walqui, A. (2007a). The development of teacher expertise to work with adolescent English Learners: A model and a few priorities. In L. Verplaetse & N. Migliacci (Eds.), *Inclusive pedagogy for English Language Learners* (pp. 107–129). New York & London: Lawrence Erlbaum Associates.

Walqui, A. (2007b, April). Becoming who we are not yet. The development of teacher expertise to work with English Learners. Paper presented at the annual meeting of the American Educational Research Association, Chicago, IL.

Walqui, A., & van Lier, L. (2010). *Scaffolding reframed. Scaffolding the academic success of adolescent English language learners: A pedagogy of promise.* San Francisco, CA: WestEd.

Wilson, S., & Berne, J. (1999). Teacher learning and the acquisition of professional knowledge: An examination of research on contemporary professional development. *Review of Research on Education, 24,* 173–209.

About the Editors and Contributors

Aída Walqui is director of the Teacher Professional Development Program at WestEd and founder and co-director of the Quality Teaching for English Learners (QTEL) initiative. She earned a Ph.D. in Language, Literacy, and Culture from Stanford University and a Masters in Sociolinguistics from Georgetown University. In addition to teaching at the university level in Peru (her home country), Mexico, England, and the United States, she has taught language arts, ESL, and social studies in both Spanish and English at the K–12 level in California. She has won multiple awards for her work on indigenous education, Spanish as a heritage language, and professional learning for teachers of English Learners, including being recognized in 2016 by the TESOL International Association as one of the 50 Most Influential Educators in the profession in the last 50 years. She was a founding partner of the Understanding Language initiative and is the author of a number of articles, white papers, and books, including *Scaffolding the Academic Success of Adolescent English Language Learners: A Pedagogy of Promise*, coauthored with Leo van Lier.

George C. Bunch is professor of education and former faculty director of teacher education at the University of California, Santa Cruz. An experienced K–12 ESL, Spanish, and social studies teacher and teacher educator, he holds a Ph.D. in educational linguistics from Stanford University and an MA in bilingual education and TESOL from the University of Maryland Baltimore County. His research on language and literacy challenges and opportunities for English Learners, and on how pedagogy, curriculum, teacher preparation, and educational policies can be improved to better serve them, has been widely published. He was a founding partner of the Understanding Language initiative, received a Spencer Foundation Midcareer Grant to serve as a visiting scholar at the Carnegie Foundation for the Advancement of Teaching, and is a former National Academy of Education/Spencer Postdoctoral Fellow. In 2017, he received the Midcareer Award from the Second Language Research Special Interest Group of the American Educational Research Association.

Elsa Billings is a senior program associate in WestEd's Quality Teaching for English Learners initiative. Prior to joining WestEd, Billings served as ELL co-advisor for the Council of Chief State School Officers, a professor in the College of Education at San Diego State University, and a consultant for Stanford University's Understanding Language. She has published numerous book chapters and articles in peer-reviewed journals. Billings received a Ph.D. in Language, Learning, and Policy from Stanford University.

Pía Castilleja is a literacy and language education associate at WestEd's Teacher Professional Development Program. Her research interests comprise the role of professional agency in the development of teacher expertise, the coherence of professional learning environments, and the role of teacher educators in professional learning. As a member of the Quality Teaching for English Learners team, she is responsible for designing and conducting learning opportunities for teachers and teacher educators.

Nicholas Catechis is a senior program associate at WestEd. Drawing on 3 decades of teaching and administrative experience, he promotes the academic success of English learners through professional development that builds teachers' pedagogical content knowledge. His expertise includes developing and implementing research-based instructional materials and workshops that help teachers deliver high-quality instruction aligned with their curriculums.

Haiwen Chu is a senior program associate in mathematics for the Quality Teaching for English Learners initiative in the Teacher Professional Development Program at WestEd. His work draws upon his experience teaching recent immigrants high school mathematics and integrating language development with curriculum design. He designs and conducts mixed methods research in partnership with districts to improve policy, programs, and praxis for English Learners. He holds a Ph.D. in Urban Education Policy from the City University of New York Graduate Center.

Tomás Galguera teaches in the Mills College School of Education and obtained his Ph.D. in Education with emphasis in Language, Literacy, and Culture from Stanford University. His publications and research interests include teacher preparation pedagogy for language development, teacher classroom research, trauma informed practice, and the role of information technology and social media on teaching and teacher education. Before Mills College, he was a Spanish bilingual teacher in the Oakland Unified School District.

Leslie Hamburger is co-director of the Quality Teaching for English Learners initiative at WestEd. She works with schools and districts in the development of educator expertise to work with English Learners in rigorous and accelerated ways. She designs mathematics curricula that weave the development of conceptual, analytic, and language practices simultaneously, and she facilitates professional learning to develop educator capacity to implement standards-based, high-challenge, high-support mathematics instruction for linguistic minority students.

Lee Hartman worked for more than a decade with newly arrived English Learner students as a high school English teacher and subsequently as a coach and mentor for teachers of English Learners. Currently, as a program associate for WestEd's Quality Teaching for English Learners, he travels the nation providing support, coaching, and professional development to teachers of English Learners with a particular emphasis on Newcomers.

Catherine Lemmi is a Ph.D. candidate in Science Curriculum and Teacher Education at Stanford University and an instructor in the Programa de Especialização Docente in São Paulo, Brazil. Her research explores the language ideologies of science teachers and how those might impact learning opportunities in multilingual communities. She has served as a science teacher in Redwood City as well as a mentor, supervisor, and instructor for preservice teachers in the Stanford Teacher Education Program.

Paolo C. Martin is a Ph.D. candidate and teacher educator at Stanford University. He studies the intersection between classroom discourse, learning technologies, and pedagogies as actors in children's experiences of their own well-being. Prior to Stanford, Paolo was a reading teacher and bench scientist in Los Angeles. He later trained teachers in science and literacy instruction at the Lawrence Hall of Science at UC Berkeley, where he received his MA in Language, Literacy, and Culture.

Sara Rutherford-Quach is a senior researcher in the Center for Educational Research and Innovation at SRI International and the former director of Academic Initiatives and Research for Understanding Language at the Stanford Graduate School of Education. A former bilingual teacher, she received her Ph.D. in Linguistic Anthropology of Education from Stanford University. Her work focuses on language and literacy practices across content areas, particularly with respect to multilingual students and their educators.

Heather Schlaman is a Ph.D. candidate in education at the University of California, Santa Cruz, and a Graduate Student Instructor in UC Santa Cruz's Writing Program. Her research focuses on the ways that school leaders shape the education of students designated as English Learners at the high school level. Prior to entering the Ph.D. program, Heather spent 20 years in high school education as an English teacher and later as a school site administrator overseeing curriculum and instruction.

Mary Schmida is a senior research associate with the Quality Teaching for English Learners initiative at WestEd. She develops instructional materials and designs and facilitates professional development nationally to enhance teacher knowledge in the areas of secondary English Language Arts teaching and pedagogy. She received a Ph.D. in Education in Language, Literacy, and Culture from the University of California, Berkeley. Her research focused on the complex linguistic, academic, and social realities of long-term English Learners.

Index

Page numbers followed by "*f*" indicate figures, "n" indicate notes, and "*t*" indicate tables.